Two Voices

Ken M. Symes
WESTERN WASHINGTON STATE COLLEGE

# TWO VOICES

## Writing About Literature

HOUGHTON MIFFLIN COMPANY · BOSTON

Atlanta   Dallas   Geneva, Ill.   Hopewell, N.J.   Palo Alto   London

Copyright © 1976 by Houghton Mifflin Company. All rights reserved. No part of this work may be reproduced or transmitted in any form or by any means, electronic or mechanical, including photocopying and recording, or by any information retrieval system, without permission in writing from the publisher.
Printed in the U.S.A.
Library of Congress Catalog Card Number: 75-31015
ISBN: 0-395-20607-3

For Linda and Brent

# Contents

| | | |
|---|---|---|
| PREFACE | | xi |
| **POETRY** | | 1 |
| ONE  PERSONIFICATIONS | | 3 |
| EXERCISE 1 Writing Personifications  3 | | |
| EXERCISE 2 Writing About Personifications  5 | | |
| TWO  DRAMATIC SITUATION | | 8 |
| EXERCISE 3 Writing Dramatic Situations  8 | | |
| EXERCISE 4 Writing About Dramatic Situations  11 | | |
| THREE  METAPHORS | | 15 |
| EXERCISE 5 Writing Images  15 | | |
| EXERCISE 6 Writing About Images  19 | | |
| FOUR  SYMBOLS | | 23 |
| EXERCISE 7 Writing About Past and Present  23 | | |
| EXERCISE 8 Writing About Symbols in Poems  26 | | |
| FIVE  THEME | | 30 |
| EXERCISE 9 Writing Memorable Sayings  30 | | |
| EXERCISE 10 Writing About Themes in Poems  34 | | |

SIX  SOUND: RHYTHM AND RHYME                    41
    EXERCISE 11 Writing About Rhythm, Past and
       Present   41
    Rhythm   44
    EXERCISE 12 Writing About Sound in Poetry   48

POETRY READINGS                                 56
    *Richard Brautigan* Adrenalin Mother   56
    *Charles Simic* Bestiary for the Fingers of My Right
       Hand   57
    *Robert Browning* Soliloquy of the Spanish Cloister   58
    *William Carlos Williams* Tract   60
    *Richard Brautigan* The Pill Versus the Springhill Mine
       Disaster   62
    *Michael Benedikt* The Energy Chest   62
    *Lucille Clifton* Good Times   63
    *James Tate* The Lost Pilot   63
    *William Childress* Lobo   65
    *William Childress* Hunting the Trolls   66
    *Diane Wakoski* No More Soft Talk   67
    *Philip Larkin* If, My Darling   69

## DRAMA                                        71

SEVEN  CHARACTER IN DRAMA                       73
    EXERCISE 13 Discovering Character in Personifications   73
    EXERCISE 14 Writing About Character in Drama   77

EIGHT  CONFLICT IN DRAMA                        81
    EXERCISE 15 Discovering Conflict in Personifications   81
    EXERCISE 16 Writing About Conflict in Drama   84

NINE  PLOT IN DRAMA                             89
    EXERCISE 17 Discovering Plot Among Personifications   89
    EXERCISE 18 Writing About Plot in Drama   92

TEN  LANGUAGE IN DRAMA                          97
    EXERCISE 19 Discovering Language for Personifications   97
    EXERCISE 20 Writing About Language in Drama   102

ELEVEN  STAGING IN DRAMA                        108
    EXERCISE 21 Writing About Staging in Drama   108

DRAMA READINGS                                  113
    Everyman *Anonymous*   113
    A Raisin in the Sun *Lorraine Hansberry*   139

# FICTION     211

**TWELVE    PLOT IN FICTION**     213
     EXERCISE 22   Discovering Plot in Survival Stories    213
     EXERCISE 23   Prewriting: Plot in Fiction    218

**THIRTEEN    CHARACTER IN FICTION**     222
     EXERCISE 24   Discovering Character in Survival Stories    222
     EXERCISE 25   Prewriting: Character in Fiction    226

**FOURTEEN    POINT OF VIEW IN FICTION**     231
     EXERCISE 26   Discovering Point of View in Survival Stories    231
     EXERCISE 27   Prewriting: Point of View in Fiction    236

**FIFTEEN    LANGUAGE IN FICTION**     242
     EXERCISE 28   Discovering Language in Survival Stories    242
     EXERCISE 29   Prewriting: Language in Fiction    245

**SIXTEEN    THEME IN FICTION**     249
     EXERCISE 30   Discovering Theme in Survival Stories    249
     EXERCISE 31   Writing a Documented Paper on Fiction    252

## FICTION READINGS     257
     Young Goodman Brown *Nathaniel Hawthorne*    257
     Gold Coast *James Alan McPherson*    268

## INDEX     287

# Preface

*Two Voices* assumes that mastering critical writing is one cornerstone of a liberal education, for the good critic has gained an appreciation of literature as well as a system for thinking.

The title *Two Voices* suggests the approach that this text takes in teaching critical writing. Each chapter asks students to discover two connected writing voices. The first is the voice of observation and experience. Students write brief, ungraded papers based upon what they have seen and done. Then they bring these papers to class and analyze them for the techniques shared with poetry, drama, and fiction written by professionals. In discovering the critic's voice, the second voice of the title, students connect what they have just learned about a technique to the way it functions in a poem, a play, or a short story. To find this second voice, they write critical papers, which are then graded. These exercises are longer and more complex than the first ones in each chapter.

These two connected assignments demonstrate the major assumption of the text—a premise that sets it off from other writing-about-literature texts: students are better able to identify and appreciate literary techniques when they can demonstrate these techniques in their own writing. For example, students best learn the function of point of view by retelling something that they have already written from another angle and by studying the way each choice affects meaning. Students, in other words, have a chance to make abstract literary terms concrete before attempting to analyze a professional writer's work. And they have another chance to visualize terms like character, rhythm, or plot when they read examples of my students' writing that illustrate both the experiential and critical kinds of writing assigned in the text.

*Two Voices* also differs from other books of its kind in that the critical writing assignments emphasize prewriting and revision. The text assumes that good thinking leads to good writing. When critical writing goes bad, it is often because students don't have the means to discover what there is to say about a poem, a play, or a short story. Or good ideas lie buried in critical papers because students don't have a system to revise them. Discussion questions in each chapter provide prewriting and revision systems. Student writing also provides illustrations of good thinking and sound revision practices.

In both experiential and critical writing, the burden is on students to produce and to discuss their own writing under the classroom supervision of the instructor. Although supervising the entire process of composition, the instructor will often see only the final draft of the revised critical paper. I find that placing the responsibility for the experiential assignment directly on the student shows excellent results when my students come to class to discuss a piece of literature, for they have a firm handle on the literary term under scrutiny and have usually begun work on a paper. Consequently, students come to class better prepared and more confident.

Another special feature of the text is that while it preserves a three-fold genre division, it offers a variety of approaches to writing. Poetry emphasizes explication in light of the techniques of personification, dramatic situation, metaphor, symbol, and sound devices found in poems. Drama introduces students to evaluative criticism, that is, each assignment gives them a chance to make a comment on how effectively character, conflict, plot, language, and staging are handled in a play. Fiction has a third writing approach. Students develop prewriting materials concerning plot, character, point of view, and language. Then in the final chapter, students are assigned a lengthy documented paper, one which draws upon the research in the earlier four chapters.

Since the text has a large variety of approaches to writing possible in its sixteen assignments, an instructor can construct a course that emphasizes a single genre or one that cuts across genre lines. For example, even though the assignments in this section are not presented in a lock-step fashion, drama can be taught as a unit, one that moves systematically from a study of character to conflict to plot to language and concludes with staging. Or choosing among the sixteen assignments, an instructor could construct a unit that focuses on a technique. For example, a course could focus on character and could begin with Chapter Two—the way that point of view reveals character in the dramatic situations of poems. The course could then move on to Chapters Seven and Eight, character and conflict in a play, and conclude with character and point of view in fiction, Chapters Thirteen and Fourteen. (I myself have at various times taught Poetry, Drama, and Fiction as single courses, and I have just concluded a course in which I stressed point of view and drew assignments from all three sections of the text.)

Even though *Two Voices* prints a selection of a dozen poems, two plays, and two short stories, the instructor will probably wish to furnish students with additional reading selections.

*Two Voices* approaches critical writing with features that students find not only attractive and fresh but also helpful and logical. With this approach the text preserves the traditional purpose of writing-about-literature texts: to introduce students to literature and to teach analysis and analytical writing. And it is hoped that this text will draw students into the study of literature beyond the introductory course.

I would like to acknowledge the help my students at Western have given me in preparing this text. Over the past three years, they have provided me with ideas and have graciously permitted me to print their writings. I have also had excellent help in preparing the manuscript from Judy Balcom, Jan McMannis, Dorothy Oliveira, Gloria Taylor, Holly Tripp, and Barbara White. And I particularly appreciate the constructive criticisms of Mary Marshall, Tallahassee Community College; George Ellenbogen, Bentley College; and Carrol L. Fry, Northwest Missouri State University.

*K.M.S.*

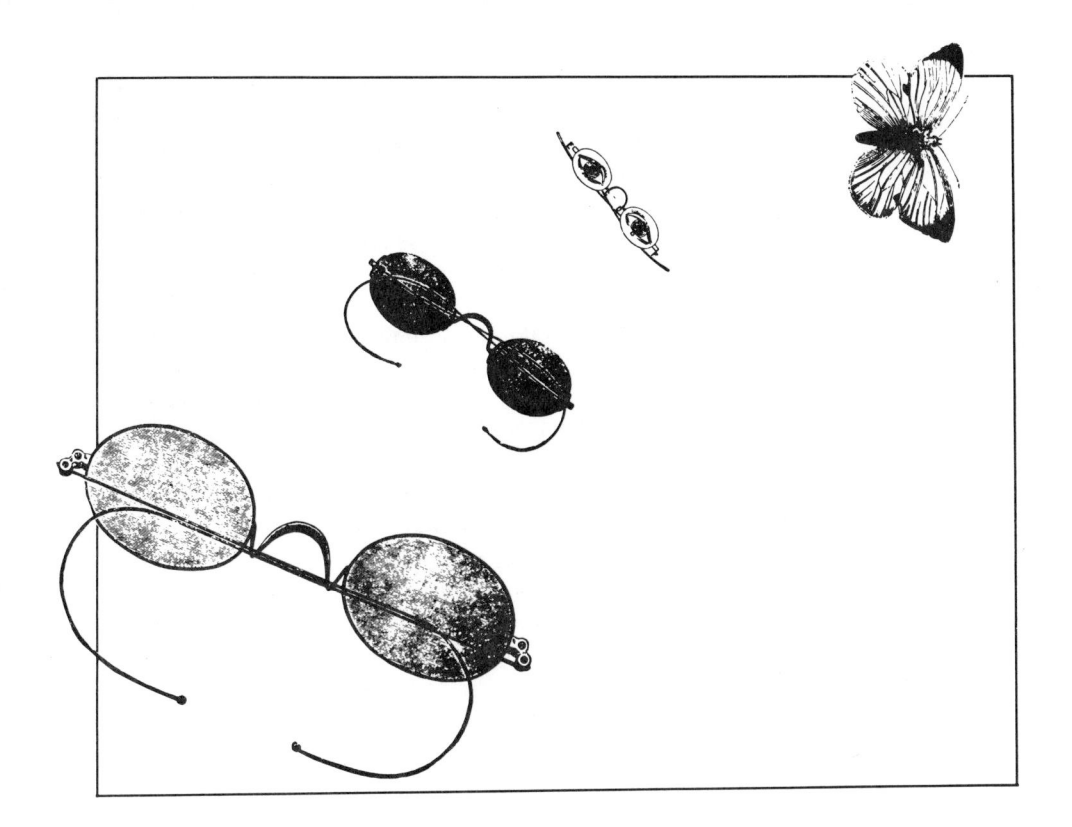

# POETRY

A student of mine once trained to be a Forest Service smoke jumper at Grand Canyon, Arizona. The first thing they taught him was how to fall. Born clumsy, he thought he knew all there was to know about falling. As an instructor drove a pickup truck round and round a baseball field, the jumpers learned to hit and roll. First at five m.p.h. Then at ten. At fifteen. Finally, they could jump and roll confidently at twenty and were ready to master other preliminaries to their first jump.

Instead of pushing you out immediately over that Grand Canyon world of poems, this text asks you to make short leaps before you plunge into the beauties, spectacles, and delights of poetry. You don't jump immediately into critical analyses of poems. Your first assignment in each chapter is always a short paper based on your own observation or experience. After analyzing that short paper for a technique like imagery or a conception like theme, you then go on to connect what you see in your own writing to the way a similar conception or technique appears in a poem. The text emphasizes critical writing, both in the time you are expected to spend on assignments and in the space the text spends in helping you master the analysis of literature. This mastery comes more easily once you have seen certain patterns in your own writing, patterns like those poets use when they compose.

The purpose of this section, then, is to show you how to become a confident and accurate reader of poetry and how to voice your observations in critical essays.

# Personifications

## 1 · WRITING PERSONIFICATIONS

*WRITING* Bring to life three or four abstract words like *Despair*. Devote a paragraph to each description as you discover human qualities in the words.

| | | | |
|---|---|---|---|
| Freedom | Duty | Greed | Error |
| Anger | Fear | Innocence | Doubt |
| Gluttony | Conscience | Deceit | Patriotism |
| Envy | Death | Love | Joy |
| Pride | Uptight | Jealousy | Fashion |

1 Would Despair be male or female?
2 How would it be dressed?
3 What would its gestures be?
4 What kind of voice would it have?

Think of the abstract word in dramatic terms — as if it were a character in a play.

5 What might Despair say?
6 In what places would it be found?
7 What would it do for pleasure?
8 To whom would it talk?
9 With whom would it conflict?

*DISCUSSION* Read your descriptions aloud in class, or prepare a ditto of them for class distribution. Discuss them in these terms:

*PERSONIFICATIONS*      3

1 What concrete things do the writers use to convey their impressions of the abstract word? What kind of clothing? Do they use body language?
2 With what other abstractions can a word be contrasted or compared? For example, does Love have any natural companions or enemies from the list above?
3 Can you improvise conversations between the conflicting or matching pairs?
4 Which of the terms might go together in a short play on war? One on courtship and marriage? One on grief?

---

## COMMENTS AND EXAMPLES

Poets often use personification (that is, they give abstract words or inanimate things human qualities) in order to define an emotion or an idea, for personifications have a way of making the invisible visible as the following two student writings illustrate:

*Despair* dressed in gray robes, old, wrinkled face, long grayish beard, eyes without sparkle, rather shaky and decrepit voice, feeble, failing frequently, fading out at the end of sentences, irregular tone.

*Linda Adamczyk*

*Despair* is a young woman, emaciated, ragged, worn, with two small children too dirty and matted for one to distinguish their sex — they are hungry and crying weakly. She seems too tired to go on. Her voice is weak, low, occasionally whiny.

*Pam Robinette*

Notice that in Linda's description Despair is male, old, and characterized partly by looks (eyes without sparkle) and largely by a weak voice. We don't have a sample of his speech, but it is easy to imagine him on stage clothed in gray robes. Despair's speaking manner is vividly described even to the way his voice fades out. Female and young, the second Despair is different from the first but is just as concrete. Pam, also, stresses Despair's weak voice but adds another dramatic quality — the dirty, indistinguishable children. Both writers convey the emotional state of despair as one of helplessness, sorrow, fatigue, and noise.

What these student writers have done is to define for us words that are hard to understand without some relation to sense experience. One of the traits of the human mind is to explain the unknown in terms of the known. Personifications make us see, hear, smell, taste, and touch what is otherwise abstract and hard to understand. Defining Despair as a whiny-voiced woman with sad children or as an old man with a decrepit voice has much more impact than saying generally, "Yesterday, I was desperate."

## 2 · WRITING ABOUT PERSONIFICATIONS

*WRITING* Now that you have looked at personifications of your own making, write one or two paragraphs analyzing the effect of personification in one of the poems that your instructor has assigned. Examine the poem in light of what you have learned about making abstractions come to life. Use the questions that follow to help you find material for your paragraph and to take notes before you write. This note taking and preliminary thinking is referred to as *prewriting* throughout the text. Prewriting should help you solve one of the biggest problems writers face — where to get material for your essays.

1 What meaning does the personified word have without the poem? (Check your dictionary.) What meanings are deepened when the word is personified?
2 Which human traits are emphasized in the personification? What sense experiences do these traits appeal to?
3 Is the personification an actor in the poem, addressed as a member of the poem's audience, or only referred to? How does its role in the drama of the poem affect what the poem says?

*DISCUSSION* Read your analyses aloud in class or have them dittoed. Give special attention to these two questions in your discussion:

1 Do the writers of the analyses give specific examples from the poem to back up their observations?
2 Do the writers capture the drama of the poem — its speaker, its audience, and its occasion or purpose? Have they caught especially the role of the personification in the drama?

## COMMENTS AND EXAMPLES

In writing analyses, you deal with two of the same major composition problems that you face in writing personifications: (1) you must be specific; and (2) you must let the reader know something about the background drama that the personification figures in. Illustrating the first point Eric Magnuson, a student writer, described how different the connotations of the word *adrenalin* are normally from its meaning in Brautigan's poem "Adrenalin Mother," included in Poetry Readings on page 56.

> Standing alone, the word "adrenalin" is a cold, clinical noun devoid of the grandiose overtones achieved through pairing it with *mother* — a term which introduces a great variety of emotional reactions because of its significance to each reader. Brautigan's images are especially vivid because "shoes of swift bird wings" makes *Adrenalin Mother* god-like, more than the human mothers most of us know.
>
> *Eric Magnuson*

Eric cites only one passage from the poem, yet his analysis of the word *mother* and its connotations allows the reader to see what he finds in the poem. This use of evidence is no different from convincing a reader of the accuracy of your description of Despair as an old man or a young girl. Details convince the reader that you have read the poem accurately.

Doug Bennion illustrates the second point — that you must let the reader know something about the background drama of the poem. As evidence that he understood the drama of "Bestiary for the Fingers of My Right Hand" (p. 57), Doug describes what the poet, Simic, made him do:

> Next, though not written down, Simic looking at his hand persuades the reader to either think back to someone of this same character that he knows or to imagine a man like this. I found myself wiggling my thumb and hoping to see the wolves it hunts with.
>
> *Doug Bennion*

This is a good account of the drama of this poem: a man contemplates his hand and the fingers come to life. As Doug suggests, the drama of a poem may be implied. Therefore, any analysis must reveal that drama so that the poem can be fully understood, and so that any presentation of the poem's details, such as Simic's personification of the fingers as animals, can be fully comprehended.

In writing analyses, however, you do face one composition problem not faced in writing personifications: you have to explain why you think a detail is important or why you think the dramatic context for the detail is significant. For example, if you say that "Brautigan gives new meanings to the effects adrenalin has on the human body," you need to say what those meanings are. Otherwise your readers will never know what the significance of "shadow of jumping fish" or "your dress of comets" was in your mind. If they don't know, readers either have to guess or go away discouraged because you took them only one step toward understanding.

But if you go on to explain the significance of the evidence that you present, then readers can follow your thought and make up their minds about the accuracy of your judgments in light of their reading of the poem. For example, T. L. Coble says this about "Bestiary for the Fingers of My Right Hand":

> The speaker uses descriptions of animals to explain some type of emotion man possesses, such as the thumb being "Rooster to his hens" — the fingers being the hens. Such a description suggests the dominating, ambitious, and adventurous spirit of men, which the unique power of the human thumb has allowed them to grasp.
>
> *T. L. Coble*

Thus T. L. presents not only the evidence but also its significance in the last sentence of her analysis. She allows us to compare our reading of the thumb's significance with hers.

Let's review, then, briefly the three basic steps in writing analyses of personifications, steps that hold for the other forms of criticism you will be doing in later exercises. First, establish the dramatic context for the poem. Who is the speaker? The audience? What is the occasion, situation, or purpose? Secondly, select representative details within the dramatic context of the poem: which ones represent best what you want to show? Thirdly, make a statement about the significance of the evidence you present. Why is it important that Brautigan addresses Mother Adrenalin thankfully, as in a prayer? What is the "something" Simic sees stirring in the weak fifth finger?

# 2

# Dramatic Situation

## 3 · WRITING DRAMATIC SITUATIONS

*WRITING* As the first step toward understanding the dramatic situations in the poems, do one of the following writing projects:

1. Describe in careful detail a photograph of yourself. Since the picture may be from the past or present, use one that you have strong feelings about or one that shows you in a characteristic action. For example, do you have a photograph that makes you cringe or feel proud when it is shown to others? Childhood nudity? Adolescent attempts at a mature pose? Or one that disguises your real feelings beneath another surface? Attempt to build into your description a sense of the person you were when the picture was taken. That is, which of your voices would speak if the picture could suddenly come to life? Would the picture "say" the same thing, or would your "voice" be the same if the picture had been taken from another angle?
2. Find a photograph or painting in a newspaper, magazine, or book that demonstrates human drama. Then describe in careful detail the nature of the scene and the people in the photograph or painting. Give special emphasis to the angle from which the painting is painted or the photograph is taken. How would changing the angle of the picture alter what it says?

    What aspect of a human voice does the picture reveal? That is, how would the people in the picture sound if they could talk? Or what would the picture "say" if it had a voice?

    Write about the picture or painting so vividly that your reader can visualize it without having seen it.

*DISCUSSION* In class read your descriptions aloud or ditto them. Discuss them in these terms:

1 From what angle is the picture taken? What details show up because this focus was chosen for the photograph?
2 Is the picture or painting described so that you can see its drama even though you haven't seen the picture?
3 Which aspects of human character are revealed either in the subject of the picture or in the angle that it was taken from?

---

## COMMENTS AND EXAMPLES

The composition of a poem has an important aspect in common with the composition of a photograph or painting, that is, its *dramatic situation*. The dramatic situation of a picture or poem includes (1) its setting or occasion; (2) its speaker or subject; (3) its audience. Before looking at some examples of student writing that demonstrate these features, let's expand this discussion of dramatic situation.

Both poems and pictures have a backdrop against which the human drama plays. Backdrops give indications of place, such as in front of a fountain or a city street, or of time, such as Elizabethan or modern, day or night. Whereas in pictures the backdrop is part of what you see, in poems you have to imagine the scenery or the time in terms of clues the writer may furnish in the language.

Both the poem and the picture have subjects, that is, actions or people that are the major focus. It is important to note that finding the center of interest of the picture or poem may require some close looking. For instance, an ad may seem to focus on a man and a woman nuzzling over two glasses of sherry, but the real focus is on the golden sherry, which is the only item in color and which contrasts with the people in black and white. Similarly, a poem may seem to focus on the drama of a monk who is pruning a monastery garden and who talks about a fellow monk he hates, but the actual center of the poem is the speaker himself, who reveals his own weaknesses as he talks. (See Robert Browning's "Soliloquy of the Spanish Cloister," pp. 58–60.)

Finally, pictures and poems directly or indirectly address an audience. That is, the photographer or poet intends for his or her work to be seen or heard. Near the table of contents of both *Playboy* and *Ms.*, the sherry ad addresses the readers of each magazine, or newsstand browsers, who may just leaf through to see what's in this month's issue. A monk in Browning's "Soliloquy of the Spanish

Cloister" is overheard talking to himself, but Browning's readers are the real listeners since the monk doesn't actually speak with his enemy. It wouldn't be difficult to pose a photograph to represent the poem's garden drama.

In this piece of student writing, notice how Rick Keck describes not only the dramatic situation of the picture but also what would be changed if the angle of the photograph were different:

> The helicopter is dropping some white people off in a remote jungle to investigate a primitive tribe. The ground-floor view, looking up past the platform made of sticks and vines, is the perspective a tribe member would have. The platform would seem to them to be a major creation; it was certainly dangerous to build and towers high over the jungle floor.
>
> Placing the helicopter next to this platform emphasizes the two cultures. Next to a flying machine, the platform becomes a primitive, ramshackle creation, similar to a young boy's tree house in his backyard.
>
> A view from the helicopter would simply place the platform in the context of the jungle and a jungle people. Here would be no contrast between our culture and theirs and the tree-top platform would be a monument built by savages and used solely by them.
>
> *Rick Keck*

Rick's sense of the setting and occasion of this photograph is clear: the jungle backdrop is necessary to understand the conflict between the two cultures. He also captures the picture's subject: even though no humans appear, the primitive platform and the helicopter become voices for the two cultures and vividly speak for the technological level of each. The picture does not, however, advocate the superiority of the culture that developed the helicopter. The picture doesn't "look down" on the primitive world being invaded. Instead it presents a view that shows the potential threat to the jungle civilization that the helicopter represents, including machines versus trees and quiet versus noise.

Notice in Paddy Chamberlain's description that the picture she writes about also has "noise" in it:

> The photographer here has done an excellent job of capturing the loudness which pictorial expression can possess. Here the undisguised disgust of the white establishment bullshit fed daily to three black students is caught in the classroom. Tired of hearing about white war heroes, white gods, and white rules, one of the young men stares down, taking himself anywhere away from where he is. A second is ricocheting apathy right back to the photographer's lens. The farthest boy glares back with distrust as if to verify that the photographer is white. If one was to change this angle of this photograph, say a straight-on shot from within the classroom, you might see more of a

hostility towards the photographer and more annoyance. These black students would react unlike white children who would mock the photographer, making faces, and acting hammish. You would also lose the perspective of their closeness, their clumping together. You might take away from the intensity of concern about them by adding additional people in the background. I feel the isolation is very effective in the original picture.

*Paddy Chamberlain*

Paddy's description convincingly captures three potential speakers who, to her mind, seem to be saying much without ever talking. The dramatic situation is clear, and the photograph becomes a speaking picture in her examination of it.

Poems also have been traditionally defined as "speaking pictures," and this phrase is helpful in defining one aspect of poetry. It furnishes us with a vivid sense of something that a composer of poetry keeps his or her eyes peeled for: the dramatic scenes from life that best capture the human voice in either a significant act of speaking or an important thought.

## 4 · WRITING ABOUT DRAMATIC SITUATIONS

*WRITING* Now go on to describe and analyze the dramatic situation of a poem, or contrast and compare the situations of two poems. Again, use these questions to prewrite your paper:

1 What is the backdrop for the drama of the poem? Is it implied or explicit? What is the importance of the setting or occasion to the poem?
2 Who is the speaker? What do you learn about his or her age and profession? What do you learn about the speaker's attitudes towards himself or herself and the subject of the poem?
3 Who is the audience of the poem? That is, who is the implied or direct listener whom the speaker tries to reach? Where do you, the reader, stand in relation to the audience of the poem? That is, are you addressed, or do you merely overhear? What is the significance of the audience to the poem?
4 If you were to photograph a scene to capture the drama of this poem, how would you set it up?

*DISCUSSION* In class, focus your discussion of these writings on this central question: Does the writer make clear (even to a reader who doesn't know the poem) what its dramatic situation is? That is, can you see the poem as a "speaking picture"?

Then work with these subordinate questions:

1 Where and when does the poem take place?
2 Who precisely is the speaker?
3 Who is listening?

---

## COMMENTS AND EXAMPLES

There are similar composition problems whether you write about pictures or poems:

1 You must describe the scene precisely so that a reader who hasn't seen the picture or read the poem can be taken to the location by words.
2 You must let the reader know not only how humans figure in the picture or poem but also how they relate to the intended audiences of the work.

Before looking at these two problems in the writing of students who have analyzed William Carlos Williams's "Tract" let's look briefly at the aspect of writing about poetry that distinguishes it from writing about pictures (see "Tract" on p. 60).

Seldom in writing about pictures do you have to worry about the title. But clearly Williams gives us an important key to the dramatic situation of "Tract" in his choice of a title. Cliff Weatherman pointed out, for example, that "the dramatic situation is one man protesting against the normal way of conducting funerals. This is the significance of the title: a leaflet in which the author is trying to put across his ideas to his 'townspeople.' The speaker's manner is one of great urgency in his presentation since he is writing a kind of propaganda." In this opening from his essay on the poem, Cliff emphasizes the significance of the title. He quotes very little from the poem, but he makes the dramatic situation clear in his definition of the word *tract*, in his citation of the people who are supposed to hear the poem, and in his suggestion that the poem imitates the manner of leaflets and propaganda.

Notice that in the following paper Laurie Day's interpretation of the dramatic situation differs from Cliff's in that she imagines a public occasion for the reading of the tract and doesn't see it as a leaflet. However, she agrees with Cliff that the poem imitates the manner of propaganda. Laurie also demonstrates how to describe the scene of a poem precisely and how to talk about audience.

> The dramatic situation is one man protesting against the normal way of conducting funerals. This is the significance of the title: the speaker is a man trying to convince some listeners. His manner is one of great urgency — he is very intense in his presentation; he is a kind of propagandist.
>
> "Tract" elicits an image of a small middle-class community, a place where everyone pretty much knows everyone else. At this particular moment people are gathered together listening to this world-weary old man trying to get across his disgust for flashy funerals. He feels all this polish (show, flowers, etc.) camouflages the meaning of the occasion. Everyone is more concerned with how the funeral will appear than with the person who has passed away. It appears that people are trying to cover up death. They are afraid to be faced with the possibility of their own deaths, and so wrap it up in an acceptable package, becoming more involved with the package than with its contents. The man feels everyone would be richer to share the fact of inevitable death and the mutual fear of it. He tells them that they have enough "ground sense" to understand their own mortality and having shared much of their lives together can share this as well. The people are still aware of the simple joys of life. They are down-to-earth people who are said to have "good sense," but haven't shown it in the way they conduct funerals.
>
> If I were to take a picture of this occasion, I would focus the attention on a small town, a small country church in the background, and a large oak tree casting shadows on the people. The townspeople would hide their children from the "crazy person" shouting his lungs out. Williams's poem "Tract" paints this sort of a picture in my mind.
>
> *Laurie Day*

Even though she doesn't analyze in depth the implications of the title, Laurie does catch the flavor of the speaker's voice, especially his disgust and his attempt to rip away the phoniness of funerals. She also dwells upon the important pun in "ground sense" — the townspeople already have, on the one hand, a sense of death in their knowledge of the "ground"; on the other hand, they have common sense in their down-to-earth attitudes. Funerals shouldn't fool them.

Finally, Laurie describes the photograph that she might pose to represent the dramatic situation, a description that nicely ties together her reading of the poem. Notice especially her reading of the relation between the speaker and the townspeople, who think he is a madman for such ranting. As audience, we as readers probably stand closer in attitude to the townspeople than to the angry speaker. But his rantings are persuasive, a quality Laurie grasps when she describes the shadows (of death) that she would have hanging over the townspeople in her posed photograph.

Seeing the poem as a speaking picture, then, is a good way to understand the relation between the voice in the poem and the poem's audience, whether that audience is someone addressed in the poem, as in "Tract," or the outside readers, as in "Soliloquy of the Spanish Cloister," where we overhear the monk.

# 3

# Metaphors

## 5 · WRITING IMAGES

*WRITING* Write some one-line comparisons like these:
 A promise is like a fortress constructed of cigarette papers.
 Working clay on a wheel is like building a basketball team; both have to be well centered.

1 Using the above one-liners as models, try five or six of your own that compare one thing to another.
2 Reach for connections which show that unlike things, like cigarette papers and promises, really do have something in common.
3 Perhaps items in this list will suggest comparisons to other items or to human conditions or states of being, such as hunger, anger, love, fatigue, elation, and so forth:

| book | egg | ice | swallow | tire | lightning |
| money | car | doorway | worm | leaf | stomach |
| beer | toe | liar | street | ear | toilet seat |
| grass | moon | garlic | child | wire | hangover |
| candle | liver | lover | flu | wolf | peanut butter |

4 During a day of observation, watch for objects or situations where things resemble one another: qualities that two people share, which you hadn't noticed before; how a building or scene familiar to your classmates reminds you of another thing; how a state of being, like shyness, is defined when compared to something else.

*DISCUSSION* Read your one-liners aloud in class. Focus your discussion on these questions:

1. What qualities do you see in the two compared items that you might not have noticed? (For example, we see clearly that promises are easily broken in the cigarette paper comparison above.)
2. What sense experiences do the comparisons appeal to? Do you immediately "feel" the connection between compared items, or does the mind have to admit finally a logical connection between them?

---

## COMMENTS AND EXAMPLES

Your one-liners have something in common with the most fundamental aspect of poetry: its use of imagery. Let's construct briefly a definition of this term and then begin to suggest its power in the language of student examples and, by extension, in poetry.

Images are pictures that present sense impressions to the mind. Your one-liners are one type of image. For example, Jerry Teagarden wrote this one-liner in response to exercise 5: "Evasion is a dark corner in a sunlit room." Jerry clarifies the abstract word *evasion* by presenting to the eye a familiar picture — light streaming into a room. Jerry's choice of sunlight as an image draws not only upon a familiar sense impression but also on a common association of ideas — light (the sunlit room) is good; dark (evasion or deceit) is bad. In other words, what begins as a sense impression ends up as an idea — a fresh insight into the nature of evasion and deceit. We may understand evasion and deceit as ideas before reading Jerry's image, but now we feel the idea at a sense level. Notice how a professional writer, C. S. Lewis, relies upon these impressions and associations concerning sunlight to talk about pleasures: "Pure and spontaneous pleasures are patches of Godlight in the woods of our experience."[1] Thus in poems, images present pictures to the mind, pictures that clarify abstractions or give us a fresh sense of an idea.

Images are effective because they appeal to the senses and because they talk about unfamiliar things in terms of familiar ones, which you have probably experienced. Even clichés began with someone's fresh image. For example, if you tell someone that you can't help him or her with a problem by saying, "No, I am hamstrung and can't do anything," the image compares your inability to deal with a situation to the state of the victim of a cat. Cats tear out their victims' hamstrings, the tendons at the back of the leg, thereby crippling them. The sense of helplessness embedded in the com-

---

1. *Letters to Malcolm: Chiefly on Prayer* (New York: Harcourt, Brace and World, 1964), p. 91.

parison is a good one because there are times when we all feel victimized by our helplessness, as if a predator had snapped our tendons. The first person to call a car a "lemon" suggested that the two classes, means of transportation and citrus fruit, have something in common not observed before. The image suggests that the performance of the car leaves a sour taste. There may also be a comparison to slot machines, which pay less when lemons come up than when other signs such as oranges, grapes, or cherries do. Our sense experience with sour lemons or gambling allows us to feel the truth of the comparison of cars to lemons before the mind admits that the image is appropriate.

Let's look at some more of Jerry Teagarden's one-liners that have a freshness lacking in clichés:

> Blue laws are like a cross-cut saw; they both go against the grain.
>
> Envy is like a new cabin boy; both are green and neither feels very good.
>
> The day after drinking is like Nagasaki and Hiroshima.
>
> Blowing trees at night are like nonconforming dancers.
>
> *Jerry Teagarden*

In these images which use *like* or *as* and are, therefore, called similes, Jerry has found surprising connections among seemingly unlike things. For example, the devastation of booze on the human system is made clearer in the comparison of hangovers to the effect of the atomic bomb. Or the sense that blue laws go against basic human tendencies (they are "against the grain") is captured in the comparison to cross-cut saws, which are designed to work against the most natural way of sawing wood, with the grain.

Another way of making comparisons is to drop the *like* or *as* and state the relationship as a fact:

> My wallet is a plush hiding place for poor air.
>
> *Jim Barlow*

In this image, which is called a *metaphor*, Jim suggests that while the wallet should be the source of rich, secret delights — in the way that a richly furnished room no one else knows about might be — it is really the house for the student's not-so-secret companion, poverty.

The following piece of student writing indicates another aspect of images that will be at the center of your analysis of a poem. Once it has seized upon a dramatic situation, the mind may uncover a wealth of comparisons, not just a single metaphor or simile that ends in the one-liner:

> Listen to the rhythm of the guards' walk. That arrogant Nazi click . . . click . . . click . . . click. . . . It turns into the tick of a metronome as

they swing back and forth past the cells, day in, day out, singing that same old refrain, "Here's breakfast, here's lunch, here's supper." Poor beat, poor rhythm. Maybe they'll change the time someday and get a three-legged guard. Maybe . . .

Remember the riddle of the Sphinx? What has four legs, two legs and three legs? Man. Four legs when he's a baby and crawls, two legs when he's a man and walks upright, and three legs when he's an old man and walks with a cane. An old man with a cane? Shuffle step tick, shuffle step tick, shuffle step tick, definitely is a good 3/4 time. Guards only walk in 2/4 time. Click clack, click clack.

If the Sphinx ever came, then I could answer his riddle and be king. King of my cell. Then I would order the kind of guard I wanted with a key signature written in the beat I like best. I'd throw away the signature and use the key to get out of here. I'd be free! Running in 6/8 time, or any time but not prison time! But until then my time is ordered by the staff, the prison staff, not the music staff. The parole director, not the orchestra conductor. When he brought his fist down to determine the beat, I was a dead beat. They threw the whole score at me.

When I leave here I'll be walking in 3/4 time. It's livelier than 2/4. Maybe . . . Just maybe three-legged people are more full of life than I think? Until then my time is contained behind bars, not musical time, not musical bars.

*Loran W. Wright*

Loran, a musician, is writing from the point of view of a prisoner. His mind draws connection after connection between his world of music and the prisoner's, and his images grow out of the dramatic situation. Prison is the backdrop — the walk of the guard, the rigidity of prison order, the bars, the keys, and the bureaucracy. The speaker, looking at this backdrop and recalling his former world as a musician, makes connections primarily between the sense experiences of prison and music and secondarily between the riddle of the Sphinx in *Oedipus Rex* and his own plight.

Fundamental to the system of human language then is the tendency to talk about one thing in terms of another, especially to define and clarify in terms of sense experience most of us have had. Poets take this tendency to make images, heighten it, and make it the cornerstone of the way that they compose.

## 6 · WRITING ABOUT IMAGES

*WRITING* Now go on to apply what you have discovered about images to a poem. In an analysis several paragraphs in length, emphasize how the images (metaphors and similes) grow out of or relate to the dramatic situation of the poem:

1 What is the backdrop for the poem? Who is the speaker? Who is the audience? What is the occasion?
2 What mood or frame of mind is the speaker in when he or she talks: angry, full of self-disgust, cynical, pleased?
3 What images or patterns of images are on the speaker's mind?
4 What does the speaker reveal about himself or herself by the chosen metaphors or similes?
5 What pictures are drawn or sense impressions appealed to in the metaphors and similes?

*Prewriting* In this prewriting exercise, attempt to do a systematic analysis of the poem before writing a rough draft. As suggested in chapter 1, often papers are unsuccessful because the student has not done enough preliminary work. In earlier assignments where you were analyzing only one aspect of a poem such as personification or dramatic situation, your job of prewriting wasn't as difficult as this one, where you have to look at both dramatic situation and figurative language, and then explain the relationship between the two.

As explained earlier, prewriting is mainly a way of taking systematic notes. You might even wish to set up a notebook or journal where you can jot down information about poems that you will be reading and analyzing for the rest of the assignments, or you may wish to take notes in the margin of this book. Copying the poem in your own handwriting, then taking specific notes between the lines, in the margins, or beneath it is another useful practice.

Successful prewriting begins with questions that efficiently help you discover significant details to fit the various topics that you are writing about. For this prewriting exercise use the questions listed above and also go back over the similar lists of questions concerning personification in chapter 1 and dramatic situation in chapter 2. It isn't necessary to follow mechanically the questions asked above. Tailor the questions to the poem, or devise new questions that are more suitable to the poem in front of you.

*DISCUSSION* After you have done the prewriting for this assignment, bring your notes in whatever form to class and work with those who are writing about the same poem as you are. Compare your individual readings of the poems as they appear in your prewritings. (This discussion is not intended to produce a consensus or group reading of a poem, but to give you a chance to see how other people go about the job of discovering material to write about.)

## COMMENTS AND EXAMPLES

Composing an analysis of a poem has something in common with a poet's techniques in creating images: once you have looked at your evidence carefully, you can begin to make connections between the details that you have discovered and a pattern for presenting those details in a paper. The ability to make connections is the poet's major power to define and clarify, the very heart of poetry. The heart of your analysis lies in a similar power: the ability to connect one piece of significant evidence that you have discovered to another piece or to an entire pattern in the poem. Let's look first at two examples of students' prewriting, on Brautigan's "The Pill Versus the Springhill Mine Disaster" (p. 62), to show how the discovery of connections begins.

Notice in Sandi Jesperson's prewriting that she describes her impressions of the mood of the poem:

> The mood of the speaker is rather depressed and sad. He compares taking a pill to a disaster, pointing out the sad, negative feeling inside *himself*. Talking of all people "lost inside of you" expresses his own feelings of alienation about the subject.
>
> *Sandi Jesperson*

This is a good start toward an analysis in that Sandi has described her perception of the speaker's sadness. In the next draft, she would have to provide evidence from the poem that this impression is accurate; that is, convince us she has read carefully. Look also at the way that she has a glimmer of an important insight into the poem: what's going on inside the woman. Glimmers, noted down after a close reading of the poem, have a way of becoming spotlights in later drafts that you can throw on the poem for the reader's benefit.

Vikki Nyborg's prewriting on the same poem likewise indicates the value of keeping track of glimpses that will prove valuable when you write a later draft:

> Brautigan, no longer poet, but man/husband talked to his wife and told her of the disaster of all the people lost inside her as each day she

swallowed a dynamite chip, the tiny white pill. As I read Brautigan's poem I felt an emotional stab, since occasionally I have felt a twinge of guilt because of the people I've imprisoned inside of me.

*Vikki Nyborg*

Especially important in Vikki's reading is the way she picks up the image drawn from coal mining at the center of the poem and explores it herself: the pill becomes a dynamite chip; it is as damaging as a coal mine disaster. Notice also how even in her first reaction to the poem, Vikki catches the importance of the dramatic situation, who's talking to whom and why. Finally, prewriting allows her to jot down a personal response to the poem. Such responses tend not to make their way into the final, polished drafts of a critical essay because it's hard to furnish evidence and reasoning to support them. Nevertheless, you should record personal feelings about the poem in your prewriting since they may furnish you with the basic insight that will open the poem up for later exploration.

Now let's look at an analysis to show how aspects discovered in prewriting dealing with figurative language and dramatic situation appear in a more polished draft. Look first at the final draft of Paddy Chamberlain's paper on "The Energy Chest" (p. 62).

> Michael Benedikt's poem, "The Energy Chest," has an eager, exciting tone. I assumed he used "the energy chest" as a metaphor for one's imagination, for it holds many ideas that never seem to run out. He also personifies "the energy chest" by giving it the capability to be "lively," "standing," and "looking," etc. "Even at night when we sleep," it doesn't stop; it seems to be groping about excited, to be working constantly.
>
> In the last two stanzas "We see it/Standing by the bedroom window/Looking out into the distant valley, just standing there/On tiptoe." Here the speaker invites us into the dramatic situation, as if to remind us that we too have seen this. This then elicits a picture of the chest, with its lid still open, straining to draw into itself all that it possibly can and to make it worth our while to dip in "with the hand of one's head" and come out with the best. We stand like parents who have come to peek in at night on a restless, creative child.
>
> *Paddy Chamberlain*

It's not hard to reconstruct what Paddy had to know about Benedickt's "The Energy Chest" to write this paper:

DRAMATIC SITUATION

1 Speaker who invites us as audience to examine the source of imagination.
2 A room where the chest, a piece of furniture, comes alive, almost like a child.

IMAGES

1. The mind is a treasure trove of feelings, ideas, associations, longings; that is, a chest of energy.
2. The energy chest is given human qualities; it is personified and possesses the ability not only to seek out things to fill itself with but also to motivate the hand to dip in and pull out materials for writing poems or other imaginative acts.

Paddy's paper, and the poem itself, nicely demonstrate the major point of this writing exercise: that as you take on more difficult tasks in writing about poems, you need to develop systematic ways of finding, keeping track of, and ordering insights and facts. Benedickt's poem suggests that details that stock the imagination need a storage place where you can dip in and retrieve them. Prewriting furnishes you with such a method.

# 4

# Symbols

## 7 · WRITING ABOUT PAST AND PRESENT

*WRITING* As you did in chapter 3, write some comparisons. This time do extended ones that look at the present in light of the past and that help you examine new aspects of imagery.

1 Write several paragraphs in which you compare how you are now with what you used to be: you used to be single, now married; once you were out of debt, now in debt; you used to travel, now stuck in one place. Follow this pattern: "Once I was . . . Now I am . . ."
2 How have your attitudes changed from the past to the present concerning parents, religion, a friend, sports, work, love, a book, or movie?
3 What in the past is different from the way it now looks? A room, a house, a street, a town or city?
4 Compare photographs from your past and present that show the person you used to be in contrast to the person you now are.
5 How do objects or words that have a special importance in the past contrast with what gives you a sense of identity now? Security blankets old and new? Words to songs or poems past and present?
6 Can you narrate an incident from your past that now has a present significance? That is, one that has come to stand for an attitude you have toward life or one that furnishes you with a clue to the human condition or to a major trait in your character?

*DISCUSSION* Once you have done exercise 7, read the papers aloud in class. Discuss them in light of these questions:

1 What does the past event or thing you described now stand for? (For example, are there incidents that suggest the kind of person you were before you were initiated into some new understanding?)
2 Are there traditional associations connected to the symbols in these papers? Or are the associations personal?

---

## COMMENTS AND EXAMPLES

Your comparisons of past and present have much in common with another important aspect of imagery in poetry, the symbol. After examining this term briefly, we will go on to look at some student writing on the subject.

In chapter 3, images were defined as "pictures that present sense impressions to the mind." Many images have traditional associations — the sunlight metaphors, we noted, often represent pleasurable and open aspects of life. Like some metaphors and similes, symbols often derive their power from something in the past that brings special meaning to the present. For example, if you comment on a friend's wild driving by saying that "Tom met his Waterloo Saturday night," you are calling up the past to explain the present: the Duke of Wellington's defeat of Napoleon at Waterloo in 1815 symbolizes how recklessness comes to justice. In other words, a symbol may furnish you with a specific picture of a nineteenth-century battle — at least at first — but then come to have a cluster of sense impressions around it that may not be connected with its original meaning. For example, *Waterloo* may symbolize simply defeat, not some loss that was justly deserved.

The past walks in the present in other examples of symbols. For example, we associate red with blood and badges with signs of military glory and rank, so Stephen Crane's title *The Red Badge of Courage* plays upon our association of red with blood and badges with authority and war.

A *symbol* then is an image in which an object or action stands for more than it is. In other words, a symbol implies a comparison that asks you to connect an established value or meaning to a circumstance at hand. Notice, for example, in this student writing how objects symbolize the difference between past and present:

> The woods aren't full of bears anymore. As children my friend and I were invaders. I never went alone down those endless, dreary trails. Carrying sticks we were prepared to protect ourselves against any *thing* that might jump out and get us.
>
> I seem to belong in the woods now, alone and mingling in with bush

and trees, hiding from the beasts of the city. My walks along the trails are always over too soon. I still carry a stick; only now I use it for walking and making patterns in the trails.

*Laurie Day*

Sticks in the past and present stand for different things: before, childhood fears; now, support and drawing. Animals also change in symbolic value: before, bears stood for unknown terrors; today, beasts symbolize the ugliness of human city life.

In this one, the student also focuses upon symbols from the past that help illuminate the present.

> I don't think I really ever conceived of parents as people. To me they just played a role. I had contact with one or the other or some adult figure constantly, but I never seemed to see beyond the apron and the briefcase. But now when I hear them talk, I pick up different sounds and deeper feelings in their words. Although I missed out on their youth experiences, I try now to pick up their adult ones. The apron and the briefcase no longer block out all their little games, their doubts, or their imperfections. Their self-knowledge, their well-deserved honor and place in life really aren't as clear-cut as I always believed. Like myself, they too have doubts; they too have bad forms of communication; they too don't stand on any pedestal.
>
> *Doug Bennion*

Parents are much more than apron or briefcase, as this person recognizes. However, these objects stand for the way the roles parents play may blind children for a while to the fact that parents are human. Part of growing up, this writer seems to say, is to discard certain symbols in place of more complex views.

Finally, in this example, a student presents a picture of disillusionment with religion. Mass once stood for something now lost:

> A past event that has a different significance to me now is going to church. I was raised with a moderate Catholic background and I went to Catholic school all of my life; and every Sunday I went to Mass because I was taught it was a mortal sin if I didn't. But that wasn't why I went to church when I was younger: Sunday was an event. We got up early, got all dressed up, went to Mass; and after church we'd gossip, go home, and have a big breakfast. But Mass was something special — a miracle. I was fervent as a child — Mass meant something to my existence.
>
> Now it all looks so different. Most people go to Mass because it's the proper thing to do. It's best to be seen in church by your neighbors and friends; otherwise you wouldn't be considered a good Catholic. Even the hierarchy of the church distresses me. All we hear when we go to church is money, money, money. I always felt religion was a personal thing — but now it's a monetary crisis.
>
> *Linda Adamzyck*

These student examples illustrate a major trait in human beings, our tendency to find significance in the past. Poets seize upon this trait as material for poems — they find symbols in their personal pasts or in history to comment on the present.

---

## 8 · WRITING ABOUT SYMBOLS IN POEMS

*WRITING* Now go on to write an analysis in which you compare and contrast two poems. Show how symbols from the speaker's personal past or from history comment on the present.

1 What is the dramatic situation for each poem? the speaker? the audience? the occasion?
2 In what ways are the dramatic situations alike or unlike in the two poems?
3 What frame of mind is each speaker in? What kinds of imagery does each speaker use?
4 How are the frames of mind and the imagery alike or unlike?
5 What event in the past has each speaker selected for its special meaning? How does the past become a symbol for the present?
6 In what ways do the two poems differ or are they similar in their use of the past as a symbol?

*PREWRITING* In your second prewriting exercise, discover ways to set the two poems side by side for preliminary analysis. For example, use the simple device of listing to aid your first look at the poems:

| POEM 1 | POEM 2 | LIKENESS OR UNLIKENESS |
|---|---|---|
| a. Dramatic Situation | a. Dramatic Situation | a. Speaker  Audience  Occasion |

Next, examine the problem of organizing a comparison and contrast paper, a scheme that presents more structural difficulties than you have faced so far in writing critical essays. Decide which of the two schemes given below is most appropriate for your paper.

### Scheme 1: Organization by topic

Using this scheme, you contrast and compare the two poems according to their like and unlike features in regard to a particular topic. For example, you could have one paragraph devoted to dramatic situation, one to imagery, and one to the past as symbol. Each poem would be contrasted and compared within the particular aspect and within the same paragraph.

### Scheme 2: Organization by poem

Using this scheme, you talk about all the major features of one poem. Then in the second section of the paper you develop parallel items. If you have talked about dramatic situation in the first paragraph of your section on Poem 1, for example, then in the initial paragraph of the discussion on Poem 2, focus also on dramatic situation.

*DISCUSSION* Bring your prewriting to class, and use it as the subject of a discussion on whether the questions in this exercise have been answered thoroughly.

---

# COMMENTS AND EXAMPLES

Writing these analyses requires you to use many of the same powers that you had to draw upon in exercise 7: discovering likenesses and unlikenesses in poems is similar to delving into your past to discover how you now differ from what you once were. Both exercises ask you to find significant contrasts and comparisons. And both ask you to think again in terms of images — the tendency to talk about one thing in terms of another is largely an act of setting items side by side to discover similarities and contrasts. Like metaphors and similes, symbols clarify the unknown, the present, in light of the experienced and now understood, the past.

Before we examine an example of student writing using this exercise, let's briefly look at the prewriting process as it aids the development of comparison and contrast papers. The poems "Good Times" by Lucile Clifton and James Tate's "The Lost Pilot" (pp. 63–64) make good examples. Notice especially the problem of speaker that each poem poses for the reader who is attempting to write about the symbolic value each speaker puts on his or her past. A side-by-side comparison of the poems is shown on page 28.

"GOOD TIMES"

1 Two voices: first two stanzas, a young child speaks in present tense.

2 Third, short, stanza: another voice (not a child, probably an adult) reflects on how children cherish "good times" when there aren't many in the ghetto. The good prevails in the speaker's memory, not the bad.

"THE LOST PILOT"

1 One voice: a searcher who has looked for his dead father, a pilot, addresses the dead man. The searcher is now an adult who has looked "once every year of my life" for the lost pilot.

2 The speaker himself reflects on the significance of his search and does not shift to an interpreting voice to understand what has happened.

LIKENESS OR UNLIKENESS

Likeness: Both speakers deal with symbolic painful experiences in the past and show how memory of the past affects the speaker's present outlook on life.

Unlikeness: One poet shifts speakers in order to interpret the experience as well as present it from the child's viewpoint. The other stays in the same adult voice and interprets as he goes.

Now let's look at an example of a student essay in which the writer had to come to terms with the problems of organizing a comparison and contrast essay. Karen Anderson wrote about the two poems by William Childress, "Lobo" and "Hunting the Trolls" (pp. 64–65). She chose to organize her paper by topic and to contrast and compare the two poems within the same paragraphs.

> There are several similarities between William Childress's two poems, "Lobo" and "Hunting the Trolls"; two of them lie in the perspective from which the poems are written and the symbols which they use.
>
> In both poems, the speaker is an adult, perhaps middle-aged, who is reviewing his childhood and recognizing the significance of certain events. He gazes on the past with wiser eyes, comprehending things which no child would understand. In "Lobo," for instance, Childress attaches new meaning to the raids of a wolf pack on Kansas farm country during his sixteenth winter; he sees something in the mysterious, savage, grey wolves which resembles an attitude in life that he is formulating. In "Hunting the Trolls" he recognizes that as a child (although he did not know it then) he was engaged in a search for his own nature; as an adult, he realizes that the fear of and attraction for trolls conceals similar fears and attraction for the speaker's qualities. It is the search which is symbolized by the hunting references in both poems.
>
> In both, the speaker is involved in an unending, irreversible hunt. There is a sense that he cannot stop or retrace his steps; in "Lobo," he says, "I had known/the family cave too long; I could/not stay"; and in "Hunting the Trolls," "Years closed behind me like latches." Both passages suggest that the boy knows he must leave — he is hunting for what he will become. Part of any search is a search for self.
>
> There is too a feeling of foreboding as he looks toward the end of the search, and a sense of despair at what he finally discovers. In "Lobo," Childress seems to be entering a hunt with no other purpose than to "kill" and "eat," his savagery his only goal. In "Hunting the Trolls" he seems to have come to the end of his quest: "and finally I walked on naked bone,/leaving behind in my hoofed tracks/only a dark unholy image/for the morning sun/to cower from." The speaker now realizes that he was as savage as the creatures he was hunting, for he left Billy Goat Gruff footprints as he left the bridge.
>
> Sometimes childhood activities, Childress seems to say, become symbols later on of the speaker's adult bleakness and despair, conditions foreshadowed in "Lobo" and realized in "Hunting the Trolls."

What Karen has nicely demonstrated in this paper is that the search of the poet's own past may be a way for him or her to come to terms with self. The past has a way of surprising us with meaning.

# 5

# Theme

## 9 · WRITING MEMORABLE SAYINGS

*WRITING* Looking back over your life, find several proverbs, sayings, lines from songs or poems, and other quotations that capture a period or mood at some stage of your life. Find short sayings that indicate and summarize a person you have been at some time in the past:

> When the going gets rough, the rough get going.
>
> If bullshit was music, he'd be a whole brass band.
>
> Birds of a feather flock together.

1 Collect several statements like these, number them, and list them on one side of a sheet of paper.
2 On the second side, comment briefly on the people or places where you encountered these statements. Also comment briefly on the dramatic situation in which they appeared. (For instance, John Cox said that "the rough get going" slogan was on the locker room wall of his high school. It represented two years of slogans and hard work under a tyrannous coach. Doug Bennion said that the "brass band" proverb was a favorite of his grandfather and was applied to whoever talked too much.)

*DISCUSSION* Bring the collections to class for reading and discussion. Focus your attention on these questions and activities:

1 Is it possible to guess the dramatic situation and speaker of the statement

even before the writer presents his or her comment on it? (For instance, does the proverb about "birds of a feather" sound like parents' advice to children, especially children of a certain age?)
2 Is it possible to group the statements into units of similar or contrasting ideas? For example, are there other slogans about winning? Or are there, for instance, contradictory statements from parents about appearances — "You are what you wear" versus "All that glitters is not gold"?
3 On the basis of your collections and discussion, put together and ditto for the class a small dictionary of proverbs organized around common ideas like habits, appearances, winning, or talking too much, or around common speakers like coaches, song writers, or parents.

---

## COMMENTS AND EXAMPLES

Even though poets often incorporate sayings into their poems, the main intention of this exercise is not to help you spot proverbs or quotations that poets use as material. Rather its purpose is to show that it is possible to put into a few memorable words a major idea, in fact an idea that may govern or at least summarize a major period of your life. This major idea in a poem is called the *theme*.

Poets thus capture, just as sayings do, a theme that serves as a basic insight into life. Often the poem makes an observation that everyone already knows but does it in such a handsome and complex way that we experience the common insight as if it were just thought of. For example, J. R. R. Tolkien, author of *The Hobbit* and *The Lord of the Rings*, says in *Beowulf: The Monsters and the Critics* that *Beowulf* has been mistreated by critics who find too many profound ideas in a poem built on one simple theme: life is transitory and all good things pass. Tolkien then goes on to point out how the Beowulf poet brings this observation to life in one of the freshest, most vigorous epics ever written: while Beowulf is young and strong, he is invincible; when old, he is vulnerable — his strength as well as his companions desert him.[1]

Just as you have shown in your collection of proverbs how we tend to distill our observations about life into short, memorable sayings, so poets tend to build their poems around their perceptions of life. These perceptions may not necessarily be conscious ideas that writers are dealing with. But the theme may be the reader's summary of a writer's work. For example, in the course I teach on Chaucer, I

1. (London: The British Academy, 1958), pp. 5–12.

often tell students that to me Chaucer says over and over again in highly complex and varied ways, "Human beings are self-deceptive. By kidding themselves, people bring on their own punishments: they are either laughed at by those they want to impress, or else their self-deceptions lead them to an even worse fate, death." This is, of course, a common insight and did not begin or end with Chaucer. Notice, for example, how the proverb "what a tangled web we weave when first we practice to deceive," originated by Sir Walter Scott, captures the same idea. But that proverb about weaving webs of deception, memorable and poetic as it may be, can't give us the complex view of human self-deception that *The Pardoner's Tale* or *The Miller's Tale* can.

One of the traits of the human mind then is to collect its thoughts into brief, memorable sayings. These comments serve as themes about life. Our minds display a similar trait when we distill poems into the various statements that they make about life. Look, for instance, at this poem by Todd Davis Jefferson for the way that he collects clichés about cows to make fun of political stereotyping.

# Cows!

### —*Todd Davis Jefferson*

It's a bag of chemicals poured into gray spongy tissues with all manner of nerve endings, blood vessels, & other sophisticated decoys to its real function. What it really does is cover this inflated piece of wet popcorn called the brain. Now what I propose is we admit that what we see on the big movie screen around us is precisely what's advertised on the marquee, & go on munching our popcorn contentedly. I've seen cows grinding their jaws, enjoying the main feature, & it appears to work.

1
Cows don't dig up fossils.
Cows never fix beef stew.
Cows have never been known to handle an M–1.
Cows are cows & proud of it,
in their own human way.
Cows, so far as we know,
have no psychoanalysts.
On the other hand, cows never write poetry.

(If cows could write, they would write poetry.)
Between no war or no poetry,
I choose no war.

2
It's a known fact that cows
are communist revolutionaries,
living & working silently among us.
They have infiltrated our entire population.
There are guerilla outposts of cows scattered
all over America's countryside. They appear to be
good workers, but they are slowly gaining control of
respectable organizations like the National Dairy Asso-
    ciation.
Cows could bring this country to its knees with a na-
    tional strike.
All cows should be registered.
Homosexual cows should be segregated.
Cow breeds should not be allowed to mix.
Children should be taught not to fraternize with cows.
I suggest we throw up a tactical nuclear ring around
all known cow gatherings of more than fifty cows.

3
I'm lying under this tree
which appears to be upside down from where I lie.
You've got to understand it is not, in fact, upside
    down.
It only appears so.
I'm waiting for the cows to come home.
They generally walk under this tree.
They'll probably stomp the shit out of me.
Though I have been told, "A decent cow will walk
    around you."
But who's to say whether that cow brain sees itself
as decent, and thus obligated. A great bovine
    philosopher
once said, "Go, mingle among cows, learn their ways.
    History
is made in the pasture, not the mind."

The theme of Jefferson's poem is that it's as silly to stereotype cows as it is to stereotype people. He uses a collection of clichés to attack clichéd thinking.

## 10 · WRITING ABOUT THEMES IN POEMS

*PREWRITING* Now that you have looked at your own collection of memorable sayings and have had a chance to think about theme, write a long paper comparing and contrasting the themes of two poems.

Pick one poem that has a woman speaker and one that has a man. Examine them first in light of what you know now about theme, and second in light of the other aspects of poetry that you have been writing about — images (personification, simile, metaphor, and symbol) and dramatic situation (speaker, audience, and occasion). Do systematic prewriting that thoroughly compares and contrasts the two poems. (Find a way of setting the poems and notes side by side as the first step of analysis.) Attempt to answer most of the following questions in note form before you sit down to do a rough draft:

1. Who is the speaker in each poem? Who is the audience? What is the occasion? What are the speaker's major ideas or attitudes toward life?
2. What is the basic pattern of imagery in each poem? How does the speaker's attitude shape that basic pattern? In other words, how does the imagery grow out of the dramatic situation? (For example, a wronged woman may compare her angry reaction to a volcano erupting. Or a man may compare a friend's view of his mind to a tidy roomful of furniture.)
3. Is the central idea or theme of the poem contained in the speaker's ideas and attitudes? Or is the theme quite different from the speaker's view of things? (For example, if a male speaker rages around and blames women for being self-deceived and helpless, the theme of the poem may be that some men project flaws onto women that the men themselves possess.)

*DISCUSSION* Bring your prewriting to class and discuss your readings of the poems with people who are writing about the same ones.

Then bring in rough drafts of your papers and give special attention to the organization of a comparison and contrast paper. (Review the Prewriting section of exercise 8 in chapter 4, where this is treated in some detail.)

1. Does the writer present a clear picture of the dramatic situation of the poem in the rough draft?
2. Is the paper organized so that the reader can view comparable or contrasting features of the two poems? Or does the organization interfere with this clear picture?
3. Which basic scheme does the writer follow: one separate section of the paper devoted to each poem? Or are the two poems set side by side

and discussed topic by topic? Should the writer find another organizational choice for his or her final draft?

## COMMENTS AND EXAMPLES

In writing about themes, you are facing new composition problems. Let's look at a couple of cases in point, two student papers that solved quite differently the problems facing writers in exercise 10, and that examine the poems "No More Soft Talk" and "If, My Darling" (pp. 67–69).

In the first instance, Linda Adamczyk attempted a rough draft without systematic prewriting. As she cheerfully admitted, the first draft was a disaster: no focus on a major idea, little sense that she had understood the complex dramatic situation of the poem, details scattered about in the paper but without relation to the paper's other parts, and a mixture of emotional reactions and interpretation.

> ("No More Soft Talk," by Diane Wakoski is an interesting poem because so many other women can relate to it.)
> 
> The speaker could possibly be a woman in her early twenties who has been terribly hurt by the man she loves. She compares her man to a brittle rock — most of the time you think of rocks as being strong — (?) But what purpose does a rock fulfill? Not a very useful one, it's just there. She labels herself as a rock "The hard rock. You can't break me." That line sets the mood for what is to follow. Without reading further I can sense that she is bitter, and that she isn't going to be very flexible in her attitude.
> 
> Then she changes her mind, sits down to cry on my shoulder — "I am trying to think how a woman/can be a rock,/when all she wants is to be soft,/to melt to the lines/her man draws for her." This tells me that she fell head over heels for some guy, maybe a first love, gave him everything he wanted, because making him happy made her happy. She is asking — "Is there anything wrong with that?" She was content being what he wanted her to be.
> 
> Then she reaches the explosion — the shock to her brain that affects her whole being. ". . . like an explosion/of flowers and blood,/staining the inside/of the skull?"
> 
> Diane Wakoski has a very unique way of expressing emotions! (It leaves an impression of pain.) It almost makes me want to grasp my head in pain.
> 
> If anyone has ever been hurt by someone they have given their all for, they can see the good with the bad, the flowers with the blood — but the blood does stain badly and it tends to make the good things look not so significant, like so what — the bad outweighs the good.
> 
> *Linda Adamzyck*

This draft doesn't indicate that the paper is going to compare Wakoski's "No More Soft Talk" with Phillip Larkin's "If, My Darling." Hence we know neither the real subject nor any of the focuses of the paper in the first six paragraphs. "No More Soft Talk" has a difficult dramatic situation that Linda hadn't solved before she tried to write. At one point, she thinks the speaker is talking to us rather than to the man she is in conversation with. The passage in question ("I am trying to think") is quite clearly in the man's voice. There are some details in this draft, but their significance isn't made clear to the reader. She says, for example, that the lines "The hard rock./ You can't break me." establish the mood for what is to follow. But she is never clear about what that mood is. Finally, the paper has a mixture of emotional reactions and interpretations inappropriate to the purpose of the essay.

Linda agreed to abandon that start, to begin again with prewriting and build a new paper. She set the two poems side by side and came up with these notes:

| WAKOSKI, "NO MORE SOFT TALK" | LARKIN, "IF, MY DARLING" |
|---|---|
| The speaker is a woman. She is, at first, speaking to a man who within the poem carries on a small conversation with her (for the first third of the poem). Then the man is silent as she talks about her hurt. The motivation is stated in the poem — she has caught her husband sleeping with another woman and her trust has been betrayed — hurt by the man she loves, tone is one of flexibility — source of the rock figures of speech. | The speaker is a man. The audience isn't quite as obvious as in Wakoski's poem. At first it sounds as if he could be talking to another man — a friend he confides in, but then possibly the audience is himself — more of a self-realization process. He has been "hurt" also but in a different way — his tone is one of open me up — look at me for what I am — I'm not really what you think I am or appear to be — he wants her — his darling — to know that he is a complex individual. So possibly what motivates him is his ego — or pride in self after realizing these things himself he decided it really isn't worth repeating to her, because it might knock her off her "unpriceable pivot." Key to other furniture figures of speech. |

Notice that in this prewriting there is already the nucleus of a solid essay. In addition to understanding the dramatic situations clearly, Linda has begun to think comparatively. Her remarks about "If, My Darling" parallel those about "No More Soft Talk": who speaks, who listens, the common feature of pain, possible motivations for the speakers, and the imagery that grows out of the dramatic situation.

Linda wrote this successful final draft largely because of her ability to do systematic prewriting, the missing step in her first attempt.

> Diane Wakoski's poem "No More Soft Talk" and Philip Larkin's poem "If, My Darling" are two examples of two different people's reactions to being hurt by a member of the opposite sex.
>
> In "No More Soft Talk" the speaker is a woman. In the first part of the poem she is speaking to one man. He asks her questions about her predicament, and that brings out her whole story. The speaker just wants to retell the situation (with all of its vivid and emotional imagery) to anyone who will listen. Her trust was betrayed by the man she loves, and her tone appears to be one of inflexibility while speaking. As she goes into her long monologue, she could be talking to all men, not just the friend she is confiding in. She is toughly realistic with him: This is what happened, and this is how it's going to be if this friend or any man happens to fall in love with her:
>
>> My rock doesn't crumble.
>> My rock is the mountain.
>> Love me
>> if you can.
>> I will not make it easy for you
>> anymore.
>
> In Philip Larkin's poem "If, My Darling," the speaker is a man. The audience isn't quite as obvious as in Diane Wakowski's poem. On first reading the poem, it sounds as if the audience could be another man, a friend that the speaker confides in; but after reading the poem over so many times, I have decided that the audience is himself — more of a self-realization process.
>
> Just like the speaker in Wakowski's poem, he too has been hurt but in a different way; his tone expresses the hurt he feels, but he tries to cover it up (his male pride shines through anyway!). He is saying to himself but wishing his darling could hear — "Open me up; look inside me for what I am; I'm not really what you think I am or appear to be." He wants his darling to see that he is a complex individual. He then decides that what he has come to understand about himself isn't worth repeating to the woman because it "Might knock my darling off her unpriceable pivot."
>
> Distinct patterns of figurative language help each speaker explain his or her hurt in the two poems. For example, in Wakowski's poem the most striking image is what takes place when she finds her husband in bed with another woman; she has the equivalent of a stroke: ". . . like an explosion/of flowers and blood,/staining the inside/of the skull?" It is a difficult image to explain — the flowers with the blood is like the good with the bad; but the blood stains so badly that it tends to

outweigh the good. All the good memories they shared are blotted out.

She then compares her experience to a volcanic eruption:

> What comes up,
> like gall in my throat,
> a river of abandoned tonsils that can no longer cry,
> a sea of gold wedding rings and smashed glasses,

She also explains her metamorphosis as a woman in terms of the volcano, this shock of new recognition. The eruption is "the lava, the crushed and melted rock/. . . now . . . bubbling out of the lips of a mountain." After trusting her husband, and being betrayed in the explosion, she could, like obsidian lava, quickly harden. But she says, "This lava,/hot and soft,/will cool someday,/and turn back into the various stones." She means it will take time to trust a man again. Her husband caused the eruption of the molten mass of pain inside of her, but the mountain (herself) will still be the same underneath the "various" colored stones.

Larkin's imagery also relates well to the dramatic situation. He wants his darling to be able to see inside his head so he draws two pictures. The first one is of a cozy, tidy room in his head that she could expect but not find:

> She would find no tables and chairs,
> No mahogany claw-footed sideboards,
> No undisturbed embers;

She expects the neat and tidy, but he wants her to see that he is disordered, complex and that his thoughts are jumbled. Instead of "small-printed books for the Sabbath" she could find a room suitable for a horror film: "A Grecian statue kicked in the privates, money,/a swill-tub of finer feelings . . ." He is truly complex, and not the picture of a programmed gentleman.

Both poems say that man and woman want to be seen for what they are or, in Wakoski's case, what the speaker has become.

There are a number of features of Linda's paper that are worth noting. In chapter 4, you looked at the alternative ways of organizing a contrast and comparison paper. From the disaster draft to this revised paper, Linda shifted from one choice to another. Her purposes are best served in the final draft where she discusses first the dramatic situation of each poem before going on to a new topic. The reader can see the comparable and contrasting aspects of the poems more clearly through this structural choice than through one where in the first section she attempted to talk about one poem, then in the second section discussed the other. Notice also that Linda arrives at a statement of theme in the last sentence of her paper as if it's a sum, a total of the parts discussed above.

As another example of contrast and comparison papers, examine this one by Judy Balcom. Unlike Linda, Judy chooses to discuss first one poem in its entirety, then goes on to the second. Judy's paper is successful in that she briefly and effectively reminds the reader what she has said about Wakoski earlier in the paper when she later talks about Larkin. Judy also makes her statements about the theme of each poem in the introduction. These statements act as hypotheses, tentative judgments, which she proves to be true in the rest of the essay.

This is Judy's paper:

> Diane Wakoski, in her poem "No More Soft Talk," contends that woman is not the weaker sex but is much more substantial than man. She says that her man *is* a rock, but only "a very brittle rock . . . one that crumbles easily," while she is "the hard rock" — the one that can't be broken but can be transformed. The man she is speaking to has stereotyped women as soft rocks: "I am trying to think how a woman/can be a rock,/when all she wants is to be soft,/to melt to the lines/her man draws for her." The woman speaker goes on to refute this idea and this figure of speech. She tells of an explosion in her brain coming from shock — of the flowers and blood spewing forth and the stains that reality leaves on her mind. This explosion was preceded by a tremor when the speaker went to her house and found the door locked, the bedroom door closed, and a woman's handbag on the couch. She explains how her transformation changed her into a better kind of rock because of the shock, the volcano in her mind. A disaster occurs just as in natural disasters: the ocean is "a sea of gold wedding rings and smashed glasses." But out of the disaster comes a tougher person. She was vulnerable when she was soft, and now the "lava, the crushed and melted rock" that was once her belief in her man have hardened into a substance she calls a mountain, and this mountain is more formidable than her previous self and she will not be so easy to love, for now she is the "hard rock."
>
> In Philip Larkin's poem, "If, My Darling," the speaker takes a view opposite to that of Diane Wakoski's speaker. In this poem it is the man who is the more substantial, and he must guard women against seeing what he and the world are really like. He says that "if my darling were to . . . not stop at my eyes," that is, not take him strictly at face value, but were to really get into his mind, she would not find a comfortable abode, but a dwelling seething with activity. "No undisturbed embers" but a roaring fire.
>
> Everything is not at peace in his mind, and he is quite different in reality from what he appears to her in his superficiality. What she would find would be various intensities of thought ("varying light") and dreams that have been exaggerated and stifled — "Delusions that shrink to the size of a woman's glove/Then sicken inclusively outwards." The floor the speaker talks of is what supports all these unappetizing descriptions of his mind, and this is the basis of his inner self. It is filthy and vile with no seeming regard for "art" or order.

Such "finer feelings" are cast aside in a "swill-tub," or refuse bucket, to be fed to the hogs.

Just as Wakoski's speaker had a shock, so the woman in Larkin's poem would suffer if she could really see inside him, but the jolt would be too much for her to handle: it would knock her off "her unpriceable pivot," her expensive, safe piece of furniture.

In both of these poems the discussion tends towards who is the stronger, the man or the woman (at least as concerns the two relationships). The speaker in Diane Wakoski's poem feels that the woman has the upper hand in that she can harden if need be to get what she wants, while the speaker in Philip Larkin's poem feels that women are too frail to really be able to cope with the world and that this chore should be left for men.

Since each writing assignment has asked you to juggle more and more terms and to attempt more difficult organizational schemes, you can see the need for the text's emphasis on prewriting. This is especially true in discussing the theme of a poem which may not be at all clear until you have looked at and lived with the poem's individual parts for a while. The central idea, in other words, may not appear until you have discovered the principles that govern the poem's dramatic situation and imagery.

# 6

# Sound: Rhythm and Rhyme

## 11 · WRITING ABOUT RHYTHM, PAST AND PRESENT

*WRITING* Describe in a paragraph a rhythm, ritual, or pulse that has organized your life. Think, for example, about daily, weekly, seasonal, or annual events that have repeated themselves. They can be pleasant or unpleasant experiences.

1 What habits, trends, arguments, traditions, illnesses, longings, frustrations, or satisfactions form rituals or rhythms in your life?
2 Can you contrast a family ritual when you were young with one now that you are grown — such as a meal or holiday?
3 To stimulate ideas of your own look, for instance, at these three pieces of student writing: one about meeting old friends, another about falling in love, and a third about the ritual of going to school.

> I see my best friend from high school about three or four times a year. On these occasions we attack each other at first sight, usually ending up on the ground laughing and exhausted. Before we catch our breath, we begin knocking down the beers, smoking the reefers, and making the plans for getting as messed up as possible. As the night progresses we talk of old times, of present times, and of how horny we are, but there really isn't much effort made to incorporate women into the festival and the party is always stag.
> 
> *John Hymas*

> I have yet to begin and end a relationship that is not either bitter or regretful. I tell myself over and over again, day in and day out, that I will

not fall in love. But do with the stranger in the library and the guy down the hall. Falling in and out of love has become a completely repetitous, inescapable ritual in my life.

*Paddy Chamberlain*

When the first day of school came around I had been preparing for it by buying three-ring binders, new crayons, a ruler, pencils and a Bonanza lunch pail. Hoss's thermos never failed to fall out the first week and break. I would cautiously shake it to hear the broken glass and milk inside. Its sound told me that my lunch pail would smell sour for a long time after and remind me of the lecture I would catch when I got home.

There was also a very special costume that went with this September ritual. It included a crisp new dress, new saddle shoes, white socks and rain gear. This outfit hung ready-to-go in my room. Everything laid out neatly, it usually took me three minutes to be ready for school on those first days. With time to kill I'd watch cartoons where Humbert, the clown, would tell me it's my first day at school for the year so I better watch out for cars when crossing the street.

Years later my old lunch pail had rusted, and I didn't drink milk. The teacher I idolized was now an old bag and school was a drag.

*Laurie Day*

DISCUSSION Bring your writings to class. Discuss them in light of these questions:

1 What organizes each person's experience into rhythm or ritual? Is the repeating pattern largely one of time? Is it the people involved? Is it the place where the ritual occurs?
2 What adds variety to the ritual? Does it happen at various times of the year and thus change? Or does it change its nature from year to year? (For example, if falling in love is one of your habits, what are the variety of ways and times it has happened?)
3 Within the writing itself what evidence is there of repetition and variety of language?
   a For example, is a phrase like "falling in love" balanced by "falling out of love"?
   b Or is there a noticeable attempt by the writer to add a rhythm to the repeated words? (For example, are there any sentences that have this kind of swing and variation — "We begin knocking down the beers, smoking the reefers, and making the plans"? In this instance, the writer has slightly distorted a normal word order to achieve his effect, but such distortion fits his comic purpose.)
   c Are there words bouncing off each other in some kind of repetition and variety? (Where milk and glass in a broken thermos are contrasted with the clause "years later . . . I didn't drink milk," for instance? Or where there are word plays such as the older student's rhyming, flip comment that the teacher "was a bag and school was a drag"?

## COMMENTS AND EXAMPLES

So far you have been writing about rhythm in a larger sense: the repeating beats, pulses, or accents that organize your experience.

And before we go on to see how rhythm in a narrower sense works in poetry, let's examine a piece of student writing that not only illustrates the pulses that order our lives, but also furnishes us a bridge to a discussion of the sound devices — rhythm and word play — that are found in poetry:

> With the arrival of December cold and my depression, I drain my motorcycle of gas and oil and callously yank out its battery. With a few mutters, curses, and disparaging remarks about how I should have sold it last summer, I abandon it to months of silence, smothered with a dirty tarp in an unfriendly garage.
>
> When March rolls around, driving out winter's chill and my bad temper, I replace my bike's life blood, tenderly insert a battery, and free it of its shroud. Then I sing the praises of this two-wheeled wonder that I had denounced as the scourge of my existence a few months before.
>
> *Eric Magnuson*

Eric's paper nicely illustrates the patterns that organize life into rhythms and rituals and that in their repetition and variety give us a sense of order. The change in seasons organizes this piece of writing — the way human attitudes are shaped by the time of year. Motorcycles are a nuisance in December, a joy in March. Contrast, then, as an organizational scheme provides the frame for other patterns of repeating and varying.

Notice, for example, that each paragraph opens with an introductory phrase or clause and that each phrase or clause mentions the time of year (December and March), the arrival or departure of winter's cold, and the speaker's corresponding moods. There are other examples as well of Eric's attempts to repeat and vary language patterns so the reader will have an easier time glancing from the way Eric sees winter to the way he views spring. He mutters, curses, and disparages the bike in December; in March, he sings its praises. The bike's gas is plainly that in December; in March, the machine has become almost human since it needs not gas, but "life blood." In the same way, the tender replacing of the battery in the spring makes the bike seem warm and human whereas the callous yanking out of it in December reminds you that the bike is a troublesome machine. Eric's brief paper, in other words, has rhythm since it repeats and varies its movement. When well done, in prose and especially in poetry, repeating and varying serve to emphasize important ideas or provide keys to ideas or things the writer wishes to contrast and compare.

# RHYTHM

Before we go further, then, in our study of poetry, it is necessary to be furnished with a technical vocabulary. After studying this section, you will be able to identify the types of sound devices in poems and to connect these discoveries with other aspects of poetry.

As you have seen in exercise 11, rhythm orders experience, and in poetry, it organizes language into regular beats where the repetition and variation in the pulse emphasize ideas and provide keys to meaning. But rhythm is not a decoration poets add to intensify meaning. Rather it is an element as integral to poetry as music is to dancing. The cadences of a poem must be shaped to its meaning. There must be a fitness of rhythm to idea.

In English poetry, the best known rhythm is discussed in terms of *meter*. That is, there are measured pulses that organize the language. These meters define the length of a line of poetry by describing how many beats are in it. They also define what kind of measures are in the line. For example, the best known meter in English poetry is *iambic pentameter*, a line with five beats. *Pentameter* is derived from the Greek word meaning "five units of measurement." In English poetry those units are called *feet*. *Iambs*, the other term in iambic pentameter, refers to a type of foot where there is a light beat on one syllable followed by a heavy one on the next. For example, "In thére!" as an exclamation illustrates how one iambic foot would look: a lightly emphasized syllable, which the u-shaped mark indicates. The angled line indicates a syllable with a heavier emphasis.

When you examine a poem whose rhythm is regularly metrical, you first count the number of syllables per line. Then you need to discern what kinds of feet those syllables are. Prince Hal in Shakespeare's *Henry IV, Part One* talks about some friends who have just left him alone on stage:

> I know you all, and will awhile uphold
> The unyoked humor of your idleness.

You find that each line has ten syllables. Then you notice in the first line that the dominant beat is one of a light, followed by a heavy accent:

> Ĭ knów / yŏu all, / aňd wíll / ăwhíle / ŭphóld

POETRY

This is easy to recognize as an iambic pentameter line where the accented syllables carry most of the weight of the line's meaning. The succeeding line also has ten syllables, but it does not work out as neatly in iambic feet:

The ún / yoḱed / humŏr / ŏf yoúr í / dlĕnéss.

If, for example, you scan the line this way, you find variations from the pattern established in the first line. These variations do not upset the basic meter of the poem, for as we have seen in exercise 11, rhythm is largely a matter of establishing a pattern then varying it for interest. In other words, an interesting tension arises from the discrepancy between the basic pattern and the deviation.

In English poetry, different kinds of feet can be substituted for the regular one to introduce variety. This line from *Henry IV, Part One* has three variations: 1) the second foot has only one syllable, an accented one; 2) the third foot has a *trochaic foot,* that is, an accented followed by an unaccented one; 3) the fourth foot has another substituted foot, this time a *dactyl,* two unaccented followed by an accented foot. To discern the meter of a poem, you determine the basic beat, then you notice how the writer achieves variety either to capture the conversational qualities of the speaker or to suggest the speaker's mood at the moment. In this speech by Prince Hal, for example, we hear him speak in verse for the first time in the play, since in the previous scene he has talked in prose, the low, joking language of his companions in the tavern. But now Hal takes a slow, reasonable look at himself in an appropriately dignified rhythm. This indicates Hal's nature and mood: he's merely waiting for a chance to shine and prove that he's not been tainted by his idle companions.

Even though the iambic foot is the one most frequently encountered in English and the one that dominates the poetry of major poets from Chaucer to Shakespeare to Pope to Wordsworth to Tennyson to Eliot and Frost, you should be able to identify the others. A convenient way to look at them is to examine Samuel Taylor Coleridge's little poem in which he demonstrates the major English feet:

Trochĕe / trips frŏm / long tŏ / short.

Frŏm long / tŏ long / iṅ sol / ĕṁn sort

Slow Spon / dee stalks; / strong foot! / yet ill / able

Evĕr tŏ / come ŭp with / Dactyl trĭ / syllablĕ.

Iamb / ics march / from short / tŏ long; —

With ă leap / and ă bound / the swift An / ăpĕsts throng.

SOUND: RHYTHM AND RHYME   45

You should also be able to identify the other types of lines besides pentameter:

|  |  |
|---|---|
| monometer: | one foot |
| dimeter: | two feet |
| trimeter: | three feet |
| tetrameter: | four feet |
| pentameter: | five feet |
| hexameter: | six feet |
| heptameter: | seven feet |

There are two other major types of rhythm in English poetry that you should be able to recognize. The first, *stressed verse,* has a more ancient claim as the basic English rhythmic pattern than does metered verse, for Anglo-Saxon and Middle English poets composed in stressed verse before Chaucer popularized meter in the fourteenth century.

Rather than being organized by feet, stressed lines have a set number of emphasized syllables per line; but these stresses can fall anywhere in the line and don't need to be separated by unaccented syllables. For example, three lines from the beginning of *Piers Plowman* look like this:

> A fair fiéld full of fólk   foúnd I there betwéen
> Of all mánner of mén,   the méan and the rích,
> Wórking and wándering   as the wórld ásks.

Notice that each line is divided to show the half-line pauses and that each half-line has two stresses. In stressed verse, the number of syllables per line is not constant; only the number of stresses per line is uniform. Stressed verse is most suitable for lofty, dignified topics. It is often the form of heroic poems, as in *Beowulf* and *Sir Gawain and the Green Knight,* although modern poets such as Hopkins or Roethke sometimes employ stressed verse. For them it has some of the conversational quality and ease of metered verse.

*Free verse,* as the name implies, has no regular metrical or stress pattern, yet it does have a rhythm corresponding to the speaker's emotion. For example, when we are angry or crying our individual words and groups of breaths tend to form a pattern shaped by the emotion. Free verse writers attempt to capture a particular speaker in a certain emotional mood. The poem "Tract," by William Carlos Williams, discussed in chapter 2, illustrates this point. In the third stanza, the angry speaker says:

> Knock the glass out!
> My God — glass, my townspeople!
> For what purpose? Is it for the dead

>     to look out or for us to see
>     how well he is housed or to see
>     the flowers or the lack of them —
>     or what?

This passage defies rhythmic analysis either as a stressed or metrical poem. What the poem does have, however, is variety and repetition used by a haranguing, sarcastic speaker, one who wants to reform his townspeople by ridiculing them. The repetition of the word *glass* in the first two lines, for instance, gives emphasis to the idea that it is silly to care about appearance at a funeral. Even though *glass* appears as the third syllable in each of the first two lines, it has special emphasis in the second since it follows the exclamation "My God." In the same way, the simple verbs *look, see,* and *see* in the long question in this stanza are placed in emphatic positions — two at the ends of succeeding lines. These verbs help us focus on the speaker's sarcastic point — since the dead can't witness their own funerals, funerals must be conducted for show. In addition, the repetition of the question "what" in lines three and seven gives a sense of the speaker's mood of exasperated anger. The repeating and varying of the mood and concepts allow Williams to give a sense of the speaker's excited, sarcastic state. In this sense, the free verse rhythms, repetitious though not regular, do contribute greatly to the impact of the poem.

Sound devices, like rhythm, make for variety as well as repetition in a poem. They serve especially to organize words so that the reader or listener attaches importance to the ideas developed in the word play. For example, the rhymes in Browning's "Soliloquy of the Spanish Cloister" (p. 58) indicate the speaker's self-righteousness, self-deception, and hypocrisy, since the words that end his lines almost invariably call attention to the speaker's pretended piety while he criticizes Brother Lawrence:

>     When he finishes refection
>     Knife and fork he never lays
>     Cross-wise, to my recollection,
>     As I do, in Jesu's praise.

The speaker's piety is all show — he makes a cross of his knife and fork to show his piety after a meal; *lays* and *praise* work well as rhymes to connect ideas that reveal the speaker's real pettiness under his proclaimed holiness.

Briefly, the other major kinds of sound device — alliteration, assonance, and internal rhyme — also establish connections between important ideas being developed by the speaker. *Alliteration* is the repetition of an initial consonant sound; *assonance* repeats a vowel;

*internal rhyme* repeats a word's sound in the same line for emphasis — if *lays* and *praise* were to appear in the same line, for example, we could call that internal rhyme.

Alliteration is so native and vital to English poetry that in the instance cited above from *Piers Plowman,* it's easy to see how the device functions to link the important ideas: "Of all manner of men, the mean and the rich . . ." Three of the four stressed words in the line alliterate since they begin with the consonant *m*. The idea in the stanza of the great scope of people at work in the fair field gets its emphasis through the clustering of *m* sounds at the beginning of three of the most important words in the line.

## 12 · WRITING ABOUT SOUND IN POETRY

*WRITING* Write a paper in which you show how rhythms and rhymes support or emphasize what the writer is trying to say. That is, show how rhythm and rhyme contribute to the dramatic situation, imagery, or theme of the poem that you wish to discuss. Before you begin, use this set of questions as a basis for your prewriting.

*Prewriting* Some questions to aid your preliminary thinking:

1 Which type of rhythm does the poem have?
    a If metrical, what is the dominant pattern of accents — iambic, trochaic, or another one? And how many feet per line — four, five, six? How does the poet vary the basic metrical pattern and for what effect?
    b If stressed verse, how many stresses per line? Does the poet use a sound device like alliteration to call attention to the stressed words?
    c If free verse, what are repetitions and variations that replace a regular rhythm? How is the speaker's mood reflected in the movement of the verse?
2 What sound devices — rhyme, alliteration, or assonance — does the poet use? Identify the types.
3 Identify the other major features of poetry in the poem: dramatic situation, pattern of images, and theme.
4 Finally, in what way do the rhythmic and sound devices contribute to the other major aspects of the poem? For instance, how is the speaker's mood reflected in the rhythm and sound devices?

## COMMENTS AND EXAMPLES

Exercise 12 culminates your study of poetry. Since the other exercises have emphasized the basics of putting a critical paper together, this one is going to stress style — how to polish a paper. This one also reviews the major aspects of studying poetry as well as the process of composing an essay.

Let's look then at how Sharon Glennon studies Roethke's "The Geranium," and examine her paper all the way from the prewriting stage to the final draft. The poem is printed with Sharon's first prewriting notes in the margin:

"The Geranium" by Theodore Roethke

| | | |
|---|---|---|
| *pure stress* | When I pút her oút,ońce, by the gárbage pail, | *most natural speaking voice:* |
| | She loóked so límp and bedrággled, | *— natural word order* |
| | So foólish and trústing, like a síck poódle, | |
| *the mistreatment; situation* | Or a wízened áster in láte Septémber, | *— phrases rather than full sentences* |
| | I broúght her báck in agáin | |
| | For a néw routíne — | |
| | Vítamins, wáter, and whátever | *— slang: sacked, hag, dumb dames, seedy, booze* |
| | Sústenance seémed sénsible | |
| | At the tíme: she'd líved | |
| | So long on gín, bóbbie pins, half-smoked cigárs, dead beer, | |
| | Hér shríveled pétals fálling | *enumeration leads to shriveled petals, dying flowers* |
| *ties lines together for ending* | On the fáded cárpet, the stale | |
| | Stéak gréase stúck to her fúzzy léaves. | |
| | (Dried-oút, she creáked like a túlip.) | |
| *personification* | The thíngs she endúred! — | |
| | The dúmb dames shríeking half the níght | |
| | Ór the twó of us, alońe, both seédy, | |
| | Mé breáthing boóze at her, | |
| | Shé leáning out of her pót toward the window. | *What kind of a fitness is there between the choice* |

Theodore Roethke, "The Geranium," copyright © 1963 by Beatrice Roethke as Administratrix to the Estate of Theodore Roethke from the book *The Collected Poems of Theodore Roethke* by Theodore Roethke. Reprinted by permission of Doubleday & Co., Inc.

SOUND: RHYTHM AND RHYME   49

*fear of closeness*   Neár the énd, she seémed álmost to heár me —   *of a speaker and subject and the rhythm?*
And thát was scáry —
So whén that snúffling crétin of a máid
Thréw her, pot and all, ínto the trásh-can,
Í said nóthing.

*realization of loneliness*   But I sácked the presúmptuous hág the next weék,   *Appropriateness — does it fit or, an ironic purpose, not fit the subject matter?*
I was thát lónely.

    Sharon's notes include comments on the dramatic situation of the speaker's mistreatment of the flower as if he were talking about a woman — and her subsequent realization from this that he fears closeness with people, yet is terribly lonely. She also has basic information that this is a stressed poem that reflects a natural speaking voice. Finally, she asks the crucial question that ties her material together: what kind of fitness is there between a choice of subject and the rhythmic and sound devices that help give voice to the idea?

    Sharon's next step of prewriting, before attempting a rough draft, was to outline a paper on the basis of her rough notes and impressions. Even though the text has not stressed outlining, in Sharon's case it works out well to give some shape to the ideas that appear fragmentary in her first notes. As is clear from her outline, the impressions in her marginal comments have led to deeper reflections. These reflections in turn emerge as ideas that later structure her paper.

  I Intro: The speaker and subject — a man who cannot accept personal relationships, his monologue of realization, but no correction of past faults. (Use as conclusion.) Rhythm of speech.
  II Devices to give rhythmical speech patterns
    A Pure stress verse
    B Variation of syllable count and number of stresses
    C Enumeration to give structure to a more irregular poem
    D A long line followed by a shorter one — first is heavily stressed, while shorter one will encapsule the idea or conclusion
    E Natural word order — not contrived
  III Structure of poem: pauses to indicate turn of thought
    A Stanza I
       1 provides situation of speaker and geranium (subject) mistreatment

      2 mid-region: short lines held together by alliteration, internal rhyme
      3 stress on "déad" rather than "beer" to show geranium's condition — then description ending with alliteration of *st* and assonance of *ea:* both dry sounds to exemplify the creaking of dying
    B Stanza II; personification of geranium
      1 continues *e* sound as continues description — *squeaks his false concern*
      2 geranium responds by leaning away — actually a natural response of growing toward the light — personal lament
    C Stanza III: shifts regularity of stresses — points out basis of speaker's problem — scared to relate personally
    D Stanza IV: Conclusion — learns nothing — for tries to remedy his loneliness by isolation from a human being.

As is clear in the two drafts of Sharon's paper, her essay develops from a rough draft that is a good statement on what she sees as the central problem to face in her essay — the fitness between rhythm and sound choices and the poem's ideas — to a first-rate paper that preserves the central focus that she found earlier. But her paper goes beyond her first insights to become a highly polished, lively paper in the final draft.

    DRAFT 1

    The speaker that Roethke has chosen for his poem "The Geranium" bemoans the loss of a living thing he has felt close to, a flower that he nearly kills through neglect and that he finally allows his maid to carry out to the trash. Despite his reference to "the dumb dames shrieking half the night" and the remnants of much partying (steak, gin, cigars, and beer), the speaker apparently has no stable human relationships. In fact, he can't even muster enough concern to keep a plant alive.
    Roethke develops as close to a natural speech rhythm as possible to present this monologue of false despair. The basic meter is four stresses per line with a natural pause after a phrase containing two stresses. To stimulate actual speech, which is not mechanically regular, Roethke has periodically varied the syllable count per line. Notice, in the opening lines, how the first line is composed of eleven syllables with five stresses, while the sixth line has diminished to five syllables with two stresses.

        When I pút her oút, ońce, by the gárbage pail,
        She loóked / so limp / and bedrággled,
        So foólish and trústing, like a síck poódle,
        Or a wízened áster in láte Septémber,
        I broúght her báck in agáin
        For a néw roútine —

Roethke uses the device of listing to give structure to lines of changing rhythm. The new routine of plant care consists of "vitamins, water, and whatever," while we are told that previously the geranium survived on "gin, bobbie pins, half-smoked cigars, dead beer." Besides giving the poem a solid cohesion this listing enables the speaker to count all the times he mistreated the geranium and further berate himself.

Musically the listing fades into a blend of alliteration and assonance:

> . . . the stale
> Steak grease stuck to her fuzzy leaves.
> (Dried-out, she creaked like a tulip.)

The alliteration of the *st* sounds contained in the phrase "stale steak grease stuck" along with the repetition of the squeaking long *e* of "grease," "leaves," and "creaked" audibly exemplify the dry sounds of parched soil and crispy rustling leaves.

In stanza two, the speaker further enumerates his sins. The continued emphasis on the long *e*, at least one word in each line, changes the personal lament into a pathetic whine of confession. What was before a cleverly conceived auditory experience becomes the reiteration of self-pity through high-pitched tones.

Roethke points our attention to the opening of stanza three by preceding a short, succinct line of regular iambs by a longer, more heavily stressed line.

> Neár the end, she seémed almóst to heár me —
> And thát was scáry

After personifying the geranium as "leaning out of her pot toward the window," as if the flower could grow against the pull of the sun, the speaker finally realizes that a living thing responds to him: "she seemed almost to hear me." However, rather than accepting and reciprocating this response, he found it "scary." The speaker, who has finally related to a living thing on a personal level, disregards this feeling, and worse yet, fears it. Roethke presents these two lines as the crux of the poem by creating a striking rhythmical pattern for them.

The concluding stanza uses the same long/short rhythm to emphasize the shallowness of the speaker's understanding.

> But I sácked the presúmptuous hág the next weék,
> I was thát lónely.

The conclusion is no more than a further realization of loneliness, once the plant is gone. The speaker realizes his loneliness for the geranium, which can't be remedied, and tries to appease his conscience by sacking "the presumptuous hag," who threw out the dead flower and pot. If the speaker had learned that loneliness is cured by acceptance of human relationships, then his final act would not have been isolation from the last remaining person involved in his life.

Roethke uses several other devices to characterize the speech patterns of the protagonist. Throughout the poem, a natural word order is followed of subject, verb, object in the active voice. Instead of many short, choppy sentences, each stanza is comprised of only a single sentence, punctuated heavily with breathing pauses after the connecting phrases. This is the way most people speak; tacking phrases together with little concern for the sentence structure, but with emphasis on the sense of what is being said.

DRAFT 2

The speaker that Roethke has chosen for his poem "The Geranium" bemoans the loss of a living thing he has felt close to, a flower that he nearly kills through neglect and that he finally allows his maid to carry out to the trash. Despite his references to the "dumb dames shrieking half the night" and to the remnants of much "partying, steak, gin, cigars, and beer," the speaker apparently has no stable human relationships. He has formed a caring attitude toward the geranium, but even this falters beneath the speaker's fear of drawing himself into love.

The dramatic situation of "The Geranium" is a comic monologue in which the speaker refers and reacts to the loss of a plant as if it were a love loss. As the monologue progresses, the speaker personifies the geranium, endowing "her" with the qualities and characteristics of a woman. He responds to this unlikely affair with melodramatic outbursts such as "The things she endured!" and also with such guilty remarks as:

> So when that snuffling cretin of a maid
> Threw her, pot and all, into the trash-can,
> I said nothing.

Roethke develops despairing speech rhythm to present his guilty feelings for neglecting his lover, the plant. The basic meter is four stresses per line with a natural pause after a phrase containing two stresses. To simulate actual speech, Roethke has periodically varied the four stresses with inclusions of longer lines with as many as seven stresses or with as few as two.

Notice in the opening lines, how the first line is composed of eleven syllables, while the sixth line has diminished to five syllables with two stresses. But lines three and four, with four stresses each, are the basic lines:

> When I pút her out, ónce, by the gárbage páil,
> She loóked so límp and bedrággled,
> So foólish and trústing, like a sík poódle,
> Or a wízened áster in láte Septémber,
> I bróught her báck in agáin
> For a néw roútine —

Since grief is not expressed in a steady, rhythmical voice, this speaker appropriately shifts from brief to long outbursts of self-recrimination and guilt.

Roethke uses the device of listing to vary his rhythmical pattern and to show the irregular cries of a sad lover. The new routine of plant care consists of "vitamins, water, and whatever sustenance seemed sensible," while we are told that previously the geranium survived on "gin, bobbie pins, half-smoked cigars, dead beer" and steak grease. Each item of the list receives one stress, and these heavily stressed lines contrast his good intentions and his bad practices. Besides supplying the poem with concrete details, this piling up of the lists lends weight to his guilt.

Musically, the listing employs another device of contrast — between the alliteration and assonance in lines 12–14:

> . . . stale
> Steak grease stuck to her fuzzy leaves.
> (Dried-out, she creaked like a tulip.)

The alliteration of the *st* sounds contained in the phrase "stale steak grease stuck" along with the repetition of the squeaking long *e* of "grease," "leaves," and "creaked" audibly exemplify the dry sounds of parched soil and crisply rustling leaves.

By using still another type of contrast at the opening of stanza three, Roethke points our attention to his loneliness and fear. In lines 20–21, the speaker uses a long line with five stresses followed by a short one with two:

> Neár the eńd, she séemed álmost to heár me —
> And thát was scáry —

After personifying the geranium as "leaning out of her pot toward the window," as if the flower could by will grow against the pull of the sun, the speaker finally realizes that a living thing responds to him: "she seemed almost to hear me." However, rather than accepting and reciprocating this response, he finds, in the short line with two stresses, the situation "scary". The speaker, who has related to a living thing on a personal level, disregards this feeling and worse yet, fears it. The short line, with its stress on "scary," fixes the impression of a lonely, guilty person, who even feels he has betrayed a sick plant.

The concluding stanza of only two lines precisely echoes this long/short rhythm of lines 20–21 and captures the same mood of self-pity, loneliness, and guilt:

> But I sacked the presumptuous hag the next week,
> I was that lonely.

The stresses of the two examples are similar, five beats in the long opening line, followed by the short phrases of only two beats.

The conclusion is no more than a further realization of loneliness once the plant is gone. The speaker realizes his loneliness for the geranium, which can't be remedied, and tries to appease his conscience by sacking "the presumptuous hag" who threw out the dead flower and pot. The pun *sacked* further adds to the comic aspects of the situation. Does the speaker fire his maid, and thereby intensify his loneliness through isolation, or does he take her to bed? One may question the desirability of sexual relations with a "snuffling maid," but loneliness can do strange things. Either way, the speaker still is not striving for a replacement of the lost love, but merely for relief of the empty, lonely feeling.

Roethke successfully presents the theme of how loneliness causes down-and-out people to find solace in plants and strange companions by portraying his speaker in a rhythmical style appropriate to the drama of the poem. The speaker is set up as a buffoon, weeping and moaning over a plant he has fallen in love with. Roethke chooses this mood for the speaker to stress, not his loneliness or loss, but the causes of them. The speaker feared a close relationship with a plant, and we are left to wonder if he will ever have one with a human being — or even if one isn't better off loving plants than the people we meet in the poem.

Notice especially how the introductions and conclusions of the papers change — the first draft wanders uncertainly into its subject and ends even more uncertainly. It concludes, for instance, by tacking on a new idea about the significance of word choices. In contrast, the second draft sharply defines its subject and concludes nicely on a humorous but touching point about loneliness and love. Notice also how the dramatic situation is much more clearly defined and discussed in the second draft, second paragraph. Once dramatic situation is established in this second draft, the paper moves naturally and gracefully to Sharon's point that Roethke develops "a despairing speech rhythm" for his speaker, an insight that has been guided by the discussion of dramatic situation and in turn guides the rest of the paper. In contrast, the rough draft is skimpy in its handling of dramatic situation; the points made about the speech rhythm have neither the clarity nor the insightfulness that they do in the final draft, where there is a fuller discussion of this aspect of the poem.

# POETRY READINGS

Adrenalin Mother

——*Richard Brautigan*

Adrenalin Mother,
with your dress of comets
and shoes of swift bird wings
and shadow of jumping fish,
thank you for touching,
understanding and loving my life.
Without you, I am dead.

Richard Brautigan, "Adrenalin Mother." From *The Pill Versus the Springhill Mine Disaster* by Richard Brautigan. Copyright © 1968 by Richard Brautigan. Used with permission of Delacorte Press/Seymour Lawrence.

# Bestiary for the Fingers of My Right Hand

—*Charles Simic*

1
Thumb, loose tooth of a horse.
Rooster to his hens.
Horn of a devil. Fat worm
They have attached to my flesh
At the time of my birth.
It takes four to hold him down,
Bend him in half, until the bone
Begins to whimper.

Cut him off. He can take care
Of himself. Take root in the earth,
Or go hunting with wolves.

2
The second points the way.
True way. The path crosses the earth,
The moon and some stars.
Watch, he points further.
He points to himself.

3
The middle one has backache.
Stiff, still unaccustomed to this life;
An old man at birth. It's about something
That he had and lost,
That he looks for within my hand,
The way a dog looks
For fleas
With a sharp tooth.

4
The fourth is mystery.
Sometimes as my hand
Rests on the table
He jumps by himself
As though someone called his name.

Charles Simic, "Bestiary for the Fingers of My Right Hand." George Braziller, Inc. From *Dismantling the Silence* by Charles Simic; reprinted with permission of the publisher. Copyright © 1971 by Charles Simic.

After each bone, finger,
I come to him, troubled.

5
Something stirs in the fifth
Something perpetually at the point
Of birth. Weak and submissive,
His touch is gentle.
It weighs a tear.
It takes the mote out of the eye.

## Soliloquy of the Spanish Cloister

*——Robert Browning*

1
Gr-r-r — there go, my heart's abhorrence!
   Water your damned flowerpots, do!
If hate killed men, Brother Lawrence,
   God's blood, would not mine kill you!
What? your myrtle-bush wants trimming?
   Oh, that rose has prior claims —
Needs its leaden vase filled brimming?
   Hell dry you up with its flames!

2
At the meal we sit together:
   *Salve tibi!* I must hear
Wise talk of the kind of weather,
   Sort of season, time of year:
*Not a plenteous cork-crop: Scarcely*
   *Dare we hope oak-galls, I doubt:*
*What's the Latin name for "parsley"?*
   What's the Greek name for Swine's Snout?

3
Whew! We'll have our platter burnished,
   Laid with care on our own shelf!
With a fire-new spoon we're furnished,
   And a goblet for ourself,
Rinsed like something sacrificial
   Ere 'tis fit to touch our chaps —
Marked with L. for our initial!
   (He-he! There his lily snaps!)

4

*Saint,* forsooth! While brown Dolores
    Squats outside the Convent bank
With Sanchicha, telling stories,
    Steeping tresses in the tank,
Blue-black, lustrous, thick like horsehairs,
    — Can't I see his dead eye glow,
Bright as 'twere a Barbary corsair's?
    (That is, if he'd let it show!)

5

When he finishes refection,
    Knife and fork he never lays
Cross-wise, to my recollection,
    As do I, in Jesu's praise.
I the Trinity illustrate,
    Drinking watered orange-pulp —
In three sips the Arian frustrate;
    While he drains his at one gulp.

6

Oh, those melons? If he's able
    We're to have a feast! so nice!
One goes to the Abbot's table,
    All of us get each a slice.
How go on your flowers? None double?
    Not one fruit-sort can you spy?
Strange! — And I, too, at such trouble,
    Keep them close-nipped on the sly!

7

There's a great text in Galatians,
    Once you trip on it, entails
Twenty-nine distinct damnations,
    One sure, if another fails:
If I trip him just a-dying,
    Sure of heaven as sure can be,
Spin him round and send him flying
    Off to hell, a Manichee?

8

Or, my scrofulous French novel
    On gray paper with blunt type!
Simply glance at it, you grovel
    Hand and foot in Belial's gripe:
If I double down its pages
    At the woeful sixteenth print,

When he gathers his greengages,
   Ope a sieve and slip it in't?

9

Or, there's Satan! — one might venture
   Pledge one's soul to him, yet leave
Such a flaw in the indenture
   As he'd miss till, past retrieve,
Blasted lay that rose-acacia
   We're so proud of! *Hy, Zy, Hine* . . .
'St, there's Vespers! *Plena gratiâ*
   *Ave, Virgo!* Gr-r-r — you swine!

# Tract

—*William Carlos Williams*

I will teach you my townspeople
how to perform a funeral —
for you have it over a troop
of artists —
unless one should scour the world —
you have the ground sense necessary.

See! the hearse leads.
I begin with a design for a hearse.
For Christ's sake not black —
nor white either — and not polished!
Let it be weathered — like a farm wagon —
with gilt wheels (this could be
applied fresh at small expense)
or no wheels at all:
a rough dray to drag over the ground.

Knock the glass out!
My God — glass, my townspeople!
For what purpose? Is it for the dead
to look out or for us to see
how well he is housed or to see
the flowers or the lack of them —
or what?

William Carlos Williams, "Tract," from *Collected Earlier Poems*. Copyright 1938 by New Directions Publishing Corporation. Reprinted by permission of New Directions Publishing Corporation.

To keep the rain and snow from him?
He will have a heavier rain soon:
pebbles and dirt and what not.
Let there be no glass —
and no upholstery! phew!
and no little brass rollers
and small easy wheels on the bottom —
my townspeople what are you thinking of?

A rough plain hearse then
with gilt wheels and no top at all.
On this the coffin lies
by its own weight.

     No wreaths please —
especially no hot house flowers.
Some common memento is better,
something he prized and is known by:
his old clothes — a few books perhaps —
God knows what! You realize
how we are about these things
my townspeople —
something will be found — anything
even flowers if he had come to that.
So much for the hearse.

For heaven's sake though see to the driver!
Take off the silk hat! In fact
that's no place at all for him —
up there unceremoniously
dragging our friend out to his own dignity!
Bring him down — bring him down!
Low and inconspicuous! I'd not have him ride
on the wagon at all — damn him —
the undertaker's understrapper!
Let him hold the reins
and walk at the side
and inconspicuously too!

Then briefly as to yourselves:
Walk behind — as they do in France,
seventh class, or if you ride
Hell take curtains! Go with show
of inconvenience; sit openly —
to the weather as to grief.

Or do you think you can shut grief in?
What — from us? We who have perhaps
nothing to lose? Share with us
share with us — it will be money
in your pockets.
                    Go now
I think you are ready.


## The Pill Versus the Springhill Mine Disaster

——*Richard Brautigan*

When you take your pill
it's like a mine disaster.
I think of all the people
   lost inside of you.


## The Energy Chest

——*Michael Benedikt*

The energy chest
One keeps dipping in

With the hand of one's head
And one's chest is seldom empty

It's lively.
Even at night when we sleep

We see it
Standing by the bedroom window

Looking out into the distant valley, just standing there
On tiptoe.

   Richard Brautigan, "The Pill Versus the Springhill Mine Disaster." From *The Pill Versus the Springhill Mine Disaster* by Richard Brautigan. Copyright © 1968 by Richard Brautigan. Used with permission of Delacorte Press/Seymour Lawrence.

   Michael Benedikt, "The Energy Chest." Copyright © 1968 by Michael Benedikt. Reprinted from *Sky*, by Michael Benedikt, by permission of Wesleyan University Press.

# Good Times

—Lucille Clifton

My Daddy has paid the rent
and the insurance man is gone
and the lights is back on
and my uncle Brud has hit
for one dollar straight
and they is good times
good times
good times

My mama has made bread
and Grampaw has come
and everybody is drunk
and dancing in the kitchen
and singing in the kitchen
oh these is good times
good times
good times

oh children think about the
good times

# The Lost Pilot

—James Tate

*for my father, 1922–1944*

Your face did not rot
like the others — the co-pilot,
for example, I saw him

yesterday. His face is corn-
mush: his wife and daughter,
the poor ignorant people, stare

Lucille Clifton, "Good Times." From *Good Times* by Lucille Clifton. Copyright © 1969 by Lucille Clifton. Reprinted by permission of Random House, Inc.

James Tate, "The Lost Pilot." From *The Lost Pilot,* 1967. Reprinted by permission of Yale University Press.

as if he will compose soon.
He was more wronged than Job.
But your face did not rot

like the others — it grew dark,
and hard like ebony;
the features progressed in their

distinction. If I could cajole
you to come back for an evening,
down from your compulsive

orbiting, I would touch you,
read your face as Dallas,
your hoodlum gunner, now,

with the blistered eyes, reads
his braille editions. I would
touch your face as a disinterested

scholar touches an original page.
However frightening, I would
discover you, and I would not

turn you in; I would not make
you face your wife, or Dallas,
or the co-pilot, Jim. You

could return to your crazy
orbiting, and I would not try
to fully understand what

it means to you. All I know
is this: when I see you,
as I have seen you at least

once every year of my life,
spin across the wilds of the sky
like a tiny, African god,

I feel dead. I feel as if I were
the residue of a stranger's life,
that I should pursue you.

My head cocked toward the sky,
I cannot get off the ground,
and, you, passing over again,

fast, perfect, and unwilling
to tell me that you are doing
well, or that it was mistake

that placed you in that world,
and me in this; or that misfortune
placed these worlds in us.

# Lobo

——*William Childress*

The winter I turned sixteen,
wolves dropped down from the Wichita hills
and slaughtered cattle for miles around.
I heard of the great three-toed lobo
who had left tracks in the snowy ground
of Beaver Creek, near one of his kills.

No one had ever seen him. His tracks
alone convinced the superstitious
that he was not a ghost. Farmers cursed
their ill-fortune and the grey wolf packs,
and set traps to no avail. When spring
arrived, I left home, feeling nothing.

Whatever hold the red dirt hills had
was broken. I could not feel where there
was nothing to be felt. I had known
the family cave too long; I could
not stay. There were things to be seen,
to be killed, eaten, and not shared.

William Childress, "Lobo." From *Lobo*. Copyright © 1972 by William Childress. Reprinted by permission of the author.

# Hunting the Trolls

### —William Childress

When I was young, I believed in trolls,
and looked for them under moss-planked bridges
and in secret orchards late at night,
when yellow fruit glowed like eyes
in the hanging moonlight.

Come deeper, deeper
whispered the orchard's trees,
until I lost myself in a maze
of shadows, where vines hung like leathery arms,
bearing fruit no animal would eat.

Years closed behind me like latches
as I prowled abandoned barns
and searched old houses with gables like tusks.
Already I half knew what I would find,
but never when or where.

I prowled the banks of Devil's Slough
where rushes clicked in the cold wind,
and always, always, I grew closer
to some thick shape, looming just out of sight.

Come deeper, deeper
murmured the dark waters, the unreal orchards,
and finally I walked on naked bone,
leaving behind in my hoofed tracks
only a dark unholy image
for the morning sun
to cower from.

William Childress, "Hunting the Trolls." From *Lobo*. Copyright © 1972 by William Childress. Reprinted by permission of the author.

# No More Soft Talk

——*Diane Wakoski*

Don't ask a geologist about rocks.
Ask me.

That man,
he said.

What can you do with him?
About him?
He's a rock.

No, not a rock,
I said.
      Well,
a very brittle rock, then.
One that crumbles easily, then.
Is crushed to dust, finally.

Me,
I said.
I am the rock.
The hard rock.
You can't break me.

I am trying to think how a woman
can be a rock,
when all she wants is to be soft,
to melt to the lines
her man draws for her.

But talking about rocks
intelligently
must be
talking about different kinds
of rock.

What happens to the brain
in shock? Is it
like an explosion

Diane Wakoski, "No More Soft Talk." From *The Motorcycle Betrayal Poems.* Copyright © 1971 by Diane Wakoski. Reprinted by permission of Simon and Schuster.

of flowers and blood,
staining the inside
of the skull?

I went to my house,
to see my man,
found the door locked,
and something I didn't plan
on — a closed bedroom door
(my bed)
another woman's handbag on the couch.
Is someone in the bedroom?

Yes, Yes,
a bed full of snakes all bearing new young,
a bed of slashed wrists,
a bed of carbines and rifles with no ammunition,
a bed of my teeth in another woman's fingers.

Then the answer to rocks,
as I sit here and talk.

The image of an explosion:
a volcanic mountain
on a deserted pacific island.
What comes up,
like gall in my throat,
a river of abandoned tonsils that can no longer cry,
a sea of gold wedding rings and smashed glasses,
the lava, the crushed and melted rock
comes pouring out now,
down this mountain you've never seen,
from this face that believed in you,
rocks that have turned soft,
but now are bubbling out of the lips of a mountain,
into the ocean raising the temperature
to 120 degrees.
If your ship were here
it would melt all the caulking.

This lava,
hot and soft,
will cool someday,
and turn back into the various stones.
None of it is
my rock.

My rock doesn't crumble.
My rock is the mountain.
Love me
if you can.
I will not make it easy for you
anymore.

# If, My Darling

*——Philip Larkin*

If my darling were once to decide
Not to stop at my eyes,
But to jump, like Alice, with floating skirt into my head,

She would find no tables and chairs,
No mahogany claw-footed sideboards,
No undisturbed embers;

The tantalus would not be filled, nor the fender-seat cosy,
Nor the shelves stuffed with small-printed books for the Sabbath,
Nor the butler bibulous, the housemaids lazy:

She would find herself looped with the creep of varying light,
Monkey-brown, fish-grey, a string of infected circles
Loitering like bullies, about to coagulate;

Delusions that shrink to the size of a woman's glove
Then sicken inclusively outwards. She would also remark
The unwholesome floor, as it might be the skin of a grave,

From which ascends an adhesive sense of betrayal,
A Grecian statue kicked in the privates, money,
A swill-tub of finer feelings. But most of all

She'd be stopping her ears against the incessant recital
Intoned by reality, larded with technical terms,
Each one double-yoked with meaning and meaning's rebuttal:

For the skirl of that bulletin unpicks the world like a knot,
And to hear how the past is past and the future neuter
Might knock my darling off her unpriceable pivot.

Philip Larkin, "If, My Darling" is reprinted from *The Less Deceived*, 1955, by permission of The Marvell Press, England.

# DRAMA

The section on drama again emphasizes the logical connection between writing from your own observation and the art of critical writing. In studying drama, you discover the important techniques of this literary form as you do brief exercises on various aspects of play writing. These discoveries are then used to examine — in critical essays — plays by professional playwrights.

Critical essays in this part differ in one significant respect from those in the poetry section: in each assignment, you are asked to comment on the credibility of the play. That is, you are asked to evaluate the success or lack of success of the playwright's method of characterization, his or her use of conflict, the plot, the language, and the directions for staging.

The purpose of these evaluative assignments on drama is to give you experience in one of the critic's main functions: to establish criteria with which to judge the worth of a piece of literature. Of all forms of literature, and of drama particularly, we often ask that these forms be "believable" or "credible." This usually means that we have a conception of reality and ask the particular work to measure up to it. However, as you compose your own plays and go on to study plays by professionals, you'll find that a conception of reality changes from age to age. To one age, reality may mean fidelity to the moral truths of the age — the hero is the man of ethical perfection. In another age, reality may mean capturing external reality and ignoring moral truths — the moth holes in the rug or the soup spots on grandfather's lapel. To a third age, reality may mean presenting faithfully a picture of psychological reality — the workings of a person's mind, which may require the characters to be Love and Pride in Christian conflict or Ego and Superego in Freudian conflict. As a reader of drama, you must be flexible enough to adjust to the playwright's vision of reality, but you must also trust your own perceptions of what motivates people, what conflicts occur between certain kinds of people, what actions grow out of certain conflicts, and what constitutes believable language and stage directions.

The drama section is organized on this principle: in the odd-numbered exercises you study the components of drama; in the even-numbered ones you do brief writings in the manner of a dramatist. For example, you will begin in the first exercise by bringing to life personifications to resemble a cast of characters. Then you apply what you have learned about characters in exercise 13 to a critical paper concerning characters in exercise 14. And each succeeding even-numbered exercise continues this pattern — it follows up and reinforces a conception from the odd-numbered assignments.

# 7

# Character in Drama

## 13 · DISCOVERING CHARACTER IN PERSONIFICATIONS

*WRITING* In exercise 1 of chapter 1, you described abstract words like *despair* so that they came to life as human beings. Go back to that list, or draw from this one for two or three abstractions that you can bring to life. (Read the discussion on character that follows before you begin to write.)

| | | | |
|---|---|---|---|
| truth | beauty | solitude | play |
| lust | humility | work | optimist |
| conceit | friendship | cynic | nature |
| sorrow | ignorance | crusader | age |
| wisdom | order | youth | haste |
| lie | sacrifice | patience | |
| disorder | company | sloth | |

Describe these abstract words for their dramatic potential. That is, what qualities might they possess that could make them interesting, lively characters on a stage? For example, would they be male or female?

1 How might they dress?
2 How might they walk? What would their typical gestures be?
3 What would they say? In what kind of voice?
4 What might they want others to know about them? What would they hide?
5 Who would be their companions?
6 Where could they be found? That is, in what dramatic setting would you be most likely to discover them and find out something about them?

*DISCUSSION* Read your descriptions aloud in class, and also reproduce them for distribution. Discuss them in terms of character revelation — behavior and language that tell us directly or indirectly what a person is like — and motivation — what drives people.

1 Character revelation: examine your personifications first for the ways characters reveal themselves. That is, of the ways that we get to know people, how many are represented in these personifications?
   a What do you infer about a person by what he or she wears?
   b What does a person's dialect indicate to you? What does voice tell you about someone?
   c What does the character reveal in language choices? In vocabulary? By frequent expressions? Does he or she use clichés, slang, obscenities?
2 Motivation: then go on to discuss what appear to be the motivations of each character on the basis of what the description reveals. That is, look at the forces that drive the character in terms of longings, desires, and goals, either hidden from or known to the character.
   a What has the character revealed about his or her desires? Ideals? Fears? Selfishness? Unselfishness?
   b What has been revealed about the character's needs? To survive? To have self-esteem? To be wanted? To belong? To have power? To be led?
   c Does the character depend on others' opinions to get started? Is the character a joiner or a loner?
   d Is the character driven by forces that he or she doesn't understand? How conscious, in other words, is the character of his or her motivations?

---

## COMMENTS AND EXAMPLES

By attributing human qualities to inanimate things like abstractions, you call attention to those aspects of character, especially how it is revealed and what motivates it, in graphic ways. To be convincing, personifications have to be carefully detailed. Look at three students' personifications, for example. Notice that it is not only possible to recognize human qualities in the figures but also to get enough information so that we could imagine someone acting out the abstractions. Mike Smith describes Gluttony in this fashion:

> Gluttony has reached the age when the accumulation of beer-drinking, roast-pork gobbling and cigarette smoking has become a burden to him; his body is collectively rounded by his indulgences in the past. While

> Gluttony is vaguely aware of his condition, it is a matter of little importance to him compared to the high price of beef. To him a 5 cent rise in the cost of Budweiser beer is a national calamity. He is forty-five, sleek and shining and oozing with carbohydrates. His attire runs along the lines of a simple oriental dressing gown; he is too lazy to dress properly every morning. He regularly takes a pinch of snuff, and combined with his nightly port, a bad cold, and too much garlic, this has caused his nose to be red and outstanding. Nevertheless, he has kept his hair and sports a halo of curls. His voice is affluent, deep, and fruity; his hands puffy and white. His Oblomovian mouth is a cavern of immense proportions, guarded by polished, sharp teeth.
> 
> He waddles. He does not walk.
> 
> *Mike Smith*

Gluttony reveals himself primarily by his looks and his habits; in fact, he reminds us of people whose primary qualities are habitual ones, in this case annoying habits that we find repulsive. This glutton doesn't know himself well — he is largely unaware of his desire to satisfy just one basic drive. The lack of awareness, Mike implies, is one of the things that makes Gluttony so repulsive. He so single-mindedly pursues food and drink that he fails to understand himself.

Just as it wouldn't be hard to play the role of Gluttony on the basis of Mike's description, so Sheryl Bailey's description of Deceitful is dramatic in the sense that it would be as easy to follow as a stage direction. It includes directions about a set of language and body gestures, a way of handling people, and a desire to fool and therefore manipulate people that an actor could follow:

> Deceitful: Mr. Deceitful is not as easily recognized as you might have guessed. He is a tall handsome man, one who assumes authority wherever he goes. He is concerned with pleasing everyone and will dress to fit the occasion. Usually he wears a nice suit, always up on the new fashions. He lures people like a magnet. They love his company. He always has something to offer to someone. In fact he pushes himself onto other people. He's a very smooth talker with seemingly a lot of wisdom. The neutral eye will view him as a beautiful person, eager to help to meet others' needs. Ninety percent of the time what he has to offer is something one wouldn't have to wait for. He believes that one must be happy every moment. He fulfills this need through all kinds of materialistic items, physical pleasures, and spiritual truths.
> 
> The problem is, that these things are all temporary. They don't quite fulfill what his visitors want, yet they always come back to see him. It's as if their eyes are blinded.
> 
> He's quite a talker, and I would warn everyone to be wary of this seemingly wise gentleman.
> 
> *Sheryl Bailey*

As we did with Gluttony, we see Deceitful mainly through his actions. Deceitful possesses a new dimension as a character, however, in that he reveals himself largely through the way he interacts with other people, which is far more appropriate to him than to Gluttony, who tends to be a solitary figure. Even the dramatic settings hinted at for these two personifications — one for a loner to satisfy his appetites and one for a joiner to manipulate people — tend to reveal their characters and furnish information about their motives.

As a final example, observe how in Wayne Olson's portrait, Duty characterizes himself in a monologue:

> DUTY. I am Duty and I tow the line. Heaven knows why you call on me; I've hardly the time to pilfer in your little play. You can't imagine the larger schemes in which I must do my bit to keep it all together for everyone else. Some, especially the younger women, say I have an ugly face and shun me as if I were a prison guard passing out shackles which are the prisoner's lot. They kick up their heels at me and prance away; it's all a riot for them, but I keep my face straight forward, as all should, and keep my mind on my work. I am an important man and know time will bend those hussies into the rigid shape they must have to do their duty.
>
> My most proud spokesmen, in fact, are the older women, who hold my ugly head aloft to scare all those who would wander astray back into their confining corners. They tell all for me to keep on the beaten track, that only evil ways lie off in the hot houses and swamps on every side.
>
> Any man who answers my demands will gain as his reward his proper lot in life. Conservative dress, with a tidy button-down collar and suit of gray flannel armor, I require from the men who obey the tasks I set out for them. The women must keep their hair tied back tight; I've no use for frivolous curls and bows.
>
> Life here on earth is a serious business. We must all obey those who give us our orders; otherwise, our comfortable world would crumble and a more disciplined race — dedicated to Duty — will prevail over us.
>
> Keep silent and heed the word from above. It wants from you proper obedience.
>
> Wayne Olson

If this monologue were to occur in a play, then we could see how well Duty knows himself. Whether or not Duty lives up to his self-analysis would be the basic means for judging him as a character — the difference between his words and his deeds.

The characters in other plays that you analyze will be more complex than personifications, which of necessity are one-dimensional. But just as you watch for behavior and motivations for your personifications that are graphic and credible so a dramatist looks for gestures, language, and motivations that correspond to people as we know them.

## 14 · WRITING ABOUT CHARACTER IN DRAMA

*WRITING* Now that you have written some personifications and have analyzed them for ways in which they resemble characters in plays, do a one-paragraph analysis of a character in a play. For this assignment, it isn't necessary to do a revised draft of the paragraph. This exercise provides practice in prewriting and writing about drama. The other assignments in the section on drama will emphasize revision.

So select one character in a play. Analyze that character in a lengthy paragraph that focuses upon three points: (1) the means by which the character is revealed; (2) the motivations that drive the character; and (3) how credibly you think the playwright has developed the character. (Read the discussion on analyzing characters on pp. 78-80 and *Raisin in the Sun* and *Everyman* on pp. 113-210 before you write.

*Prewriting* Use these questions as prewriting for your paragraph. Note that you are asked to include information about how successfully the dramatist has revealed and motivated his characters.

1 How does the character reveal himself or herself? What are the specific actions, language, gestures, or things said about him or her that indicate what the character is like?
2 Are the characters and their motivations consistent and credible? That is, do they continue to reveal themselves in the same manner throughout the play? If a character changes, has the reader been prepared for these changes and are they believable? (For example, if a stingy man becomes generous at the end of the play, whatever caused his change will have to be believable.)
3 How would you describe the character's major motivations? That is, what seem to be the driving forces behind the character you are studying? Desire for money or for fame? Need for power? Dependent upon or independent of society's moral judgments? Conscious or unconscious of what drives him or her?

*DISCUSSION* Go over your paragraphs in class. Since you won't be asked to do a polished draft of this first character sketch, spend your time on the techniques of prewriting that led to these short sketches. (Keep your notes and papers from this assignment, as they may be useful in succeeding ones.) Use these questions to organize a class discussion:

1 Compare and contrast your prewriting notes with your drafts of the character

sketches. What refinements in prewriting or writing can you learn from them?
2 Has the writer specified the means by which the character is revealed?
3 Has the writer specified the characters' motivations?
4 Has the writer commented on the reasons why a character is effectively or ineffectively presented? That is, are the prewritings and sketches truly evaluative?

---

## COMMENTS AND EXAMPLES

In writing about character in drama, you are asked to perform a critical task not asked for in the poetry section — to make an evaluative statement about the success or lack of success of the characterization. These evaluations usually take the form of statements about the believability of the characters in light of your own experience with people. As mentioned in the introduction to Drama, part of our test for the validity of a literary statement is to confront it with human experience. Look now at how students have handled exercise 14, the paragraph assignment that examines the revelation, motivation, and credibility of characters.

The first two examples analyze characters in *Everyman,* a play in which personifications have to behave like people in order to be believed. Notice that Perry Bedard even imagines physical characteristics for Kindred and that Shannon Flynn pays special attention to Fellowship's conversations. Both writers, in other words, attempt to square these characters with their experience of how people reveal themselves through behavior and language.

### KINDRED

Kindred in *Everyman* is believable as a relative because he gives Everyman a great deal of support until Everyman asks Kindred to accompany him to death. Kindred offers to help out only if it requires little of him. Kindred is a very shallow character — one gets a picture of a short, fat man, very jovial. He well could have flunked out of Santa Claus school for not having inner feelings. He is willing to give materialistic things but not himself. He tells Everyman to cheer up in one breath and not to expect any help from him in the next. His character is certainly consistent for his brief stay (being so shallow he probably could not endure any more exposure) and his sudden departure; and he is true-to-life in that he shows how fair-weather relatives are tested at the time of one's difficulties.

*Perry Bedard*

FELLOWSHIP

> In "Everyman," Fellowship is typical of the proverbial fair-weather friend. His assurances of good faith and undying loyalty are entirely inconsistent with his actions. Fellowship voices idealistic promises and speaks noble words, "I will not forsake thee by the way." However, when he is actually called upon to put his theory into practice, he concedes to his own more fickle emotions and cannot give what he so fervently promised: "Sir, I say as I will do indeed. . . . Promise is duty; but . . . it should be to my pain; Also it maketh me afeard." Fellowship is then a credible character: one of those friends you can't count on during times of trouble; only to share good times.
>
> *Shannon Flynn*

Notice that Perry focuses more on Kindred's act of desertion than on what Kindred says to Everyman. In other words, Kindred reveals his fickle nature and his motivation to live for pleasure by the way he behaves.

In much the same way that Perry views Kindred, Shannon sees Fellowship as a believable character — both students use the phrase "fair-weather" — to describe people who are apparently close but drift away when stormy times occur. Shannon dwells more, however, on the discrepancy between what Fellowship promises and what he delivers than on other aspects of evaluation.

Another student, Mike Smith, writes about Walter in *A Raisin in the Sun,* and is especially interested in Walter's development as a character:

> *A Raisin in the Sun* would not be quite so wrinkled if not for the character of Walter Lee Younger. Perhaps the one word which best describes him is *pride* — he is a proud man. Realizing the low position life has given him, he feels compelled to escape it using the only tool available, his father's savings. Placing trust in a misguided friend, Willy, he loses much of the money and a large part of his pride. It is only later when he must choose between it and regaining a portion of the money, that he remembers why he needed the money in the first place. This concept of money and pride prevails throughout Walter's growth as a character. Early in the play when his son, Travis, needs fifty cents for school, for example, Walter is too proud to admit they can't afford it. Then, just to show they aren't "poor," he gives Travis an extra fifty cents for taxi fare. Walter's comments on his job of chauffeur raise the same issue. He is tired of being a yes man, of opening other people's car doors, of telling his son stories about rich white people. He sees his future before him, and it looks just like his past. He has become motivated by money because it is an escape from this future. This need for pride is consistent throughout the play. In the final act, when he has called Karl Lindner, a representative from white neighbors to come and do business, he says he will get down on his knees. He is depressed and discouraged. When Lindner arrives the moment of decision has arrived. Will he accept

the bribe and let the white neighborhood buy him off? Walter gives up his false pride in gaining wealth and finds his true source of pride — his family's reputation. For when Lindner arrives, Mama keeps Travis in the room. She would never have let Travis stay had she thought there was the slightest chance Walter would beg. Perhaps the pressure of Travis being present also helped to sway Walter's feelings toward true pride. Given Walter's desire to keep face with Travis (the taxi money episode in Act I), his change to a truer kind of pride is consistent and believable. For people are concerned not only about their children's welfare but also about their children's respect. Walter's growth is therefore credible on the basis of what he wants for Travis.

*Mike Smith*

Mike makes a precise distinction between the two types of pride driving Walter, the first a false kind deriving from his quest for money and from his desire to misuse it. The second, a pride in family, replaces the first, and Walter's character undergoes a credible change once he recognizes, as his family has all along, that the first type brings him nothing but pain and loss. Mike focuses on two actions that reveal the two types of pride in Walter — the scene concerning Travis's taxi money and Walter's rejection of Lindner's bribe. Then Mike goes on to judge Walter to be a credible character on the basis of parents' feelings for their children.

Even though these paragraphs lack the polish of papers that have been revised, they do provide models of what this chapter wishes to establish concerning writing about drama: (1) identifying a single character; (2) specifying motivation and means of revelation; and (3) commenting on the success of the characterizations. From chapter 8 on, the text emphasizes ways to revise and polish first drafts.

# 8

# Conflict in Drama

## 15 · DISCOVERING CONFLICT IN PERSONIFICATIONS

*WRITING* Exercise 13 asked you to create a personification as if it were a character in a play. In this exercise, create another personification, but this time imagine two or three other abstract words that would be its companions and enemies. Build these friendships and animosities into the description. For example, watch for competing pairs of characters or those with conflicting loyalties. For instance, what different assumptions about the law would Pessimism and Optimism have if each were a lawyer in a courtroom battle?

Or you could construct a personification to show a set of inner conflicts. Take a case where Duty, a father, tries to decide whether or not to turn in his criminal son, Deceit, and where you examine the father's inner conflicts in loyalty: is his duty to his blood ties or to the law? (Read the discussion that follows the assignment on discovering conflict in personifications before you begin to write.)

*DISCUSSION* Use the following questions to discuss your personifications:

1 Does each writer have a lively situation (such as a courtroom or family scene) for his personification to act in? Are there opposite types represented in the description, or natural antagonisms between a pair? Youth-age, idealists-cynics, country-city, learned-unlearned, foreigner-native, male-female, and so forth?

2 Do the characters fit the situation? Given the situation are there new ones that need to be invented?
3 Do the descriptions as they now stand clearly reveal most facets of the characters: habits, gestures, language, friends, etc.? What do you learn from watching and listening to a character named Crusader in a military scene? What might you learn additionally by hearing others like Duty, Sloth, or Disorder talk about Crusader?
4 Do the descriptions indicate the primary or conflicting motivations of a character? For example, is Uptight attempting to live a hip life? With what other characters would she come in conflict? How would their motivations differ? What inner conflicts would Uptight possess as she tries to gain acceptance in a new world?
5 Can you invent an impromptu dialogue between two of the characters?

## COMMENTS AND EXAMPLES

The conflicts that occur between people are the very soul of drama. Think, for example, of the large number of dramatic plots like the plot of Shakespeare's *Romeo and Juliet:* conflict occurring when an older generation tries to block two members of a younger one from marrying. Characters can disagree over ideas or morals, over how to wage a war, over whom to marry, over how to spend an inheritance, over what is the best route to salvation, and so on. But the disagreements bring out character traits and get actions going. Conflict, the divisions that exist or arise among people and that serve to reveal character and to get actions started, may be between political or moral systems, between characters' competing self-interests, or it may be internal: between the tendencies or motivations inside one character. Observe how two students have pointed out some potential conflicts in their personifications written for exercise 15. Perry Bedard describes Pride, her conflicts and companions; while Cole Flegel writes about Cynicism's friends and enemies.

> Pride is a female human. She's about 5' 6", slender, beautiful and sexually desirable. Her constant companions are Greed, Jealousy and Fashion. Like Greed, and Jealousy, she sees the world as centering around herself. Like Fashion she has placed her appearance as being about the most important aspect of her person. Her main habit is turning every conversation into an I-centered one. When talking about herself her voice is calm and self-assured; and when talking about others it's bored. She betrays herself when she talks with her friend Jealousy because at these times Pride's voice is high, uptight, and tense.

She is likely to be found in any habitat, although her favorite places are parties in chic apartments, or shopping in the "best" boutiques in town.

Her worst enemies are Duty and Conscience. When selecting a companion these two are last on her list.

*Perry Bedard*

Cynicism has a tendency to appear whenever Love or Innocence are present. He is a fairly tall, thin man, who habitually slouches when sitting or standing. As Love and Innocence are speaking, he frequently yawns in a huge parody of boredom. Occasionally when the other characters are showing signs of deep emotional involvement in their speeches, he snickers, or even laughs out loud. When Patriotism, Pride or Greed speaks, he smiles and nods in approval. Cynicism himself has nothing to say — he merely makes it hard to attend to the gentler emotions, and gives nonverbal signs of approval to the more "worldly" figures. Love and Innocence can occasionally work together to literally force him from the stage, but a guard must be left to kill him off, which reduces the forces left to fight against Pride, Greed, *et al*. Eventually, the guard must abandon his post, and when he does, Cynicism immediately returns. Only a firm alliance under Joy can banish him, but such an alliance is difficult if not impossible to form.

*Cole Flegel*

Notice that a dramatic situation is implied for Pride: surrounded by Greed, Jealously, and Fashion, she is most comfortable shopping or at parties. She is in conflict with Duty and Conscience; if either of these two were to show up at one of Pride's most comfortable locations, conflict would follow.

In Cole's paper, Cynicism is an intruder into any happy occasion: one can imagine a civil observance like a Fourth of July speech, a family occasion like a wedding, or even a private occasion like rejoicing in a picture well painted, or even a game well played, where a cynical attitude would damage the happiness. Notice that Cynicism's sneering animosity — even nonverbal — is directed against Love and Innocence. His allies are Pride and Greed. As in the case of the description of Pride in the previous paragraph, one can almost begin to imagine conversations between the characters given, let's say, an engagement between Love and Innocence when Pride and Greed show up to help Cynicism destroy the good feelings.

Conflict then is that set of forces dividing people or those forces inside one person dividing him- or herself. Action in drama begins in conflict: Pride finds Duty's company distasteful, hence she will avoid her and Conscience at any cost. Now go on and study a play in which you identify and analyze conflict within a character or among characters; conflict that will be much more complex than these single-dimensional personifications possess.

# 16 · WRITING ABOUT CONFLICT IN DRAMA

*WRITING* Your second paper on drama asks you to identify and analyze how and how successfully a play presents a conflict. This paper should be longer than your first essay on drama, which was only one paragraph in length. Also, this one should be revised once you have done a rough draft.

Begin by selecting a conflict in the play and by using the following prewriting questions to discover as much as you can about it before you set pen to paper. Then as you develop a rough draft, focus your attention on (1) identifying the kind of conflict in this play, (2) relating the way the character is revealed and his or her motivations to your discussion of conflict, and (3) stating how believably the playwright handles the conflict given the situation and the characters. (Read the section of Comments and Examples that follows this assignment before attempting your paper.)

*Prewriting* Use the following questions to generate material for the paper you are going to write about conflict.
1 Are there pairs of opposites in the play that you are working on; pairs that might help you identify a major conflict? What characters are differently motivated? Does a parent conflict with a child? Does an idealist, a traditionalist, or a dutiful person disagree with a cynical or rebellious one? Does someone with knowledge or power compete with one having none of these gifts? Are men and women competitive in the play? Do two members of one sex vie for the love of one or another?
   a Is there conflict on the level of ideas? Do a religious and nonreligious person disagree? Is a socialist pitted against a capitalist? Is race behind any trouble in the play? Is freedom of the will argued by one character and blind destiny by another? Is there a discrepancy between what two characters hold to be true about life — each thinks the other has sold out to a system of illusions and has missed the reality underneath?
   b Is the question raised of women's role in life (duties, powers, nature)?
   c Can you discover a character with an inner conflict, that is, one torn between two ideas, two people, or two motivations?
   d Or is there a character trying to decide what choice to make on another important matter?
2 After you have identified a conflict using question 1, explain in what characters and how this conflict is revealed.
   a What ideas or forces drive the characters to have different views or

  to behave differently? What different forces are driving characters with inner conflicts? In other words, what motivates the conflicting characters?
 b Are the conflicts revealed by the characters themselves in conversation or action? By what other characters say about them? By manners and gestures? By hints from the playwright about staging? In short, how do the conflicting characters reveal themselves?
3 Then attempt to identify the main conflict or issue in the play. Is it over who is going to marry whom? Is there a great decision at stake — how, for example, to spend an inheritance? Does it concern whose idea of order or justice will win? Is the basic issue whether a person will save his soul or integrity? Is the major conflict one between competing religious or political theories? Often even the major focus of a play will be debatable. Have confidence in and be able to defend your perception of the main conflict.

*DISCUSSION* Wait until you have completed a rough draft to discuss your essay on conflict. Bring your prewriting notes along with you as you talk over your first draft. Watch for these qualities in the rough draft:

1 In this draft, has the writer begun to fulfill the three basic purposes of the assignment: (1) to identify a conflict; (2) to relate that conflict to motivation and revelation of the characters; (3) to state how credibly the playwright handles conflict?
2 Has the basic argument been supported adequately by conversations and by paraphrases of action from the play?
3 Is each bit of evidence introduced in the paper so that you understand who speaks the lines or who participates in the action? In other words, is the writer so familiar with the play that he or she may skip over references to the play that a reader not familiar with the play may need in order to locate a speech or an action?
4 Does each paper evaluate the credibility of the conflicts in the play?

---

# COMMENTS AND EXAMPLES

  Your first essay on drama didn't emphasize revision. This one, however, stresses refining your basic insights into a polished, well-argued paper. Compare, for example, Holly Walker's rough draft with her second, polished version of a paper on Everyman's inner conflict:

FIRST DRAFT

There is only one major conflict in *Everyman* and that is the conflict within Everyman himself. He encounters and disagrees with many other personifications, but these are mere disagreements at a certain time and place, not a major conflict. Everyman is fighting with himself. His mind is in turmoil; and in desperation he goes to all the temporary things in life: friends, relatives, goods. In this way he is fighting for life itself, by clinging to the passing things. He is searching for the help the temporal world can offer. He asks, "For help in this world whither shall I resort?" But as he encounters each supposed friend or relative, he discovers that none of these can or will help him. For example, Fellowship says, "In prosperity men friends may find,/Which in Adversity be unkind." Goods refuses him too, and Everyman laments, "Alas, I have thee loved, and had great pleasure/All my life-days on good and treasure." But the conflict begins to turn at this point, and Everyman goes to Good Deeds. He begins to stop fighting with himself. He is more of a man in a daze, prepared to do anything he is told to do. He says, for example, "My Good Deeds, gramercy!/I am well content, certainly,/With your words sweet." He begins to realize that those forgotten sacraments (penance, etc.) are the solution to his problem: "For now I will my penance begin;/This hath rejoiced and lighted my heart." He is so sure of his readiness at this time that he says, "And let us go now without tarrying." With the company of his new friends (Beauty, Five Wits, etc.) he is happy until they all leave at which point he despairs, until he discovers the only things that count, "they that I loved best do forsake me,/Except my Good Deeds that bideth truly." Thus he goes to the grave with Good Deeds who will support him, and the conflict has come to an end.

*Holly Walker*

SECOND DRAFT

"They that I loved best do forsake me,/Except my Good Deeds that bideth truly" is the outcome of Everyman's conflict. Throughout the first part of the play, Everyman is fighting within himself. He is trying to cling to all the transient things of this world rather than let go, and to grasp the one thing that can help him go before the judgment seat since Death has just read him his sentence. Since he slowly discovers that the passing things won't help him, he begins his search for another companion. He wonders "For help in this world whither shall I resort?" He makes one stubborn attempt after another, each failing. But soon after Goods enters, Everyman makes a statement that marks a turning point, "Alas, I have thee loved, and had great pleasure/All my life-days on good and treasure." Everyman himself states his problem: all his life he has valued material things rather than the higher things in life.

At this point, Everyman lets go of his previous material security and stops fighting with himself. He is more than willing to do whatever he is told; for after some advice from Good Deeds, he remarks, "I am well content, certainly,/With your words sweet." Knowledge guides

Everyman to Confession, who sets the conflict in Everyman to such rest that Everyman rejoices in lightness of heart and is so assured of his salvation that he feels full ready to face the "Judge": "And let us go now without tarrying." Everyman has learned his lesson, a lesson which enabled Good Deeds, Everyman's only support, to rise and stand with him before the throne of God.

While having a person's inner-conflicts come to life may not be believable, it is very credible to see a person torn between material security and the higher things in life. Peace, the play says, comes when one settles for the higher things and rejects the material.

*Holly Walker*

While Holly's first draft has some insightful comments, such as her opening perception that the conflict in the play is centered in Everyman himself, the paper itself scatters worthwhile comments about. It doesn't focus, however, the insights carefully nor does it connect them smoothly so that the paper is persuasive. Notice, for instance, that at midpoint in the paper Holly sees Everyman's vision changed by Goods' rejection and by the necessity of turning to Good Deeds: "He begins to stop fighting with himself. He is more of a man in a daze." In this first draft, Holly doesn't make it clear that Everyman has finally deserted earthly pleasures and that this resolves his conflict because he turns to a new source of inner strength, Good Deeds. So while she has defined a conflict and has a basic sense of how to support it, Holly fails to provide clear connections between her subordinate argument about the importance of Everyman's change of heart and his initial conflict. In the second draft, however, this same passage becomes one of Holly's most convincing ones when she says about Goods' rejection that Everyman himself perceives his problem of valuing "material things rather than the higher things in life. At this point, Everyman lets go of material security and stops fighting with himself."

Likewise, Holly introduces quotations choppily in draft one but smoothly in draft two. She talks about Everyman's crucial lines in this way in the first draft: "Alas, I have thee loved, and had great pleasure/All my life-days on good and treasure," by saying that it occurs after the refusal of Goods! In the second draft, however, she introduces it with this: "soon after Goods enters, Everyman makes a statement that marks a turning point." Then she quotes the crucial line. Such an introduction not only stresses its significance to the thesis of the paper, but also sets the reader straight as to the location of the speech in the play.

Finally, the first draft has no comment on credibility, whereas the second one makes a nice point about the believability of the conflict of the play; a connection between Everyman's realization and what might bring peace of mind to many people with inner conflicts.

Another student, Sheryl Bailey, writes about an external conflict in *A Raisin in the Sun.* The conflict is between Walter and his sister Beneatha.

"What do you want from me, brother — that I quit school or just drop dead? Which!" This question directed at Walter very early in *A Raisin in the Sun* illustrates the deep conflict between Walter and the speaker of this quoted passage, his sister, Beneatha.

Beneatha is dead set on becoming a doctor while Walter expresses the thoughts that she should "be a nurse like other women — or just get married and be quiet." His male chauvinist attitudes expresses the jealousy he feels for his sister. She is young; she has a far-reaching goal that will take her farther than most *white* women would ever get. Above all, her goal is approved of by Mama. Walter feels that if Beneatha were to settle down like most young women, perhaps his goals would get precedence, and he would get Mama's approval.

Beneatha has no faith in her brother's investment of buying a liquor store. She feels that he would lead the family from one bad situation to another just as bad, or worse. She expresses this thought in the middle of the first scene when she says about one of Walter's wild schemes: "And there are all those prophets who would lead us out of the wilderness — into the swamps!"

Beneatha continues to hold this lack of faith until practically the end of the last scene. She feels that money is actually so important to Walter that he would go ahead and sell the house back to the white community! She has given up all hope for her brother making the right decision when she cries "Oh God! Where is the bottom! Where is the real honest-to-God bottom so he can't go any further!"

These conflicts are universal and highly credible in a brother-sister rivalry. Each is vying for the approval and support of the parent figure; each feels that his or her ideas and plans are more important. This is illustrated several times throughout the play when Beneatha asks Mama to "be on my side for once!"; or when Walter screamed out in scene two, "Will someone please listen to me!"

Beneatha's attitude toward her brother changes at the end of the play. She is happy with his final decision to keep the house and not sell it. This feeling is shown at the end of the play when she retorts to Lindner and backs up Walter's decision to keep the house: "That's what the man said!"

For the first time throughout the play, Walter and Beneatha are in unison as brother and sister.

*Sheryl Bailey*

Sheryl's paper exhibits the strengths of a well-argued paper on conflict: a careful definition of the conflict under consideration; solid, smoothly introduced evidence from the play to support her main and subordinate points; and a fine analysis of the believability of the brother-sister rivalry in the play.

# 9

# Plot in Drama

## 17 · DISCOVERING PLOT AMONG PERSONIFICATIONS

*WRITING* Develop two or three personifications that have some conflict between them. Then find them a situation where they can react according to their natures and conflicts. For example, how would Fear, Rebellion, and Joy behave as wedding guests or at a funeral? In other words, find a situation — plot — suitable for the invented characters. By *plot,* we mean the main action of a play and also the chain of events that leads up to the main action: the chain of events that almost thwarts but finally leads up to a marriage; that causes a death; that conceals the identity of a criminal for a while; or that precedes and justifies taking revenge.

Describe in a paragraph a possible plot for the characters you have invented or, better yet, write a page-long scene for them. (Be sure to look over the section of Comments and Examples that follows this assignment before you write.)

Use these questions to get started:

1 How would your group of characters with their assorted motivations and conflicts behave as a family at a funeral, a birth, a marriage, or some other important occasion? What traits, conflicts, and conversations would emerge?
2 How would they behave as a group of citizens at some local political gathering: the censorship league; a meeting where some ecological issue is at stake; a group planning a trip to Washington, D.C. to protest

a new national policy? Who would emerge as leader and center of the plot?
3 How would they behave in a crisis situation: a fire, a flood, a ship or plane wreck? What character would become the focal one?
4 What other situation would most likely generate conflict among your set of characters?

DISCUSSION Once you have settled on a situation and main action, read and discuss your papers in class. Use these questions to guide the discussion:

1 Do the plots grow out of character conflicts and motivations?
2 Has a central character emerged who will be the focus for the plot? Do the major events in the chain emerge from his or her character or involve him or her?
3 Which of the remaining characters in the group are useful to the plot? Which must be dropped?

## COMMENTS AND EXAMPLES

Look at two pieces of student writing that demonstrate the development of plot in drama.

Plots in drama grow out of characters and their conflicts. People make things happen because of the kinds of natures they have or because their conflicts and natures draw them into certain situations. Observe, for example, how this process works in a group-written play by Mark Jones, Sue Campbell, Wayne Olsen, and Holly Walker. Their play "Another Day in the Death," a scene from which is printed in chapter 10, looked like this after they had completed exercise 17 on discovering a plot:

CHARACTERS

Mr. Average (the dead man)      Greedy (a thief)
Apathy (an indifferent citizen)  Guilt (Mrs. Average)
Concern (a tender-hearted woman) Duty (police)
Innocence (daughter of Concern)

SITUATION AND ACTION

Busy street in big city during rush hour, Mr. Average drops dead. Concern and Innocence are first to notice and run up to him, as Apathy stumbles over him muttering (checking his watch). Greedy comes up to rob Average's pockets. Duty comes up to do his duty. And as the end approaches, Guilt comes.

CONFLICTS

Guilt — inner conflict, gave him wrong pills that morning, thinks of all other details that might have caused his death. (No hot breakfast; forgot hat and umbrella, etc.)

Concern conflicts with Apathy, Greedy, and Duty. Apathy, Greedy, and Duty are concerned for themselves and facts (intellect). Concern is emotion-centered and selfless.

As you'll see in the final draft, this first attempt at a plot was too ambitious, and the writers dropped Guilt and Innocence from the play. Instead, they continued to focus on the street scene and kept family out of it. The plot finally concerns how these personifications react to another's death, and it shows how their natures cause them to behave in certain ways given the situation.

Holly did a short play of her own based on the behavior of a husband and wife, Optimism and Pessimism, trying to organize a picnic. Notice how the preparations for the outing — the plot of the sketch — go forward or are impeded by the characters' natures and the resulting conflicts:

> OPTIMISM. Successful businessman, tall and slender, large expressive hands, walks with a sure step, husband of Pessimism.
> PESSIMISM. Housewife, short and quite thin, large bug eyes, wringing hands, takes quick short steps, wife of Optimism.
> (*The two are mismatched and seem barely to like each other. They are in the car on the way to a campground via a grocery store. It's pouring down rain.*)
> PESSIMISM. Look at this awful rain, what an awful day, maybe we should go next week.
> OPTIMISM. Oh, it'll clear up.
> PESSIMISM. What if the campground is full, and we run out of gas and can't get back home, or get a flat tire—
> OPTIMISM. The campground won't be full on a Tuesday.
> PESSIMISM. I think I forgot the toothpaste.
> OPTIMISM. We'll buy some at the store.
> PESSIMISM. Oh, but I'm sure their prices are higher.
> OPTIMISM. Doesn't matter; we'll buy some anyway. (*Arrive and enter grocery store.*)
> OPTIMISM. Let's buy some delicious fruit and hamburger and buns for dinner tonight.
> PESSIMISM. Their prices are so high, and their fruit probably isn't fresh, ohhh, and this hamburger looks old—
> OPTIMISM. It won't kill us.
> PESSIMISM. Oh, I don't know.
> (*After an hour of decision-making the shopping is done. They continue on their trip and enter the campground.*)

OPTIMISM. Hey, there's a terrific campsite over there!
PESSIMISM. It might be too sunny.
OPTIMISM. Here's a good one!
PESSIMISM. Oh, the people next door might have noisy children.
OPTIMISM. Well, let's take this one.
PESSIMISM. I don't know, we might be sorry.
OPTIMISM. Ah, it'll be fine and we'll have a terrific time anyway, after all it's my vacation.
PESSIMISM. Oh, what if it doesn't stop raining —

*Holly Walker*

Once Holly has found her characters and has a basic description of each, a description which implies a view of life and a motivation, she discovers a suitable plot which reveals them as it develops their conflict: a husband, Optimism, and a wife, Pessimism, trying to plan something. The first is encouraging and hopeful; the second, discouraging and reluctant. The divisions between them are the very center of Holly's sketch just as conflict lies at the heart of all action in drama.

---

## 18 · WRITING ABOUT PLOT IN DRAMA

*WRITING* To be credible, drama plots must grow out of character and conflict — people set events in motion. Beginning with this assumption about plot, this third paper asks you to identify both a major and a minor action of a play and to show how the minor is related to the main plot.

As you have done in the other papers on drama, also focus part of your attention in this assignment on evaluating the success or lack of success of the plot. That is, be able to show whether or not a minor action connects to a major one, and be able to say how credible both actions are. For example, if the play you are studying has as its main plot a poor black family trying to decide how to spend a ten thousand dollar inheritance, you could examine any number of subordinate actions that show how individual family members dream of using money. For example, a woman with one child dreams of better housing than her mother-in-law's ghetto apartment, where the family now lives. An important minor action concerns this woman's second pregnancy: should she abort the child when it looks as though the hopes for the new house have been dashed? Is that choice she faces, as a minor action in the play, well connected to the main inheritance plot? How does her choice complicate the main plot, and what light does it shed on the characters who are involved in the decisions? Do both the subordinate and main actions emerge out of the characters and conflicts of the woman and her family?

That is, is it believable that in this circumstance (the inheritance after years of poverty and disappointment), this woman as revealed in the play would contemplate abortion?

These are the kinds of questions that one must ask, then, in order to think through a paper on plot. You should consider the following topics when you do your first draft: first, identify the main plot by stating a description of it as briefly as you can. Secondly, identify a minor action and examine its connection to the major one. Finally, consider the credibility of the actions as they grow out of character and conflict. (Be sure to read through the section of Comments and Examples that follows this assignment before beginning your paper.)

*Prewriting* These questions are intended to help you discover the means to think through your paper and to provide you with material for the first draft of your essay.

1. First identify the central characters and the central conflicts in the play. What are the different motivations of the characters, and how do these motivations come into conflict?
2. What is the main action of the play — a marriage, a death, a victory, a defeat, a discovery, an act of vengeance or reconciliation? (Attempt to state the main plot in a sentence or two. Get at its essence.)
3. What are the subordinate actions, the chain of events, that complicate, hinder, or further the main action? Is a character refused help by a person he or she had counted on? Do two characters fall in love with the same person? Is a character hindered from revenge by his or her conscience? Does a major character get conflicting advice on how to solve an issue like whom to marry, how to react to defeat, and so forth?
4. Does the play make a convincing connection between the main plot and the subordinate action, between the major action and one of the links in the chain of events? For example, is a parent's attempt to block a marriage between two young people convincingly motivated? Given that parent as the play reveals him or her, would he or she attempt to hinder a marriage for the reasons the play offers?
5. Does what happens in a play, in terms of main and subordinate actions, convincingly grow out of character? If a person near to them died, would these characters respond this way in conversation and action? Are you given a chance to see them in other emotions besides grief? Are their emotional reactions consistent?

*DISCUSSION* Rather than bringing your prewriting to class for discussion, wait until you have done a rough draft. Look at these discussion questions as you discuss your rough draft and again when you write your polished draft.

1 Have the main action and a subordinate action been clearly identified?
    a Have you established a connection between the two with which to begin your analysis and evaluation?
2 If in the rough draft stage, the paper isn't confident in its identification of two kinds of action in the play, check the rough draft with the prewriting. Has the prewriting been thorough enough? Are there hints in prewriting that could help the writer unfold his or her paper more clearly?
3 Pay careful attention to beginnings and endings of the rough drafts. Does the paper begin on a dramatic, eye-catching note? Does the paper end smoothly and not leave some major new idea, introduced right at the end, dangling without supporting evidence?
4 Is evidence offered for each generalization made in the paper?
5 Is each citation of evidence (either a direct quotation or paraphrase of the play) smoothly connected to the text of the paper?
6 Does the paper make a statement evaluating the success or lack of success of the plot?

---

## COMMENTS AND EXAMPLES

Exercise 18 has emphasized a set of cumulative tasks, applying what you have learned about character and conflict in drama to a study of plot. Observe how Wayne Olsen's paper on *A Raisin in the Sun* develops from prewriting through a polished draft to accomplish the purposes of this assignment.

Wayne's prewriting may look a bit fragmentary in this form, but his thoroughness shows up when you see his first and second drafts. Here are his prewriting notes:

Main plot — get out of the rut of ghetto life.
Minor plot — plant never dies but never grows because of lack of air, light, and room.

{ Plant has to get into fresh sun and air to grow — more plant environment.
Family has to get out of ghetto into a more family environment.

{ Hazy small window for light and air.
Walter drives south and sees steel mills.

{ The light is the only source of life for plant.
Hope is the only source of life for family.

> Mama's first action is to attend plant as her main purpose in the play is to attend to keeping everyone's hopes up.

Note that Wayne begins to make immediate connections between the minor plot (the plant) and the main plot (to spend the inheritance). Notice also that he ties both actions to a central motivation of a major character, Mama's hope for a new life symbolized in the plant.

In Wayne's rough draft, only part of which is printed here, his opening statement is on the clumsy side since his excellent prewriting insights haven't quite emerged: "The plight in *A Raisin in the Sun* of a small ghetto family trying to obtain a state of pride and contentment is nicely reflected in a struggle of a small potted plant trying to survive." Likewise at times in the rough draft, Wayne makes a bold generalization and fails to support it with evidence: "The family is living in a small apartment under very difficult living conditions." Finally, the rough draft lacked a statement about the credibility of the minor and main plots.

Following the questions outlined in the discussion section above, Wayne then did a revised draft of his essay, one which capitalizes on the fine insights of the prewriting and one which corrects the flaws of the rough draft — the weak introduction, the occasional lack of support for a major idea, and the failure to provide a statement about credibility:

> The main plot of *Raisin in the Sun* — of a small ghetto family trying to obtain a state of pride and contentment through an inheritance — is nicely mirrored in a minor action, the struggle of a small potted plant to survive. Mama's first action in the play is to check her plant. Her hope is the driving force of herself and her family; to find a better way of life so the family can survive is what she wants: "Lord, if this little old plant don't get more sun than it's been getting it ain't never going to see spring again." Mama's quote suggests the family imperative to get into the sun soon, for the family is living in a lousy little apartment which has one bathroom for their apartment and another family. There are cockroaches everywhere, and there just isn't enough room for five people in three rooms. Walter is totally discouraged with his job; Ruth is unfortunately pregnant; in other words, the family is falling apart. Comparatively the plant is living in a pot with only one small window to expose it to life-supporting light. Whereas the dim Chicago sun rays are what keeps the plant alive, Mama's hope is the thin thread holding the family together.
>
> Mama's last action, grabbing the plant from the dining room, illustrates how she forcefully influenced Walter's decision not to sell the house. Her fixation on the plant is also a credible aspect of her character and actions, a rural woman by birth wanting once again to

have the space and the hope that contact with sun and out-of-doors provides.

*Wayne Olson*

Like Wayne's paper on *A Raisin in the Sun,* Esther Winebarger's paper on plot in *Everyman* also provides a good example of how to develop an essay on drama. Notice especially: (1) how smoothly she introduces the minor plot as a topic, and also leads into Goods' crucial conversation in the third paragraph; (2) how her conclusion catches up the idea of Everyman's need to bring his "book of count" with him to death when Esther discusses the plot's credibility; and (3) how carefully she provides the reader with enough information to understand the context of Everyman's encounter with Goods as a minor but significant action in the play.

> The main plot of Everyman is how to get to heaven. The problem is how to live one's life — or in other words, how to face death. Everyman, the person, illustrates the struggle between virtue and vice and how that struggle relates to how to live.
>
> Everyman is refused help from everyone he has counted on when he faces Death. Death has told him to "bring his book of count," that is, to tell of the good and bad he has done. Everyman sees that he needs some help before he can stand for judgment.
>
> First his false friends, those that he has accumulated along with his wealth, appear eager to help; but then learning of his plight, they turn away. Part of this is illustrated, by a minor action in the middle of the play, the one I want to focus on, the scene with Goods and Everyman. Goods, the wealth that Everyman loved and cherished the most, says that he can't help Everyman and that "Nay Everyman, I sing another song / I follow no man in such voyages." This brief rejection scene connects with the main plot in that it shows how the material things that Everyman loved best are of no value.
>
> It is with this rejection that Everyman turns to Good Deeds, not Goods, for help. This is a believable change in that in hours of stress we do have to turn to inner-strength, not to outside help. Good Deeds represents one aspect of inner-strength — self-worth gathered from helping other people.
>
> Thus Everyman learns in this crucial encounter with Goods that it is not what you have that counts in Death's book of reckoning but what you have done.
>
> *Esther Winebarger*

As Wayne's and Esther's papers demonstrate, the study of plot in drama is largely a matter of carefully identifying both a main action and a significant minor one and then connecting those actions to the characters whose behavior initially caused them.

# 10

# Language in Drama

## 19 · DISCOVERING LANGUAGE FOR PERSONIFICATIONS

*WRITING* Develop some conversations among a set of personifications whom you can imagine in a situation like a wedding or a funeral and who are in conflict. For example, let's return to a situation in chapter 8 in which a father named Duty discovers that his son Deceit is a criminal. The father can't decide whether his duty lies in turning the son over to the law or in protecting his own blood from punishment. Imagine the two personifications in a scene — a jail cell or the son's room — where the father and son have their first chance to talk about the boy's crime. (Look over the Comments and Examples following this assignment in plays before you begin to write.)

Use these questions to generate dialogue for a scene and then to discuss language aspects in your sketch.

1 What is the situation for this piece of dialogue? Are the scene and backdrop clearly visible?
2 Given what you know about the characters, is the dialogue credible? Do they speak in a language that fits them?
3 Is there dramatic irony? Do the characters reveal more of themselves than they are conscious of? If so, what effect does this revelation have on the characters or their conflicts?
4 Do any of the characters have particularly colorful language? Slang? Dialect? Is it full of homely, down-to-earth comparisons? Learned references or witty phrases?

## COMMENTS AND EXAMPLES

Language in drama, to be credible, has to have an authentic ring. The characters, given their education, place in society, and background, and given the dramatic situation of the play, must not only be individuals but also be consistent once they are established. You can't have a lawyer, for example, go into a ghetto and begin to speak dialect unless you establish that the lawyer comes from such a background or that through work with people who live in the ghetto, he has mastered their language.

Pay special attention to the way in which characters unwittingly reveal facts about themselves. This device in plays is called *dramatic irony:* that is, the audience or perhaps another character is aware of a meaning in the character's speech that is now hidden from the character but may later be revealed. Perhaps the most famous instance is in *Oedipus Rex,* where Oedipus, who most of us know will soon be blind, makes many references early in the play to sight and light. Dramatic irony operates in our own sense of language when we are aware of something they are not. Say, for example, you have a friend who is a tough talker: who is cynical about love, about friendship, who says other people's sensitivities are foolish, yet you have caught this friend in soft moments when he or she has betrayed through a generous act, another kinder, more optimistic, more idealistic side. So you judge the friend by his or her actions, not by the feigned cynicism. The audience of a play, like you with your friend, judges a character largely by differences between what the character says and what he or she does, or between what the character says to one person and what he or she says to another.

Drama, then, takes advantage of an important aspect of our everyday language in its employment of dramatic irony: the reversals in language that reveal people's natures and that lead us to judge them.

Observe how the following scene from "Another Day in the Death" strives to capture the authentic voices of people at the death of a man on a busy downtown street.

### ANOTHER DAY IN THE DEATH

Scene: Typically busy downtown street in any large city. The stage is the sidewalk, with a concrete business building in the background. As the curtain rises the sidewalk is busy with faceless businessmen identically dressed in gray suits, hats shadowing their faces, and briefcases.

They all walk in a swift rhythm of unconcern. This scene is held for several seconds, until the metropolitan mood is set.

Our star, Mr. Average, enters dressed identical to everyone else on stage. He is probably first noticed when he breaks the street rhythm by slowing down near center stage. He stops then and drops motionless. The street rhythm continues without noticing him. One pedestrian reading a newspaper trips over the body dropping his newspaper, almost falling.

APATHY. Hell! Some people are as considerate as a hole in the wall. (*Picking up the newspaper*) Now where was that article on degenerate Americans? (*He checks his watch, picks the paper up, and exits quickly*) (*Sidewalk traffic continues*)

Greedy enters looking at the ground and walking a bit slower than the constant rhythm of traffic. His hands are in his pockets seeming to hold his pants up. He walks past the body, shiftily looks both ways to see if anyone is watching. No one is. Greedy kneels next to the body, takes Mr. Average's belt off and puts it on. Standing he finds it's a nice fit. He smiles with satisfaction. Checking both ways again he kneels and pulls out Mr. Average's billfold, takes the money out and stuffs it into his pocket. Then continues to investigate it further. Concern enters; her waddling walk is in direct contrast with the rhythmic traffic. She sees Greedy and Mr. Average.

CONCERN. (*Surprised*) Oh dear! (*Her voice startles Greedy; he drops the billfold*) What's happened to your friend?

GREEDY. (*Stuttering*) Ah, er, he's fainted; yah, he just fainted. I'm trying to bring him to. It's nothing serious.

CONCERN. (*Informatively*) Fainting can be serious if the proper steps aren't taken. I took a Red Cross course once. Here, raise his legs, loosen his tie. He looks so pale. Mouth-to-mouth, that's what's needed. (*She bends to revive Mr. Average. When her lips touch his mouth, she reels back, shocked*) He's dead! He's as cold as the sidewalk.

GREEDY. Ridiculous. (*Checking Mr. Average he notices no pulse but he does notice his watch*) I—I think you're right, he is dead.

(*During the moment Concern is stunned, Greedy removes Mr. A's watch*)

CONCERN. (*Snapping to*) Heart massage! That's what he needs now. Pound as hard as you can right here on his chest.

GREEDY. No way, lady. I don't need no murder rap.

CONCERN. My name is Concern.

GREEDY. (*Not noticing her comment. Jumps up looks both ways and begins to exit quickly*) I'll go get help! There's a phone booth around the corner. I'll call for help there.

(*Concern turns her attention to the body while Greedy is exiting; however, before he can get off stage he runs into a policeman who just steps on stage. Their eyes meet in a brief display of fear and suspicion*)

DUTY. What seems to be the trouble? (*He directs Greedy back to Mr. A. and Concern. As they approach, Concern looks up*)

CONCERN. Thank God, you've brought help. This man needs help. He's dead!
DUTY. (*Routinely looking the body over and giving it a kick*) Yep.
CONCERN. (*Impatiently*) You've got to do something; this is a human life here.
DUTY. (*Unimpressed*) Was a life you mean. (*Pulling out his notebook*) Anyone got a pencil? (*Concern gives him a pen*) What time did he die?
CONCERN. Just now. (*She looks at Greedy and he nods in agreement*) Maybe there's something we can do. There's still hope.
DUTY. (*He glances at the body*) Na. What time is it anyway? Anyone got a watch?
GREEDY. Four-fifteen, on the dot.
DUTY. (*Looking to Concern*) Who is he?
CONCERN. (*Points to Greedy*) I don't know; ask his friend.
GREEDY. (*Startled*) I've never seen him before. I was just walking by, don't know the man, and don't want to.
DUTY. (*Spying the billfold lying next to Mr. A*) I wonder how this got here? (*Picking the billfold up*)
CONCERN. Oh dear, he's been mugged. There's proof.
DUTY. (*Looking to Greedy as a potential mugger*) Na. What do you think?
GREEDY. I couldn't say; I was just walking by. I didn't see a thing.
DUTY. (*Giving Greedy a penetrating look*) We-ll if no one saw him drop, there's a chance for murder, so, there'll be an investigation. And the Lord knows an investigation means filling out forms and more forms.
GREEDY. (*Getting the message*) Oh, now that you mention it; it all happened so fast. I was walking along and he just dropped; there weren't a soul near him. (*The cop begins to go through the billfold*) Yep, that's what happened, I was just —
DUTY. Why this is Barry Johnson! He's a big wheel down at City Hall. (*Pause*) This is news. (*Posing as if having picture taken*) Maybe I'll get my picture in the paper. Or a promotion.
CONCERN. (*Looking down at the body and shaking her head*) He was such a good man!
DUTY. (*Smile turns to a frown; then he grabs Greedy and pushes him to the wall*) You murdered the wrong person, buster. (*He begins to frisk Greedy*)
CONCERN. He was just trying to help. You have no proof. (*Her voice changes from defensive to angry*) I don't like you; you're a cold man.
GREEDY. (*Pleadingly*) She's right; I was just trying to help. I haven't done anything wrong.
DUTY. (*Pulling money from Greedy's pockets*) Trying to help yourself you mean. You're as innocent as a killer wolf.
CONCERN. (*Angry now*) That's no proof. You just said it wasn't a mugging. Now what's changed your mind?
DUTY. New evidence, besides it's my job to be suspicious, lady.
CONCERN. My name is Concern.
DUTY. (*Looking back to Greedy*) By the way, what's your name?

GREEDY. I ain't saying nothin' till I see a lawyer. (*He shuts his eyes and mouth tight*)
DUTY. Don't be ridiculous; your only way out of this is to plead insanity and the sanest thing you can do right now is to clam up.
GREEDY. (*Opening his eyes*) Oh. Ah, Fred Greedy, and I don't remember anything.
DUTY. (*Begins to whistle while he hands Concern his notepad and handcuffs Greedy*) Here, write down your name and address, and what you saw. I'll get in touch with you later.
(*While Greedy mumbles in despair, Duty finishes cuffing and takes the notepad back from Concern. He puts the pad and pen in his pocket; Concern takes her pen out of Duty's pocket. Duty and Greedy begin to leave*)
CONCERN. What about this man here? You just can't have human bodies lying in the street.
DUTY. When you're as cold as a cucumber, you may as well be one. Nothing is going to hurt him anyway.
CONCERN. What about your duty now?
DUTY. (*Turning all his attention to Concern*) My duty is not lugging bodies out of the streets. I'm here to protect the people. (*Greedy once again looks both ways and then sneaks off stage*) And I can't protect people like you while I'm lugging bodies around. There are certain responsibilities and priorities we have to follow. Rules are the backbone of society. (*Turning to let Greedy in on his lecture*) Now see what you've done! (*Cop runs off stage after prisoner. As lights dim, a street sweeper enters, sees the body, and sweeps his pile of dirt under our star, Mr. Average, as Concern watches, horrified.*)

*Mark Jones, Sue Campbell, Wayne Olson, and Holly Walker*

If you write plays, you can't intrude as a dramatist and say what a character is like or why he behaves the way he does. Character traits and behavior have to be shown in actions and especially in believable dialogue. Characters like Greedy and Concern in "Another Day in the Death" are, of course, exaggerated and lacking in depth, but we do demand consistency even of them. Greedy must be shifty and selfish in both language and deed. Concern must be consistently kind-hearted and selfless in her words and behavior. If they aren't consistent and if they don't speak in accordance with their natures or social backgrounds, characters lack authenticity, and the playwright has trouble making us believe in his or her characters' language.

# 20 · WRITING ABOUT LANGUAGE IN DRAMA

*WRITING* This exercise calls for another sharply focused paper: analyze the language of a main character in a play. Other aspects of the character must be examined in order to analyze language; thus, as have the other essays on drama, this one gives you three tasks to do: (Read the section of Comments and Examples that follows before going on with this assignment.)

1 identify a main character and look at his or her motivations and conflicts;
2 discuss the principal language features of that character;
3 comment on the credibility of the character's language and nature.

*Prewriting* Begin with a systematic study of a character in light of his or her traits, conflicts, and function in the plot. Then go on to analyze the character's language in relation to these aspects:

1 What are the character's major motivations, and in what way besides language is the character revealed?
2 What are the character's conflicts, either with others or within himself or herself?
3 How does this character contribute to the action of the play?
4. What is the principal feature that individualizes this character's speech? Is it slang? Dialect? Does it show education? Does he or she have the ability to persuade others or are the characters easily persuaded?
5 Is there dramatic irony present in this character's speech? That is, does this character make slips in speech that reveal himself or herself in ways that the character may not want to disclose? Does something the character says unconsciously anticipate an event later in the play? (For example, Oedipus' sight references, anticipating his blinding.)
6 Is the character's speech barren of or rich in comparisons? What does the presence or absence of imagery tell you about his or her character or function in the play?
7 Is the character's speech believable given his or her station in life and given the circumstances of the play?

*DISCUSSION* As your papers develop, look first in class at your prewriting evidence:

1 Has the character been thoroughly researched in regard to motivation, revelation, conflicts, role in plot, and type of language?
2 What are the language qualities that individualize the characters?

Once you have done a rough draft, then examine the essays in light of these questions:

1. Does each writer justify his or her evaluation of a character's language as successful or unsuccessful?
2. Has the writer presented specific, smoothly introduced examples of the character's language (individualizing qualities, dramatic irony, or imagery)?

---

## COMMENTS AND EXAMPLES

You have already been exposed throughout this section on drama to the process of prewriting and revising critical essays of evaluation. The following two student essays, by Tim Budd on *Everyman* and by Teresa Tucker on *A Raisin in the Sun,* are offered as models of another important quality in critical writing: the art of convincing a reader that your judgments are accurate.

### WALTER'S LANGUAGE IN *A RAISIN IN THE SUN*

In Lorraine Hansbury's *A Raisin in the Sun* the character Walter has an urgent need to assert himself as an individual to his family and the world and thus establish his own self-worth. It is this need and his defense of this need that ignites the situation and action of this play and transforms it into drama.

Walter is frustrated, an ambitious man bound by the low expectations of those around him and basically unsure of his own abilities. Truly American, he sees wealth and status as the great indicators of personal value. Possessing neither of these attributes, his self-esteem rests upon unstable foundations, largely his dreams of success.

His personality is stamped with the volatile impatience of the ambitious dreamer. Hindering his ambitious longing is an impractical and naive perception of the world that leaves him vulnerable to eventual disappointment when his little inheritance is stolen by an unscrupulous friend.

Walter's personality is revealed through his dialogue in two ways: the individual's speech characteristics (his verbal style) and what he says (the content). If either element were lacking, then the development of Walter would suffer. Leave out verbal style and any character becomes one-dimensional, a stick figure lacking any credibility. If content is absent then the character, however charming he may appear, lacks consequence. When this happens the audience is unable to identify deeply with him and his fate becomes a trivial matter. Walter, however, has both credible style and content.

Walter's style of speaking gains its strength from being colorful and

*LANGUAGE IN DRAMA*     103

rhythmic. It is captivating even as a purely listening experience. This occurs through the use of repetition which has an almost hypnotic effect on the ear. For example, Walter is a dreamer who wants his family to believe in his dreams and his successful friends. In this speech, he rebukes his family for downgrading his friends and his dreams of wealth: "Anybody who talks to me has got to be a good-for-nothing loud mouth, ain't he? And what you know about who is just a good-for-nothing loud mouth? Charlie Atkins was just a 'good for nothing loud mouth' too, wasn't he! When he wanted me to go into the dry cleaning business with him. And now — he's grossing a hundred thousand a year. A hundred thousand dollars a year! You can still call him a loud mouth!"

"Good-for-nothing loud mouth" occurs as an expression three times, "loud mouth" four times. The effect of this repetition, far from being mere redundancy, establishes an ordered rhythm that heightens the effect of a statement that could have been expressed by a single sentence.

The chant-like effect of Walter's speech also underlines his role as the dreamer. His speech becomes almost song-like, for he talks out loud expounding, idealizing, questing just as his daydreams must sound. In this speech, he accuses his family of holding him back from wealth.

Lorraine Hansberry does not stop there, however. She links the repetitious rhythm with content that is believable. Walter's dialogue is credible to his status and circumstance both socially and emotionally. For he is always building worlds of images with his speech. As they reel hypnotically off his tongue, the audience is allowed to participate in Walter's dream which for him is more actual than the things and people that do indeed surround him. He's a black, surrounded by ugly circumstances, so he dreams of being like his sister's suitor George, a wealthy black, one who has escaped circumstances.

*Teresa Tucker*

## LANGUAGE IN *EVERYMAN*

In studying the literary works of the medieval English period, the major obstacle to overcome is the language itself. Not many of us are fluent in Middle English, and even in translation the subtle shades of meaning and changes in tone may entirely escape us.

With these warnings firmly planted in my mind I now wish to go on to discuss the nature of language in the play *Everyman*. In particular, I wish to concentrate on a single character, the person of Death.

Acting as a liaison between God and Man, Death occupies a central position of importance in the divine hierarchy that we see presented in the play. We know this to be fact from the first conversation God has with Death:

> DEATH. Almighty God, I am here at your will,
>   Your commandment to fulfill.
> GOD. Go thou to Everyman,
>   And show him, in my name . . .

So we see very clearly that immediately everybody is put in their place, God above Death, and Death above man.

Acting as a messenger from God, Death initiates the action throughout the entire play. Since he is empowered to "cruelly outsearch both great and small," he then sets out to find Everyman. As a note here, we should not stumble over the word *cruel* as it is used in this context. Looking to the *Oxford English Dictionary* we find that, at this time, "cruelly" meant "with haste and thoroughness" and also "with indifference." It should not in any case be taken to represent the medieval picture of God, as a cruel, in the sense of heartless, being.

The next person that Death meets after leaving God is Everyman. He informs Everyman that God desires "A reckoning . . ./Without any longer respite."

Thus Death sets in motion the machinery that will move throughout the play until the very end when Everyman manages salvation.

Death appears to be fully cognizant about the power he holds, and he seems to be truly interested in the fate of those he lords it over. He lets Everyman have one day to get his matters straight, apparently without consulting with his superiors about the propriety of these actions. That just makes us, as readers, feel all the more certain that he really isn't a bad fellow; he just has a job to do.

As I mentioned in the beginning, it is very hard to tell one character's language in style from another's. There may be subtle dialects or changes in tone, but they are lost to the modern reader.

When Death says: "It is God's commandment/That all to me should be obedient"; and when Everyman responds by saying "Oh Death, thou comest when I had thee least in mind," I cannot tell the style of the latter from that of the former. But the tone of the words in the two characters are very different. All throughout the first part of the play Everyman is afraid, turning every way at once to seek help. Death, on the other hand, seems self-assured, seems to have everything in control since he obeys God. Obedience is what Everyman lacks, and it shows in his language.

For instance, we see this in the exchange:

EVERYMAN. Yea, a thousand pound shalt thou have,
  And defer this matter till another day.
DEATH. Everyman, it may not be, by no way.
  And again:
EVERYMAN. . . . whither shall I flee . . .
  . . . gentle Death, spare me till tomorrow . . .
DEATH. Nor no man will I respite.

Acting, as Death does, as the major strength and backbone of the opening scenes in the play, even without ever appearing again on stage, Death then becomes a symbol of the strength and fairness of God's ultimate justice, and his influences are felt to the very end. So it is a credible language used in *Everyman* to establish the differences between a respectful figure, Death, who carries out his duty, and a disrespectful character, Everyman, who in the course of the play must leave his duty even as he is sentenced to death. The language choices help support this important statement on obedience in the play.

Tim Budd

Throughout the text, you have been urged to trust your own perceptions of a piece of literature once you have thoroughly analyzed it and have done at least two drafts of a paper. The insightfulness of your perceptions may, however, be misunderstood if you have communicated them ineffectively. The text assumes that good thinking and careful preparation precede good writing, and that effective communication begins early in the process. But in the sequence of composition, moving from prewriting to rough draft to polished version, you must also be aware that critical writing necessitates convincing a reader of the accuracy of your judgments. There are three steps in the convincing process, as the papers just quoted illustrate. We will now analyze them:

1. The writer begins with a perception or judgment about the work that may be the covering idea for the paper and follows with supporting perceptions; ones that help convince the reader that the main idea is sound. For example, Teresa offers as a basic idea that Walter represents the "frustrated . . . ambitious . . . American," one who "sees wealth and status as the great indicators of personal value." This notion she supports with a look at Walter's version of this American vision as revealed by his chanting, dreamlike language, a language which supports his illusions.

2. The writer offers evidence from the work in support of the basic contention or from one of the subordinate ideas. For instance, Teresa offers a lengthy speech by Walter, one in which he defends his new friend Willy and his old friend Charlie Atkins: "Anybody who talks to me has got to be a good-for-nothing loud mouth, ain't he?" In other words, each general statement needs to be pinned down in your papers so that the reader doesn't have to search his or her mind for the proof that the writer should provide. The reader has to set his own reading of the play against the critic's, and judge how well and how fairly he or she has selected evidence as support.

3. Finally, once the general assertion has been made and evidence offered to support it, the writer's last step is to analyze the evidence and to say why that piece of evidence is significant to his or her reading of the play. This final step, the act of interpretation of the evidence, often distinguishes the least successful from the most successful papers. Notice, for instance, in Tim's essay how he continues to follow up his citation of Death's function and language in *Everyman:* Death is "em-

powered to 'cruelly outsearch both great and small.' " Tim goes on to point out that *cruel* in Middle English doesn't have our sense of heartless but does have a sense of indifference and of haste and thoroughness. Without this final step, Tim's citation would have been flat. As it is, his analysis contributes to the excellence and thoroughness of his paper, the quality that convinces us that he has justified his perceptions of the play.

While we may not change our minds about a play after reading someone else's arguments about it, we may wish to admit that the person had a well-supported, keen insight into the play and that we have to consider that perception as an alternative to our own.

# 11

# Staging in Drama

## 21 · WRITING ABOUT STAGING IN DRAMA

*WRITING* This assignment combines the individual experience paper and critical paper into one exercise. It gives you a choice of three topics on staging, two of them a bit freer than the critical essays you have been writing. Each topic gives you a chance not only to imagine directing a scene from a play, but also to see how such aspects as character, conflict, plot, and language can be brought alive on stage.

Write on one of the following three topics:

Topic I Develop a critical essay, much like those in the first four chapters of the drama section, in which you give a scene a close reading and argue how it might best be staged. For example, you could concentrate on Everyman's first encounter with Death or Good Deeds; or the scene where the Youngers first meet Karl Lindner in *A Raisin in the Sun*. Consider these aspects of staging as possible subtopics for your paper:
  a What scenery would you use?
  b What type of actors would you seek? (Perhaps you can draw upon familiar ones like Charles Bronson, Richard Roundtree, or Barbra Streisand as models.)
  c How would you block the characters? That is, where would you have them stand and where would you have them move within your scenery?
  d What gestures and voice tones would you emphasize in your staging of the play?

Topic II   If the play you are working with is an old play, like *Everyman,* give it an appropriately modern setting.
  a  Suggest an overall plan for updating the play, or
  b  Give one scene an expanded reading with director's suggestions for staging, in light of your idea for updating it.
Topic III   Write a new scene in which two characters from the play meet in another setting. For example, Tom Stoppard a few years ago wrote *Rosencrantz and Guildenstern Are Dead* as a takeoff on *Hamlet.* In your new scene, give careful directions about scenery, blocking, and gestures.

*DISCUSSION*  Examine your papers in light of how well the writers have preserved the credibility of the characters, conflicts, plot, and language of each play.

## COMMENTS AND EXAMPLES

In staging a play, a director emphasizes what he or she sees significant in it. Interpretations may vary widely since each director's personal vision will be imposed on the drama. This variation is what gives theater its vitality. There's always a new *Midsummer Night's Dream* possible, because either the changing cultural climate or a fresh reading by an imaginative director will bring out aspects unseen before the new production.

Here are three fresh looks at *Everyman*. Two of them imagine an overall modern plan for the play; the third gives one scene a close reading in a modern setting.

### MODERN SETTING FOR *EVERYMAN*

*Everyman* would take place in a bus station — a big ugly one such as Greyhound's in Seattle. Everyman would be sitting in a TV chair watching "Let's Make a Deal" when Death appears on the screen.

All the characters would then appear in sequence on the screen, and Everyman would talk to them as he continued to sit in his chair. No one in the station would notice; they would keep on buying tickets and drinking coffee.

In the end, Everyman himself would descend in death into the screen as he goes off to justice with Good Deeds. Then as if she has been waiting her chance, a fat sweaty woman would leap into the chair, slip in a quarter, and watch "Search for Tomorrow."

*Rhonda Rinne*

A PRESENT-DAY *EVERYMAN*

In presenting the play *Everyman,* I would move the time period into the present. The setting would be on a road, in a very influential residential area of a large city.

A Lincoln Continental Mark IV drives by with Everyman at the wheel. He appears to be dressed for a night out on the town, wearing brown wool pants, small plaid sport coat and a creamy colored long-sleeved shirt. His age seems to be early fifties. His hair is flecked with grey (Grecian Formula 49 keeps a lot more from showing). His face over the years has gradually become very distinguished, with wrinkles in all the right places. His manner is confident, capable of getting everything he wants. He is humming the song that is playing on his tape deck, lightly tapping the steering wheel with his fingers.

Ahead he sees a young man walking along the road. For no apparent reason Everyman pulls over and asks him if he needs a ride.

The young man gets in the car. His age is twenty to twenty-five. His clothing is clean. He is wearing faded blue jeans, a blue denim work shirt and cowboy boots. His hair is light brown, wavy and of medium length. He has a quiet manner, but his presence is commanding.

Everyman pulls the car away from the curb and continues driving. They ride in silence for a few minutes. Then a polite impersonal conversation begins. The usual, about the weather and what a nice day it has been. They then exchange names.

"I'm Everyman."

The young man turns toward Everyman and replies, "And I am Death; I come seeking you. Do you have your accounts in order?"

The play begins at this point. Everyman, being taken by surprise, loses control of the car; it plunges over the bank. Everyman is unconscious and seriously injured. Death then merges into Everyman's mind and begins to tell him what he needs and must do.

*Esther Winebarger*

MODERN SCENE: EVERYMAN AND DEATH

Setting: X-Rated movie theatre in a big city. In the back of the theatre sits Everyman, of medium height, slight beer belly, toupé on his head. He is a middle-class businessman, owning a large house, sailboat, two sportscars, etc. He is thoroughly enjoying the movie and is holding a can of beer in his hand.

Enter: Death — tall, slender, dark, weatherworn but kindly face (Abraham Lincoln style) strides quickly and confidently down the aisle and sits down next to Everyman. (As play goes on, Death should age and fade out till at the end he is white-haired and bearded, stooping low)

DEATH. (*Urgently*) Everyman, sit still, What are you doing so happily? Have you forgotten your Maker?

EVERYMAN. (*Sitting up and forward in his seat; indignantly*) What do you want?

DEATH. (*Earnestly*) I'll tell you; I've been sent to you from God.
EVERYMAN. (*Thinking it a joke*) What?
DEATH. Yes, you may have forgotten him, but He's thinking about you. You'll understand when we leave.
EVERYMAN. (*Playing along*) What does God want me for?
DEATH. This: He wants a reckoning from you without further delay.
EVERYMAN. (*Not quite believing, but realizing that Death is serious*) I'd need more time for a reckoning. I don't quite understand all this.
DEATH. There's a long trip you have to take —
EVERYMAN. (*Tired of this game, sitting back in his seat*) Well, I'm not ready for any reckoning. I don't even know you, Who are you anyway?
DEATH. I am Death . . .
EVERYMAN. (*Suddenly realizing it is not a game, that Death is really* Death, *he sits on the edge of his seat, quickly shoving his beer to the side and behind him. In a desperate tone*) Death! Of all times I was least expecting you now! . . . (*reaching for his wallet, thumbing through his bills, he hands Death a thousand dollars*) I'll give you a thousand dollars, anything! to put this off till another day.
DEATH. (*Pushing aside the money, and impatiently*) . . . I can't give you any help. Now come on, stop delaying.
(*They get up and start walking up the aisle*)
EVERYMAN. (*With hands out to side, pleafully*) Wait till I can get some help . . .
DEATH. (*Unable to give an inch*) . . . man must die, it's natural.
EVERYMAN. (*In a vain and failing hope*) . . . I will be coming back soon, won't I?
DEATH. (*Feeling a little sorry for Everyman continues slightly in front of Everyman, looking a little older, walking slower*) No, of that you can be sure.
EVERYMAN. (*More to himself than to Death, almost prayerfully*) Won't I have anyone to go with me?
(*They approach the door opening onto the sidewalk, just before going out, they stop, Death turns to Everyman searching his eyes*)
DEATH. Yes, if anyone *will* go with you . . . (*Seeing Everyman's vanity, in exasperation*) Did you think your life was yours, and your possessions, too?
EVERYMAN. (*In honesty*) Yes, I did.
DEATH. (*Pitying Everyman*) No, no, they were only yours for awhile . . . You should do something while you have a chance, because I come without warning.
EVERYMAN. (*In a last effort*) Give me just one more day to get ready!
DEATH. (*In a more authoritative tone than before, mysteriously*) I can't give you that . . . no one can escape from me. (*And he disappears into a dark corner. Everyman follows the shadow, and then hopelessly turns around, walking out into the street in a dream-like state*)
EVERYMAN. (*Groaning*) I should be torn apart! I have no one, no one at all to help me . . .
(*Enter Fellowship*)

*Holly Walker*

All three of these versions of *Everyman*, despite their differences, stress the same aspects of character, conflict, and plot as the original play does — that excessive stress on worldly concerns is vanity; man must pay for misdirecting his energies. Holly's paper, the most elaborate of the three, gives you not only a modern scene (the X-rated movie) but also careful stage descriptions about the looks, language, blocking, and gestures of her modern Death and Everyman. Making a play credible, she realizes, is partly the director's job: to provide an audience with an identifiable setting and set of characters, so that the director can proceed to interpret the play on grounds familiar to the audience.

# DRAMA READINGS

## EVERYMAN

—— *Anonymous*

CHARACTERS

| | | |
|---|---|---|
| God | Cousin | Strength |
| Messenger | Goods | Discretion |
| Death | Good Deeds | Five Wits |
| Everyman | Knowledge | Angel |
| Fellowship | Confession | Doctor |
| Kindred | Beauty | |

Here beginneth a treatise how the High Father of Heaven sendeth

Anonymous, "Everyman," from *Everyman and Medieval Miracle Plays* Edited by A. C. Cawley. Published in 1959 by E. P. Dutton & Co., Inc., and used with their permission.

Death to summon every creature to come and give account of their lives in this world, and is in manner of a moral play.

MESSENGER. I pray you all give your audience,
   And hear this matter with reverence,
   By figure a moral play:                           *in form*
   The *Summoning of Everyman* called it is,
5   That of our lives and ending shows
   How transitory we be all day.                      *always*
   This matter is wondrous precious,
   But the intent of it is more gracious,
   And sweet to bear away.
10  The story saith: Man, in the beginning
   Look well, and take good heed to the ending,
   Be you never so gay!
   Ye think sin in the beginning full sweet,
   Which in the end causeth the soul to weep,
15  When the body lieth in clay.
   Here shall you see how Fellowship and Jollity,
   Both Strength, Pleasure, and Beauty,
   Will fade from thee as flower in May;
   For ye shall hear how our Heaven King
20  Calleth Everyman to a general reckoning:
   Give audience, and hear what he doth say.  [*Exit.*

*God speaketh:*

GOD.  I perceive, here in my majesty,
   How that all creatures be to me unkind,        *ungrateful*
   Living without dread in worldly prosperity:
25  Of ghostly sight the people be so blind,
   Drowned in sin, they know me not for their God;
   In worldly riches is all their mind,
   They fear not my righteousness, the sharp rod.
   My law that I showed, when I for them died,
30  They forget clean, and shedding of my blood red;
   I hanged between two, it cannot be denied;
   To get them life I suffered to be dead;
   I healed their feet, with thorns hurt was my head.
   I could do no more than I did, truly;
35  And now I see the people do clean forsake me:
   They use the seven deadly sins damnable,

   8 But the purpose of it is more devout.
   25 In spiritual vision.
   32 I consented to die.

|   |   |   |
|---|---|---|
|    | As pride, covetise, wrath, and lechery | *covetousness* |
|    | Now in the world be made commendable; |  |
|    | And thus they leave of angels the heavenly company. |  |
| 40 | Every man liveth so after his own pleasure, |  |
|    | And yet of their life they be nothing sure: |  |
|    | I see the more that I them forbear |  |
|    | The worse they be from year to year. |  |
|    | All that liveth appaireth fast; | *degenerates* |
| 45 | Therefore I will, in all the haste, |  |
|    | Have a reckoning of every man's person; |  |
|    | For, and I leave the people thus alone | *if* |
|    | In their life and wicked tempests, | *tumults* |
|    | Verily they will become much worse than beasts; |  |
| 50 | For now one would by envy another up eat; |  |
|    | Charity they do all clean forget. |  |
|    | I hoped well that every man |  |
|    | In my glory should make his mansion, |  |
|    | And thereto I had them all elect; |  |
| 55 | But now I see, like traitors deject, | *abject* |
|    | They thank me not for the pleasure that I to them meant, | *for* |
|    | Nor yet for their being that I them have lent. |  |
|    | I proffered the people great multitude of mercy, |  |
|    | And few there be that asketh it heartily. | *earnestly* |
| 60 | They be so cumbered with worldly riches |  |
|    | That needs on them I must do justice, |  |
|    | On every man living without fear. |  |
|    | Where art thou, Death, thou mighty messenger? |  |

*[Enter Death]*

|   |   |   |
|---|---|---|
|    | DEATH. Almighty God, I am here at your will, |  |
| 65 | Your commandment to fulfill. |  |
|    | GOD. Go thou to Everyman, |  |
|    | And show him, in my name, |  |
|    | A pilgrimage he must on him take, |  |
|    | Which he in no wise may escape; |  |
| 70 | And that he bring with him a sure reckoning |  |
|    | Without delay or any tarrying. *[God withdraws.]* |  |
|    | DEATH. Lord, I will in the world go run overall, | *everywhere* |
|    | And cruelly outsearch both great and small; |  |
|    | Every man will I beset that liveth beastly |  |
| 75 | Out of God's laws, and dreadeth not folly. |  |

41 And yet their lives are by no means secure.

He that loveth riches I will strike with my dart,
His sight to blind, and from heaven to depart — *separate*
Except that alms be his good friend —
In hell for to dwell, world without end.
80 Lo, yonder I see Everyman walking.
Full little he thinketh on my coming;
His mind is on fleshly lusts and his treasure,
And great pain it shall cause him to endure
Before the Lord, Heaven King.

[*Enter Everyman*]

85 Everyman, stand still! Whither art thou going
Thus gaily? Hast thou thy Maker forget?
EVERYMAN. Why asketh thou?
Wouldest thou wit? *know*
DEATH. Yea, sir; I will show you:
90 In great haste I am sent to thee
From God out of his majesty.
EVERYMAN. What, sent to me?
DEATH. Yea, certainly.
Though thou have forget him here,
95 He thinketh on thee in the heavenly sphere,
As, ere we depart, thou shalt know.
EVERYMAN. What desireth God of me?
DEATH. That shall I show thee:
A reckoning he will needs have
100 Without any longer respite.
EVERYMAN. To give a reckoning longer leisure I crave;
This blind matter troubleth my wit. *obscure*
DEATH. On thee thou must take a long journey;
Therefore thy book of count with thee thou bring, *account*
105 For turn again thou cannot by no way. *return*
And look thou be sure of thy reckoning,
For before God thou shalt answer, and show
Thy many bad deeds, and good but a few;
How thou hast spent thy life, and in what wise,
110 Before the chief Lord of paradise.
Have ado that we were in that way,
For, wit thou well, thou shalt make none attorney.
EVERYMAN. Full unready I am such reckoning to give.
I know thee not. What messenger art thou?

111 i.e., let's see about making that journey.
112 No one [your] advocate.

DEATH. I am Death, that no man dreadeth,   *arrest*
    For every man I rest, and no man spareth;
    For it is God's commandment
    That all to me should be obedient.
EVERYMAN. O Death, thou comest when I had thee
        least in mind!
    In thy power it lieth me to save;
    Yet of my good will I give thee, if thou will be   *goods*
        kind:
    Yea, a thousand pound shalt thou have,
    And defer this matter till another day.
DEATH. Everyman, it may not be, by no way.
    I set not by gold, silver, nor riches,   *care not for*
    Ne by pope, emperor, king, duke, ne princes;
    For, and I would receive gifts great,   *if*
    All the world I might get;
    But my custom is clean contrary.
    I give thee no respite. Come hence, and not tarry.
EVERYMAN. Alas, shall I have no longer respite?
    I may say Death giveth no warning!
    To think on thee, it maketh my heart sick,
    For all unready is my book of reckoning.
    But twelve year and I might have abiding,
    My counting-book I would make so clear
    That my reckoning I should not need to fear.
    Wherefore, Death, I pray thee, for God's mercy,
    Spare me till I be provided of remedy.
DEATH. Thee availeth not to cry, weep, and pray;
    But haste thee lightly that thou were gone that
        journey,
    And prove thy friends if thou can;
    For, wit thou well, the tide abideth no man,   *time*
    And in the world each living creature
    For Adam's sin must die of nature.
EVERYMAN. Death, if I should this pilgrimage take,
    And my reckoning surely make,
    Show me, for saint charity,
    Should I not come again shortly?
DEATH. No, Everyman; and thou be once there,

115 Who fears no man.
123 If you defer.
135 If I could stay for just twelve more years.
141 But set off quickly on your journey.
145 In the course of nature.
148 In the name of holy charity.

>     Thou mayst never more come here,
>     Trust me verily.
> EVERYMAN. O gracious God in the high seat celestial,
>     Have mercy on me in this most need!
> 155 Shall I have no company from this vale terrestrial
>     Of mine acquaintance, that way me to lead?
> DEATH. Yea, if any be so hardy
>     That would go with thee and bear thee company.
>     Hie thee that thou were gone to God's magnif-
>         icence,
> 160 Thy reckoning to give before his presence.
>     What, weenest thou thy life is given thee,       *suppose*
>     And thy worldly goods also?
> EVERYMAN. I had wend so, verily.                      *supposed*
> DEATH. Nay, nay; it was but lent thee;
> 165 For as soon as thou art go,                       *gone*
>     Another a while shall have it, and then go
>         therefro,                                     *from it*
>     Even as thou hast done.
>     Everyman, thou art mad! Thou hast thy wits five,
>     And here on earth will not amend thy life;
> 170 For suddenly I do come.
> EVERYMAN. O wretched caitiff, whither shall I flee,
>     That I might scape this endless sorrow?
>     Now, gentle Death, spare me till to-morrow,
>     That I may amend me
> 175 With good advisement.                             *reflection*
> DEATH. Nay, thereto I will not consent,
>     Nor no man will I respite;
>     But to the heart suddenly I shall smite
>     Without any advisement.
> 180 And now out of thy sight I will me hie;
>     See thou make thee ready shortly,
>     For thou mayst say this is the day
>     That no man living may scape away.   [*Exit Death.*
> EVERYMAN. Alas, I may well weep with sighs deep!
> 185 Now have I no manner of company
>     To help me in my journey, and me to keep;        *guard*
>     And also my writing is full unready.
>     How shall I do now for to excuse me?
>     I would to God I had never be get!               *been born*
> 190 To my soul a full great profit it had be;

159 Hurry up and go.
187 *writing:* i.e., the writing of Everyman's accounts.

>           For now I fear pains huge and great.
>           The time passeth. Lord, help, that all wrought!
>           For though I mourn it availeth nought.
>           The day passeth, and is almost ago;                      *gone*
> 195       I wot not well what for to do.
>           To whom were I best my complaint to make?
>           What and I to Fellowship thereof spake,                  *if*
>           And showed him of this sudden chance?
>           For in him is all mine affiance;                         *trust*
> 200       We have in the world so many a day
>           Be good friends in sport and play.
>           I see him yonder, certainly.
>           I trust that he will bear me company;
>           Therefore to him will I speak to ease my sorrow.
> 205       Well met, good Fellowship, and good morrow!
>
>                   *Fellowship speaketh:*
>
>           FELLOWSHIP. Everyman, good morrow, by this day!
>              Sir, why lookest thou so piteously?
>              If any thing be amiss, I pray thee me say,
>              That I may help to remedy.
> 210       EVERYMAN. Yea, good Fellowship, yea;
>              I am in great jeopardy.
>           FELLOWSHIP. My true friend, show to me your mind;
>              I will not forsake thee to my life's end,
>              In the way of good company.
> 215       EVERYMAN. That was well spoken, and lovingly.
>           FELLOWSHIP. Sir, I must needs know your heaviness;       *sorrow*
>              I have pity to see you in any distress.
>              If any have you wronged, ye shall revenged be,
>              Though I on the ground be slain for thee —
> 220          Though that I know before that I should die.
>           EVERYMAN. Verily, Fellowship, gramercy.
>           FELLOWSHIP. Tush! by thy thanks I set not a straw.
>              Show me your grief, and say no more.
>           EVERYMAN. If I my heart should to you break,             *open*
> 225          And then you to turn your mind from me,
>              And would not me comfort when ye hear me speak,
>              Then should I ten times sorrier be.
>           FELLOWSHIP. Sir, I say as I will do indeed.
>           EVERYMAN. Then be you a good friend at need:
> 230          I have found you true herebefore.

206 *by this day,* an asseveration.

FELLOWSHIP. And so ye shall evermore;
   For, in faith, and thou go to hell,
   I will not forsake thee by the way.
EVERYMAN. Ye speak like a good friend; I believe you well.
235    I shall deserve it, and I may.    *repay*
FELLOWSHIP. I speak of no deserving, by this day!
   For he that will say, and nothing do,
   Is not worthy with good company to go;
   Therefore show me the grief of your mind,
240    As to your friend most loving and kind.
EVERYMAN. I shall show you how it is:
   Commanded I am to go a journey,
   A long way, hard and dangerous,
   And give a strait count, without delay,    *strict account*
245    Before the high Judge, Adonai.
   Wherefore, I pray you, bear me company,
   As ye have promised, in this journey.
FELLOWSHIP. That is matter indeed. Promise is duty;
   But, and I should take such a voyage on me,
250    I know it well, it should be to my pain;
   Also it maketh me afeard, certain.
   But let us take counsel here as well as we can,
   For your words would fear a strong man.    *frighten*
EVERYMAN. Why, ye said if I had need
255    Ye would me never forsake, quick ne dead,
   Though it were to hell, truly.
FELLOWSHIP. So I said, certainly,
   But such pleasures be set aside, the sooth to say;
   And also, if we took such a journey,
260    When should we come again?
EVERYMAN. Nay, never again, till the day of doom.
FELLOWSHIP. In faith, then will not I come there!
   Who hath you these tidings brought?
EVERYMAN. Indeed, Death was with me here.
265 FELLOWSHIP. Now, by God that all hath bought,    *redeemed*
   If Death were the messenger,
   For no man that is living to-day
   I will not go that loath journey —    *loathsome*
   Not for the father that begat me!
270 EVERYMAN. Ye promised otherwise, pardie.    *by God*
FELLOWSHIP. I wot well I said so, truly;

245 *Adonai*, a Hebrew name for God.
248 That is a good reason indeed [for asking me].

  And yet if thou wilt eat, and drink, and make good cheer,
  Or haunt to women the lusty company,
  I would not forsake you while the day is clear,
275   Trust me verily.
EVERYMAN. Yea, thereto ye would be ready!
  To go to mirth, solace, and play,
  Your mind will sooner apply,     *attend*
  Than to bear me company in my long journey.
280 FELLOWSHIP. Now, in good faith, I will not that way.
  But and thou will murder, or any man kill,
  In that I will help thee with a good will.
EVERYMAN. O, that is a simple advice indeed.
  Gentle fellow, help me in my necessity!
285   We have loved long, and now I need;
  And now, gentle Fellowship, remember me.
FELLOWSHIP. Whether ye have loved me or no,
  By Saint John, I will not with thee go.
EVERYMAN. Yet, I pray thee, take the labour, and do so much for me
290   To bring me forward, for saint charity,   *escort me*
  And comfort me till I come without the town.
FELLOWSHIP. Nay, and thou would give me a new gown,
  I will not a foot with thee go;
  But, and thou had tarried, I would not have left thee so.
295   And as now God speed thee in thy journey,
  For from thee I will depart as fast as I may.
EVERYMAN. Whither away, Fellowship? Will thou forsake me?
FELLOWSHIP. Yea, by my fay! To God I betake thee.   *faith; commend*
EVERYMAN. Farewell, good Fellowship; for thee my heart is sore.
300   Adieu for ever! I shall see thee no more.
FELLOWSHIP. In faith, Everyman, farewell now at the ending;
  For you I will remember that parting is mourning.

      [*Exit Fellowship.*

273 Or frequent the pleasant company of women.
274 Until daybreak.

EVERYMAN. Alack! shall we thus depart indeed— *part*
　　Ah, Lady, help!—without any more comfort?
305　Lo, Fellowship forsaketh me in my most need.
　　For help in this world whither shall I resort?
　　Fellowship herebefore with me would merry make,
　　And now little sorrow for me doth he take.
　　It is said, "In prosperity men friends may find,
310　Which in adversity be full unkind."
　　Now whither for succour shall I flee,
　　Sith that Fellowship hath forsaken me? *since*
　　To my kinsmen I will, truly,
　　Praying them to help me in my necessity;
315　I believe that they will do so,
　　For kind will creep where it may not go.
　　I will go say, for yonder I see them. *essay, try*
　　Where be ye now, my friends and kinsmen?

*[Enter Kindred and Cousin]*

KINDRED. Here be we now at your commandment.
320　Cousin, I pray you show us your intent
　　In any wise, and do not spare.
COUSIN. Yea, Everyman, and to us declare
　　If ye be disposed to go anywhither; *anywhere*
　　For, wit you well, we will live and die together.
325 KINDRED. In wealth and woe we will with you hold, *side*
　　For over his kin a man may be bold.
EVERYMAN. Gramercy, my friends and kinsmen kind.
　　Now shall I show you the grief of my mind:
　　I was commanded by a messenger,
330　That is a high king's chief officer;
　　He bade me go a pilgrimage, to my pain,
　　And I know well I shall never come again;
　　Also I must give a reckoning strait,
　　For I have a great enemy that hath me in wait,
335　Which intendeth me for to hinder.
KINDRED. What account is that which ye must render?
　　That would I know.
EVERYMAN. Of all my works I must show
　　How I have lived and my days spent;

---

316 For kinship will creep where it cannot walk; i.e., blood is thicker than water.
321 Without fail, and do not hold back.
326 For a man may be sure of his kinsfolk.
334 A great enemy (i.e., the devil) who has me under observation.

| | | |
|---|---|---|
| 340 | Also of ill deeds that I have used | *practised* |
| | In my time, sith life was me lent; | |
| | And of all virtues that I have refused. | |
| | Therefore, I pray you, go thither with me | |
| | To help to make mine account, for saint charity. | |
| 345 | COUSIN. What, to go thither? Is that the matter? | |
| | Nay, Everyman, I had liefer fast bread and water | |
| | All this five year and more. | |
| | EVERYMAN. Alas, that ever I was bore! | *born* |
| | For now shall I never be merry, | |
| 350 | If that you forsake me. | |
| | KINDRED. Ah, sir, what ye be a merry man! | |
| | Take good heart to you, and make no moan. | |
| | But one thing I warn you, by Saint Anne — | |
| | As for me, ye shall go alone. | |
| 355 | EVERYMAN. My Cousin, will you not with me go? | |
| | COUSIN. No, by our Lady! I have the cramp in my toe. | |
| | Trust not to me, for, so God me speed, | |
| | I will deceive you in your most need. | |
| | KINDRED. It availeth not us to tice. | |
| 360 | Ye shall have my maid with all my heart; | |
| | She loveth to go to feasts, there to be nice, | *wanton* |
| | And to dance, and abroad to start: | |
| | I will give her leave to help you in that journey, | |
| | If that you and she may agree. | |
| 365 | EVERYMAN. Now show me the very effect of your mind: | *tenor* |
| | Will you go with me, or abide behind? | |
| | KINDRED. Abide behind? Yea, that will I, and I may! | |
| | Therefore farewell till another day. [*Exit Kindred.* | |
| | EVERYMAN. How should I be merry or glad? | |
| 370 | For fair promises men to me make, | |
| | But when I have most need they me forsake. | |
| | I am deceived; that maketh me sad. | |
| | COUSIN. Cousin Everyman, farewell now, | |
| | For verily I will not go with you. | |
| 375 | Also of mine own an unready reckoning | |
| | I have to account; therefore I make tarrying. | |
| | Now God keep thee, for now I go. [*Exit Cousin.* | |
| | EVERYMAN. Ah, Jesus, is all come hereto? | |

346 I had rather fast on bread and water.
351 What a merry man you are!
359 It is no use trying to entice us.
362 Go out and about.

Lo, fair words maketh fools fain;
380 They promise, and nothing will do, certain.
My kinsmen promised me faithfully
For to abide with me steadfastly,
And now fast away do they flee:
Even so Fellowship promised me.
385 What friend were best me of to provide?
I lose my time here longer to abide.
Yet in my mind a thing there is:
All my life I have loved riches;
If that my Good now help me might,    *Goods*
390 He would make my heart full light.
I will speak to him in this distress —
Where art thou, my Goods and riches?

[*Goods speaks from a corner*]

GOODS. Who calleth me? Everyman? What!
    hast thou haste?
I lie here in corners, trussed and piled so high,
395 And in chests I am locked so fast,
Also sacked in bags. Thou mayst see with thine eye
I cannot stir; in packs low I lie.
What would ye have? Lightly me say.    *quickly*
EVERYMAN. Come hither, Goods, in all the haste thou
    may,
400   For of counsel I must desire thee.
GOODS. Sir, and ye in the world have sorrow or
    adversity,
That can I help you to remedy shortly.
EVERYMAN. It is another disease that grieveth me;    *trouble*
In this world it is not, I tell thee so.
405 I am sent for, another way to go,
To give a strait count general
Before the highest Jupiter of all;
And all my life I have had joy and pleasure in thee,
Therefore, I pray thee, go with me;
410 For, peradventure, thou mayst before God Almighty
My reckoning help to clean and purify;
For it is said ever among

385 To provide myself with.
400 For I must entreat your advice.
412 For it is sometimes said.

That money maketh all right that is wrong.
GOODS. Nay, Everyman, I sing another song.
    I follow no man in such voyages;
    For, and I went with thee,
    Thou shouldst fare much the worse for me;
    For because on me thou did set thy mind,
    Thy reckoning I have made blotted and blind,    *obscure*
    That thine account thou cannot make truly;
    And that hast thou for the love of me.
EVERYMAN. That would grieve me full sore,
    When I should come to that fearful answer.
    Up, let us go thither together.
GOODS. Nay, not so! I am too brittle, I may not endure;
    I will follow no man one foot, be ye sure.
EVERYMAN. Alas, I have thee loved, and had great pleasure
    All my life-days on good and treasure.
GOODS. That is to thy damnation, without leasing,
    For my love is contrary to the love everlasting;
    But if thou had me loved moderately during,
    As to the poor to give part of me,
    Then shouldst thou not in this dolour be,    *distress*
    Nor in this great sorrow and care.
EVERYMAN. Lo, now was I deceived ere I was ware,    *aware*
    And all I may wite misspending of time.
GOODS. What, weenest thou that I am thine?
EVERYMAN. I had wend so.    *supposed*
GOODS. Nay, Everyman, I say no.
    As for a while I was lent thee;
    A season thou hast had me in prosperity.
    My condition is man's soul to kill;    *nature*
    If I save one, a thousand I do spill.    *ruin*
    Weenest thou that I will follow thee?
    Nay, not from this world, verily.
EVERYMAN. I had wend otherwise.
GOODS. Therefore to thy soul Good is a thief;
    For when thou art dead, this is my guise —    *practice*
    Another to deceive in this same wise
    As I have done thee, and all to his soul's reprief.    *shame*

429 Without a lie; i.e., truly.
431–2 But if you had loved me moderately during your lifetime, so as to give part of me to the poor.
436 And I may blame it all on the bad use I have made of my time.

EVERYMAN. O false Good, cursed may thou be,
  Thou traitor to God, that hast deceived me
  And caught me in thy snare!
GOODS. Marry, thou brought thyself in care,
  Whereof I am glad;                                455
  I must needs laugh, I cannot be sad.
EVERYMAN. Ah, Good, thou hast had long my
      heartly love;                                   *heartfelt*
  I gave thee that which should be the Lord's above.
  But wilt thou not go with me indeed?
  I pray thee truth to say.                           460
GOODS. No, so God me speed!
  Therefore farewell, and have good day.

                    [*Exit Goods.*

EVERYMAN. O to whom shall I make my moan
  For to go with me in that heavy journey?
  First Fellowship said he would with me gone;    *go*
  His words were very pleasant and gay,
  But afterward he left me alone.
  Then spake I to my kinsmen, all in despair,
  And also they gave me words fair;
  They lacked no fair speaking,
  But all forsook me in the ending.
  Then went I to my Goods, that I loved best,
  In hope to have comfort, but there had I least;
  For my Goods sharply did me tell
  That he bringeth many into hell.
  Then of myself I was ashamed,
  And so I am worthy to be blamed;
  Thus may I well myself hate.
  Of whom shall I now counsel take?
  I think that I shall never speed
  Till that I go to my Good Deed.
  But, alas, she is so weak
  That she can neither go nor speak;    *walk*
  Yet will I venture on her now.        *gamble*
  My Good Deeds, where be you?

      [*Good Deeds speaks from the ground*]

GOOD DEEDS. Here I lie, cold in the ground;
  Thy sins hath me sore bound,
  That I caannot stir.

126    *DRAMA*

EVERYMAN. O Good Deeds, I stand in fear!
    I must you pray of counsel,
    For help now should come right well.
GOOD DEEDS. Everyman, I have understanding
    That ye be summoned account to make
    Before Messias, of Jerusalem King;
    And you do by me, that journey with you will I take.
EVERYMAN. Therefore I come to you, my moan to make;
    I pray you that ye will go with me.
GOOD DEEDS. I would full fain, but I cannot stand, verily.
EVERYMAN. Why, is there anything on you fall?    *befallen*
GOOD DEEDS. Yea, sir, I may thank you of all;    *for*
    If ye had perfectly cheered me,
    Your book of count full ready had be.
    Look, the books of your works and deeds eke!    *also*
    Behold how they lie under the feet,
    To your soul's heaviness.
EVERYMAN. Our Lord Jesus help me!
    For one letter here I cannot see.
GOOD DEEDS. There is a blind reckoning in time of distress.
EVERYMAN. Good Deeds, I pray you help me in this need,
    Or else I am for ever damned indeed;
    Therefore help me to make reckoning
    Before the Redeemer of all thing,
    That King is, and was, and ever shall.
GOOD DEEDS. Everyman, I am sorry of your fall,
    And fain would I help you, and I were able.
EVERYMAN. Good Deeds, your counsel I pray you give me.
GOOD DEEDS. That shall I do verily;
    Though that on my feet I may not go,
    I have a sister that shall with you also,
    Called Knowledge, which shall with you abide,
    To help you to make that dreadful reckoning.

---

491 For help would now be very welcome.
495 If you do as I advise.
501 If you had encouraged me fully.
508 i.e., a sinful person in his hour of need finds that the account of his good deeds is dimly written and difficult to read.
520 The meaning of Knowledge here is "acknowledgment or recognition of sins."

[*Enter Knowledge*]

KNOWLEDGE. Everyman, I will go with thee, and be thy guide,
In thy most need to go by thy side.
EVERYMAN. In good condition I am now in every thing,
525 And am wholly content with this good thing,
Thanked be God my creator.
GOOD DEEDS. And when she hath brought you there
Where thou shalt heal thee of thy smart,    *pain*
Then go you with your reckoning and your Good Deeds together,
530 For to make you joyful at heart
Before the blessed Trinity.
EVERYMAN. My Good Deeds, gramercy!
I am well content, certainly,
With your words sweet.
535 KNOWLEDGE. Now go we together lovingly
To Confession, that cleansing river.
EVERYMAN. For joy I weep; I would we were there!
But, I pray you, give me cognition    *knowledge*
Where dwelleth that Holy man, Confession.
540 KNOWLEDGE. In the house of salvation:
We shall find him in that place,
That shall us comfort, by God's grace.

[*Knowledge takes Everyman to Confession*]

Lo, this is Confession. Kneel down and ask mercy,
For he is in good conceit with God Almighty.    *esteem*
545 EVERYMAN. O glorious fountain, that all uncleanness doth clarify,
Wash from me the spots of vice unclean,
That on me no sin may be seen.
I come with Knowledge for my redemption,
Redempt with heart and full contrition;
550 For I am commanded a pilgrimage to take,
And great accounts before God to make.
Now I pray you, Shrift, mother of salvation,    *confession*
Help my Good Deeds for my piteous exclamation.

540 i.e., in the church.
549 Redeemed by heartfelt and full contrition.
553 In answer to my piteous cry.

CONFESSION. I know your sorrow well, Everyman.
555 Because with Knowledge ye come to me,
I will you comfort as well as I can,
And a precious jewel I will give thee,
Called penance, voider of adversity;                      *expeller*
Therewith shall your body chastised be,
560 With abstinence and perseverance in God's service.
Here shall you receive that scourge of me,
Which is penance strong that ye must endure,
To remember thy Saviour was scourged for thee
With sharp scourges, and suffered it patiently;
565 So must thou, ere thou scape that painful pilgrimage.
Knowledge, keep him in this voyage,
And by that time Good Deeds will be with thee.
But in any wise be siker of mercy,                         *sure*
For your time draweth fast; and ye will saved be,          *if*
570 Ask God mercy, and he will grant truly.
When with the scourge of penance man doth him bind,        *himself*
The oil of forgiveness then shall he find.
EVERYMAN. Thanked be God for his gracious work!
For now I will my penance begin;
575 This hath rejoiced and lighted my heart,                  *lightened*
Though the knots be painful and hard within.
KNOWLEDGE. Everyman, look your penance that ye fulfil,
What pain that ever it to you be;
And Knowledge shall give you counsel at will
580 How your account ye shall make clearly.
EVERYMAN. O eternal God, O heavenly figure,
O way of righteousness, O goodly vision,
Which descended down in a virgin pure
Because he would every man redeem,
585 Which Adam forfeited by his disobedience:
O blessed Godhead, elect and high divine,                  *divinity*
Forgive my grievous offence;
Here I cry thee mercy in this presence.
O ghostly treasure, O ransomer and redeemer,
590 Of all the world hope and conductor,
Mirror of joy, and founder of mercy,
Which enlumineth heaven and earth thereby,                 *besides*

569 Draws quickly to an end.
576 Though the knots [of the scourge] be painful and hard to my body.
588 In the presence of this company.

EVERYMAN   129

  Hear my clamorous complaint, though it late be;
  Receive my prayers, of thy benignity;
595  Though I be a sinner most abominable,
  Yet let my name be written in Moses' table.
  O Mary, pray to the Maker of all thing,
  Me for to help at my ending;
  And save me from the power of my enemy,
600  For Death assaileth me strongly.
  And, Lady, that I may by mean of thy prayer
  Of your Son's glory to be partner,
  By the means of his passion, I it crave;
  I beseech you help my soul to save.
605  Knowledge, give me the scourge of penance;
  My flesh therewith shall give acquittance:
  I will now begin, if God give me grace.
 KNOWLEDGE. Everyman, God give you time and
   space!           *opportunity*
610  Now may you make your reckoning sure.
 EVERYMAN. In the name of the Holy Trinity,
  My body sore punished shall be:
  Take this, body, for the sin of the flesh!

      [*Scourges himself.*

  Also thou delightest to go gay and fresh,     *as*
615  And in the way of damnation thou did me bring,
  Therefore suffer now strokes and punishing.
  Now of penance I will wade the water clear,
  To save me from purgatory, that sharp fire.

   [*Good Deeds rises from the ground*]

 GOOD DEEDS. I thank God, now I can walk and go,
620  And am delivered of my sickness and woe.
  Therefore with Everyman I will go, and not spare;
  His good works I will help him to declare.
 KNOWLEDGE. Now, Everyman, be merry and glad!
  Your Good Deeds cometh now; ye may not be sad.

596 Medieval theologians regarded the two tables given on Sinai as symbols of baptism and penance respectively. Thus Everyman is asking to be numbered among those who have escaped damnation by doing penance for their sins.
599 i.e., from the devil.
601–3 And, Lady, I beg that through the mediation of thy prayer I may share in your Son's glory, in consequence of His passion.
606 *acquittance,* satisfaction (as a part of the sacrament of penance).

625     Now is your Good Deeds whole and sound,
Going upright upon the ground.
EVERYMAN. My heart is light, and shall be evermore;
Now will I smite faster than I did before.
GOOD DEEDS. Everyman, pilgrim, my special friend,
630     Blessed be thou without end;
For thee is preparate the eternal glory.    *prepared*
Ye have me made whole and sound,
Therefore I will bide by thee in every stound.    *trial*
EVERYMAN. Welcome, my Good Deeds; now I hear thy voice,
635     I weep for very sweetness of love.
KNOWLEDGE. Be no more sad, but ever rejoice;
God seeth thy living in his throne above.
Put on this garment to thy behoof,    *advantage*
Which is wet with your tears,
640     Or else before God you may it miss,
When ye to your journey's end come shall.
EVERYMAN. Gentle Knowledge, what do ye it call?
KNOWLEDGE. It is a garment of sorrow:
From pain it will you borrow;    *release*
645     Contrition it is,
That geteth forgiveness;
It pleaseth God passing well.    *exceedingly*
GOOD DEEDS. Everyman, will you wear it for your heal?    *salvation*
EVERYMAN. Now blessed be Jesu, Mary's Son,
650     For now have I on true contrition.
And let us go now without tarrying;
Good Deeds, have we clear our reckoning?
GOOD DEEDS. Yea, indeed, I have it here.
EVERYMAN. Then I trust we need not fear;
655     Now, friends, let us not part in twain.
KNOWLEDGE. Nay, Everyman, that will we not, certain.
GOOD DEEDS. Yet must thou lead with thee
Three persons of great might.
EVERYMAN. Who should they be?
660     GOOD DEEDS. Discretion and Strength they hight,    *are called*
And thy Beauty may not abide behind.
KNOWLEDGE. Also ye must call to mind
Your Five Wits as for your counsellors.    *senses*
GOOD DEEDS. You must have them ready at all hours.
665     EVERYMAN. How shall I get them hither?
KNOWLEDGE. You must call them all together,
And they will hear you incontinent.    *immediately*

EVERYMAN. My friends, come hither and be present,
Discretion, Strength, my Five Wits, and Beauty.

[*Enter Beauty, Strength, Discretion, and Five Wits*]

670 BEAUTY. Here at your will we be all ready.
What will ye that we should do?
GOOD DEEDS. That ye would with Everyman go,
And help him in his pilgrimage.
Advise you, will ye with him or not in that *consider*
voyage?
675 STRENGTH. We will bring him all thither,
To his help and comfort, ye may believe me.
DISCRETION. So will we go with him all together.
EVERYMAN. Almighty God, lofed may thou be! *praised*
I give thee laud that I have hither brought
680 Strength, Discretion, Beauty, and Five Wits.
Lack I nought.
And my Good Deeds, with Knowledge clear,
All be in my company at my will here;
I desire no more to my business. *for*
STRENGTH. And I, Strength, will by you stand in
distress,
685 Though thou would in battle fight on the ground.
FIVE WITS. And though it were through the world
round,
We will not depart for sweet ne sour.
BEAUTY. No more will I unto death's hour, *until*
Whatsoever thereof befall.
690 DISCRETION. Everyman, advise you first of all;
Go with a good advisement and deliberation. *reflection*
We all give you virtuous monition *forewarning*
That all shall be well.
EVERYMAN. My friends, harken what I will tell:
695 I pray God reward you in his heavenly sphere.
Now harken, all that be here,
For I will make my testament
Here before you all present:
In alms half my good I will give with my hands
twain
700 In the way of charity, with good intent,

687 i.e., in happiness or adversity.
701–2 The meaning seems to be that Everyman's immovable property (i.e., his body) will lie at rest in the earth.

And the other half still shall remain
In queth, to be returned there it ought to be. *bequest; where*
This I do in despite of the fiend of hell,
To go quit out of his peril
705     Ever after and this day.
KNOWLEDGE. Everyman, harken what I say:
Go to priesthood, I you advise,
And receive of him in any wise *without fail*
The holy sacrament and ointment together.
710     Then shortly see ye turn again hither;
We will all abide you here.
FIVE WITS. Yea, Everyman, hie you that ye ready were
There is no emperor, king, duke, ne baron,
That of God hath commission *authority*
715     As hath the least priest in the world being; *living*
For of the blessed sacraments pure and benign
He beareth the keys, and thereof hath the cure *charge*
For man's redemption — it is ever sure —
Which God for our soul's medicine
720     Gave us out of his heart with great pine. *suffering*
Here in this transitory life, for thee and me,
The blessed sacraments seven there be:
Baptism, confirmation, with priesthood good,
And the sacrament of God's precious flesh and blood,
725     Marriage, the holy extreme unction, and penance;
These seven be good to have in remembrance,
Gracious sacraments of high divinity.
EVERYMAN. Fain would I receive that holy body,
And meekly to my ghostly father I will go. *spiritual*
730     FIVE WITS. Everyman, that is the best that ye can do.
God will you to salvation bring,
For priesthood exceedeth all other thing:
To us Holy Scripture they do teach,
And converteth man from sin heaven to reach;
735     God hath to them more power given
Than to any angel that is in heaven.
With five words he may consecrate,
God's body in flesh and blood to make,

704–5 To go free out of his power to-day and ever after.
712 Hurry and prepare yourself.
728 i.e., the sacrament.
737 *five words:* i.e., *Hoc est enim corpus meum.*

|     | And handleth his Maker between his hands. |     |
| --- | --- | --- |
| 740 | The priest bindeth and unbindeth all bands, |     |
|     | Both in earth and in heaven. |     |
|     | Thou ministers all the sacraments seven; | *administer* |
|     | Though we kissed thy feet, thou were worthy; |     |
|     | Thou art surgeon that cureth sin deadly: |     |
| 745 | No remedy we find under God |     |
|     | But all only priesthood. |     |
|     | Everyman, God gave priests that dignity, |     |
|     | And setteth them in his stead among us to be; |     |
|     | Thus be they above angels in degree. |     |

[*Everyman goes to the priest to receive the last sacraments*]

| 750 | KNOWLEDGE. If priests be good, it is so, surely. |     |
| --- | --- | --- |
|     | But when Jesus hanged on the cross with great smart, |     |
|     | There he gave out of his blessed heart |     |
|     | The same sacrament in great torment: |     |
|     | He sold them not to us, that Lord omnipotent. |     |
| 755 | Therefore Saint Peter the apostle doth say |     |
|     | That Jesu's curse hath all they |     |
|     | Which God their Savior do buy or sell, |     |
|     | Or they for any money to take or tell. | *count out* |
|     | Sinful priests giveth the sinners example bad; |     |
| 760 | Their children sitteth by other men's fires, I have heard; |     |
|     | And some haunteth women's company |     |
|     | With unclean life, as lusts of lechery: |     |
|     | These be with sin made blind. |     |
|     | FIVE WITS. I trust to God no such may we find; |     |
| 765 | Therefore let us priesthood honour, |     |
|     | And follow their doctrine for our souls' succour. |     |
|     | We be their sheep, and they shepherds be |     |
|     | By whom we all be kept in surety. |     |
|     | Peace, for yonder I see Everyman come, |     |
| 770 | Which hath made true satisfaction. |     |
|     | GOOD DEEDS. Methink it is he indeed. |     |

[*Re-enter Everyman*]

740 Matt. xvi. 19.
746 Except only from the priesthood.
750 *it is so:* i.e., that they are above the angels.
755–8 The reference here is to the sin of simony (Acts viii. 18 ff.)
760 i.e., illegitimate children.

EVERYMAN. Now Jesu be your alder speed!
  I have received the sacrament for my redemption,
  And then mine extreme unction:
775  Blessed be all they that counselled me to take it!
  And now, friends, let us go without longer respite;
  I thank God that ye have tarried so long.
  Now set each of you on this rood your hand,    *cross*
  And shortly follow me:
780  I go before there I would be; God be our guide!
STRENGTH. Everyman, we will not from you go
  Till ye have done this voyage long.
DISCRETION. I, Discretion, will bide by you also.
KNOWLEDGE. And though this pilgrimage be never so
    strong,    *grievous*
785  I will never part you fro.    *from you*
STRENGTH. Everyman, I will be as sure by thee
  As ever I did by Judas Maccabee.

[*Everyman comes to his grave*]

EVERYMAN. Alas, I am so faint I may not stand;
  My limbs under me doth fold.
790  Friends, let us not turn again to this land,
  Not for all the world's gold;
  For into this cave must I creep
  And turn to earth, and there to sleep.
BEAUTY. What, into this grave? Alas!
795 EVERYMAN. Yea, there shall ye consume, more and less.
BEAUTY. And what, should I smother here?
EVERYMAN. Yea, by my faith, and never more appear.
  In this world live no more we shall,
  But in heaven before the highest Lord of all.
800 BEAUTY. I cross out all this; adieu, by Saint John!
  I take my cap in my lap, and am gone.
EVERYMAN. What, Beauty, whither will ye?
BEAUTY. Peace, I am deaf; I look not behind me,
  Not and thou wouldest give me all the gold in thy
    chest.    [*Exit Beauty.*
805 EVERYMAN. Alas, whereto may I trust?

772 Be the helper of you all.
786-7 I will stand by you as steadfastly as ever I did by Judas Maccabaeus (1 Macc. iii).
795 Decay, all of you.
800 I cancel all this: i.e., my promise to stay with you.
801 I doff my cap [so low that it comes] into my lap.

EVERYMAN     135

Beauty goeth fast away from me;
She promised with me to live and die.
STRENGTH. Everyman, I will thee also forsake and deny;
Thy game liketh me not at all. *pleases*
810 EVERYMAN. Why, then, ye will forsake me all?
Sweet Strength, tarry a little space. *while*
STRENGTH. Nay, sir, by the rood of grace!
I will hie me from thee fast,
Though thou weep till thy heart to-brast. *break*
815 EVERYMAN. Ye would ever bide by me, ye said.
STRENGTH. Yea, I have you far enough conveyed.
Ye be old enough, I understand,
Your pilgrimage to take on hand;
I repent me that I hither came.
820 EVERYMAN. Strength, you to displease I am to blame;
Yet promise is debt, this ye well wot.
STRENGTH. In faith, I care not.
Thou art but a fool to complain;
You spend your speech and waste your brain.
825 Go thrust thee into the ground! [*Exit Strength.*
EVERYMAN. I had wend surer I should you have found.
He that trusteth in his Strength
She him deceiveth at the length.
Both Strength and Beauty forsaketh me;
830 Yet they promised me fair and lovingly.
DISCRETION. Everyman, I will after Strength be gone;
As for me, I will leave you alone.
EVERYMAN. Why, Discretion, will ye forsake me?
DISCRETION. Yea, in faith, I will go from thee,
835 For when Strength goeth before
I follow after evermore.
EVERYMAN. Yet, I pray thee, for the love of the Trinity,
Look in my grave once piteously.
DISCRETION. Nay, so nigh will I not come;
840 Farewell, every one! [*Exit Discretion.*
EVERYMAN. O, all thing faileth, save God alone —
Beauty, Strength, and Discretion;
For when Death bloweth his blast,
They all run from me full fast.
845 FIVE WITS. Everyman, my leave now of thee I take;
I will follow the other, for here I thee forsake.

820 I am to blame for displeasing you.

EVERYMAN. Alas, then may I wail and weep,
   For I took you for my best friend.
FIVE WITS. I will no longer thee keep;
   Now farewell, and there an end. [*Exit Five Wits.*
EVERYMAN. O Jesu, help! All hath forsaken me.
GOOD DEEDS. Nay, Everyman; I will bide with thee.
   I will not forsake thee indeed;
   Thou shalt find me a good friend at need.
EVERYMAN. Gramercy, Good Deeds! Now may I true friends see.
   They have forsaken me, every one;
   I loved them better than my Good Deeds alone.
   Knowledge, will ye forsake me also?
KNOWLEDGE. Yea, Everyman, when ye to Death shall go;
   But not yet, for no manner of danger.
EVERYMAN. Gramercy, Knowledge, with all my heart.
KNOWLEDGE. Nay, yet, I will not from hence depart
   Till I see where ye shall become.
EVERYMAN. Methink, alas, that I must be gone
   To make my reckoning and my debts pay,
   For I see my time is nigh spent away.
   Take example, all ye that this do hear or see,
   How they that I loved best do forsake me,
   Except my Good Deeds that bideth truly.
GOOD DEEDS. All earthly things is but vanity:
   Beauty, Strength, and Discretion do man forsake,
   Foolish friends, and kinsmen, that fair spake —
   All fleeth save Good Deeds, and that am I.
EVERYMAN. Have mercy on me, God most mighty;
   And stand by me, thou mother and maid, holy Mary.
GOOD DEEDS. Fear not; I will speak for thee.
EVERYMAN. Here I cry God mercy.
GOOD DEEDS. Short our end, and minish our pain;
   Let us go and never come again.
EVERYMAN. Into thy hands, Lord, my soul I commend;
   Receive it, Lord, that it be not lost.
   As thou me boughtest, so me defend,
   And save me from the fiend's boast,

863 What shall become of you.
878 Shorten our end, and diminish our pain.

885 That I may appear with that blessed host
That shall be saved at the day of doom.
*In manus tuas,* of mights most
For ever, *commendo spiritum meum.*

[*He sinks into his grave.*

KNOWLEDGE. Now hath he suffered that we all shall endure;
The Good Deeds shall make all sure.
890 Now hath he made ending;
Methinketh that I hear angels sing,
And make great joy and melody
Where Everyman's soul received shall be.
ANGEL. Come, excellent elect spouse, to Jesu!
895 Hereabove thou shalt go
Because of thy singular virtue.
Now the soul is taken the body fro,
Thy reckoning is crystal-clear.
Now shalt thou into the heavenly sphere,
900 Unto the which all ye shall come
That liveth well before the day of doom.

[*Enter Doctor*]

DOCTOR. This moral men may have in mind.
Ye hearers, take it of worth, old and young,        *value it*
And forsake Pride, for he deceiveth you in the end;
905 And remember Beauty, Five Wits, Strength, and Discretion,
They all at the last do every man forsake,
Save his Good Deeds there doth he take.        *unless*
But beware, for and they be small
Before God, he hath no help at all;
910 None excuse may be there for every man.
Alas, how shall he do then?
For after death amends may no man make,
For then mercy and pity doth him forsake.
If his reckoning be not clear when he doth come,
915 God will say: "*Ite, maledicti, in ignem eternum.*"

886–7 Into thy hands, most mighty One for ever, I commend my spirit.
894 Bride of Jesus (a common medieval metaphor to express the idea of the soul's union with God).
915 Depart, ye cursed, into everlasting fire (Matt. xxv. 41).

And he that hath his account whole and sound,
High in heaven he shall be crowned;
Unto which place God brings us all thither,
That we may live body and soul together.
Thereto help the Trinity!
Amen, say ye, for saint charity.
　　Thus endeth this moral play of Everyman

# A RAISIN IN THE SUN

——*Lorraine Hansberry*

What happens to a dream deferred?
Does it dry up
Like a raisin in the sun?
Or fester like a sore —
And then run?
Does it stink like rotten meat?
Or crust and sugar over —
Like a syrupy sweet?

Maybe it just sags
Like a heavy load.

*Or does it explode?*

　　　　　　　　　　—*Langston Hughes*

The action of the play is set in Chicago's Southside, sometime between World War II and the present.

## Act One

SCENE 1　Friday morning.

SCENE 2　The following morning.

　Lorraine Hansberry, *A Raisin in the Sun.* Copyright © 1958, 1959, 1966 by Robert Nemiroff as Executor of the Estate of Lorraine Hansberry. Reprinted by permission of Random House, Inc.
　Langston Hughes, "Dream Deferred." Copyright 1951 by Langston Hughes. Reprinted from *The Panther and the Lash,* by Langston Hughes, by permission of Alfred A. Knopf, Inc.

## Act Two

SCENE 1 Later, the same day.

SCENE 2 Friday night, a few weeks later,

SCENE 3 Moving day, one week later.

## Act Three

An hour later.

## Act I

SCENE ONE

The Younger living room would be a comfortable and well-ordered room if it were not for a number of indestructible contradictions to this state of being. Its furnishings are typical and undistinguished and their primary feature now is that they have clearly had to accommodate the living of too many people for too many years — and they are tired. Still, we can see that at some time, a time probably no longer remembered by the family (except perhaps for Mama) the furnishings of this room were actually selected with care and love and even hope — and brought to this apartment and arranged with taste and pride.

That was a long time ago. Now the once loved pattern of the couch upholstery has to fight to show itself from under acres of crocheted doilies and couch covers which have themselves finally come to be more important than the upholstery. And here a table or a chair has been moved to disguise the worn places in the carpet; but the carpet has fought back by showing its weariness, with depressing uniformity, elsewhere on its surface.

Weariness has, in fact, won in this room. Everything has been polished, washed, sat on, used, scrubbed too often. All pretenses but living itself have long since vanished from the very atmosphere of this room.

Moreover, a section of this room, for it is not really a room unto itself, though the landlord's lease would make it seem so, slopes backward to provide a small kitchen area, where the family prepares the meals that are eaten in the living room proper, which must also serve as dining room. The single window that has been provided for these "two" rooms is located in this kitchen area. The sole natural light the family may enjoy in the course of a day is only that which fights its way through this little window.

At left, a door leads to a bedroom which is shared by Mama and her daughter, Beneatha. At right, opposite, is a second room (which in the beginning of the life of this apartment was probably a breakfast room), which serves as a bedroom for Walter and his wife, Ruth.

Time: Sometime between World War II and the present.

Place: Chicago's Southside.

At Rise: It is morning dark in the living room. Travis is asleep on the make-down bed at center. An alarm clock sounds from within the bedroom at right, and presently Ruth enters from that room and closes the door behind her. She crosses sleepily toward the window. As she passes her sleeping son she reaches down and shakes him a little. At the window she raises the shade and a dusky Southside morning light comes in feebly. She fills a pot with water and puts it on to boil. She calls to the boy, between yawns, in a slightly muffled voice.

Ruth is about thirty. We can see that she was a pretty girl, even exceptionally so, but now it is apparent that life has been little that she expected, and disappointment has already begun to hang in her face. In a few years, before thirty-five even, she will be known among her people as a "settled woman."

She crosses to her son and gives him a good, final, rousing shake.

RUTH. Come on now, boy, it's seven thirty! (*Her son sits up at last, in a stupor of sleepiness*) I say hurry up, Travis! You ain't the only person in the world got to use a bathroom! (*The child, a sturdy handsome little boy of ten or eleven, drags himself out of the bed and almost blindly takes his towels and "today's clothes" from drawers and a closet and goes out to the bathroom, which is in an outside hall and which is shared by another family or families on the same floor. Ruth crosses to the bedroom door at right and opens it and calls in to her husband*) Walter Lee! ... It's after seven thirty! Lemme see you do some waking up in there now! (*She waits*) You better get up from there, man! It's after seven thirty I tell you. (*She waits again*) All right, you just go ahead and lay there and next thing you know Travis be finished and Mr. Johnson'll be in there and you'll be fussing and cussing round here like a mad man! And be late too! (*She waits, at the end of patience*) Walter Lee — it's time for you to get up!

(*She waits another second and then starts to go into the bedroom, but is apparently satisfied that her husband has begun to get up. She stops, pulls the door to, and returns to the kitchen area. She wipes her face with a moist cloth and runs her fingers through her sleep-disheveled hair in a vain effort and ties an apron around her housecoat. The bedroom door at right opens and her husband stands in the doorway in his pajamas, which are rumpled and mismated. He is a lean, intense young man in his middle thirties, inclined to quick nervous movements and erratic speech habits — and always in his voice there is a quality of indictment*)

WALTER. Is he out yet?
RUTH. What you mean *out*? He ain't hardly got in there good yet.
WALTER. (*Wandering in, still more oriented to sleep than to a new day*) Well, what was you doing all that yelling for if I can't even get in there yet? (*Stopping and thinking*) Check coming today?
RUTH. They *said* Saturday and this is just Friday and I hopes to God you ain't going to get up here first thing this morning and start talking to me 'bout no money — 'cause I 'bout don't want to hear it.
WALTER. Something the matter with you this morning?
RUTH. No — I'm just sleepy as the devil. What kind of eggs you want?
WALTER. Not scrambled. (*Ruth starts to scramble eggs*) Paper come? (*Ruth points impatiently to the rolled up* Tribune *on the table, and he gets it and spreads it out and vaguely reads the front page*) Set off another bomb yesterday.
RUTH. (*Maximum indifference*) Did they?
WALTER. (*Looking up*) What's the matter with you?
RUTH. Ain't nothing the matter with me. And don't keep asking me that this morning.
WALTER. Ain't nobody bothering you. (*Reading the news of the day absently again*) Say Colonel McCormick is sick.
RUTH. (*Affecting tea-party interest*) Is he now? Poor thing.
WALTER. (*Sighing and looking at his watch*) Oh, me. (*He waits*) Now what is that boy doing in that bathroom all this time? He just going to have to start getting up earlier. I can't be being late to work on account of him fooling around in there.
RUTH. (*Turning on him*) Oh, no he ain't going to be getting up no earlier no such thing! It ain't his fault that he can't get to bed no earlier nights 'cause he got a bunch of crazy good-for-nothing clowns sitting up running their mouths in what is supposed to be his bedroom after ten o'clock at night . . .
WALTER. That's what you mad about, ain't it? The things I want to talk about with my friends just couldn't be important in your mind, could they?

(*He rises and finds a cigarette in her handbag on the table and crosses to the little window and looks out, smoking and deeply enjoying this first one*)

RUTH. (*Almost matter of factly, a complaint too automatic to deserve emphasis*) Why you always got to smoke before you eat in the morning?
WALTER. (*At the window*) Just look at 'em down there. . . . Running and racing to work. . . . (*He turns and faces his wife and watches her a moment at the stove, and then, suddenly*) You look young this morning, baby.
RUTH. (*Indifferently*) Yeah?

WALTER. Just for a second — stirring them eggs. It's gone now — just for a second it was — you looked real young again. (*Then, drily*) It's gone now — you look like yourself again.
RUTH. Man, if you don't shut up and leave me alone.
WALTER. (*Looking out to the street again*) First thing a man ought to learn in life is not to make love to no colored woman first thing in the morning. You all some evil people at eight o'clock in the morning.

> (*Travis appears in the hall doorway, almost fully dressed and quite wide awake now, his towels and pajamas across his shoulders. He opens the door and signals for his father to make the bathroom in a hurry*)

TRAVIS. (*Watching the bathroom*) Daddy, come on!
(*Walter gets his bathroom utensils and flies out to the bathroom*)
RUTH. Sit down and have your breakfast, Travis.
TRAVIS. Mama, this is Friday. (*Gleefully*) Check coming tomorrow, huh?
RUTH. You get your mind off money and eat your breakfast.
TRAVIS. (*Eating*) This is the morning we supposed to bring the fifty cents to school.
RUTH. Well, I ain't got no fifty cents this morning.
TRAVIS. Teacher say we have to.
RUTH. I don't care what teacher say. I ain't got it. Eat your breakfast, Travis.
TRAVIS. I *am* eating.
RUTH. Hush up now and just eat!

> (*The boy gives her an exasperated look for her lack of understanding, and eats grudgingly*)

TRAVIS. You think Grandmama would have it?
RUTH. No! And I want you to stop asking your grandmother for money, you hear me?
TRAVIS. (*Outraged*) Gaaaleee! I don't ask her, she just gimme it sometimes!
RUTH. Travis Willard Younger — I got too much on me this morning to be —
TRAVIS. Maybe Daddy —
RUTH. *Travis!*

> (*The boy hushes abruptly. They are both quiet and tense for several seconds*)

TRAVIS. (*Presently*) Could I maybe go carry some groceries in front of the supermarket for a little while after school then?
RUTH. Just hush, I said. (*Travis jabs his spoon into his cereal bowl viciously, and rests his head in anger upon his fists*) If you through eating, you can get over there and make up your bed.

> (*The boy obeys stiffly and crosses the room, almost mechanically, to the bed and more or less carefully folds the covering. He carries the bedding into his mother's room and returns with his books and cap*)

TRAVIS. (*Sulking and standing apart from her unnaturally*) I'm gone.

RUTH. (*Looking up from the stove to inspect him automatically*) Come here. (*He crosses to her and she studies his head*) If you don't take this comb and fix this here head, you better! (*Travis puts down his books with a great sigh of oppression, and crosses to the mirror. His mother mutters under her breath about his "slubbornness"*) 'Bout to march out of here with that head looking just like chickens slept in it! I just don't know where you get your slubborn ways . . . And get your jacket, too. Looks chilly out this morning.

TRAVIS. (*With conspicuously brushed hair and jacket*) I'm gone.

RUTH. Get carfare and milk money — (*Waving one finger*) — and not a single penny for no caps, you hear me?

TRAVIS. (*With sullen politeness*) Yes'm.

(*He turns in outrage to leave. His mother watches after him as in his frustration he approaches the door almost comically. When she speaks to him, her voice has become a very gentle tease*)

RUTH. (*Mocking; as she thinks he would say it*) Oh, Mama makes me so mad sometimes, I don't know what to do! (*She waits and continues to his back as he stands stock-still in front of the door*) I wouldn't kiss that woman good-bye for nothing in this world this morning! (*The boy finally turns around and rolls his eyes at her, knowing the mood has changed and he is vindicated; he does not, however, move toward her yet*) Not for nothing in this world! (*She finally laughs aloud at him and holds out her arms to him and we see that it is a way between them, very old and practiced. He crosses to her and allows her to embrace him warmly but keeps his face fixed with masculine rigidity. She holds him back from her presently and looks at him and runs her fingers over the features of his face. With utter gentleness —*) Now — whose little old angry man are you?

TRAVIS. (*The masculinity and gruffness start to fade at last*) Aw gaalee — Mama . . .

RUTH. (*Mimicking*) Aw — gaaaaalleeeee, Mama! (*She pushes him, with rough playfulness and finality, toward the door*) Get on out of here or you going to be late.

TRAVIS. (*In the face of love, new aggressiveness*) Mama, could I *please* go carry groceries?

RUTH. Honey, it's starting to get so cold evenings.

WALTER. (*Coming in from the bathroom and drawing a make-believe gun from a make-believe holster and shooting at his son*) What is it he wants to do?

RUTH. Go carry groceries after school at the supermarket.

WALTER. Well, let him go . . .

TRAVIS. (*Quickly, to the ally*) I *have* to — she won't gimme the fifty cents . . .

WALTER. (*To his wife only*) Why not?

RUTH. (*Simply, and with flavor*) 'Cause we don't have it.
WALTER. (*To Ruth only*) What you tell the boy things like that for? (*Reaching down into his pants with a rather important gesture*) Here, son —
  (*He hands the boy the coin, but his eyes are directed to his wife's. Travis takes the money happily*)
TRAVIS. Thanks, Daddy.
  (*He starts out. Ruth watches both of them with murder in her eyes. Walter stands and stares back at her with defiance, and suddenly reaches into his pocket again on an afterthought*)
WALTER. (*Without even looking at his son, still staring hard at his wife*) In fact, here's another fifty cents . . . Buy yourself some fruit today — or take a taxicab to school or something!
TRAVIS. Whoopee —
  (*He leaps up and clasps his father around the middle with his legs, and they face each other in mutual appreciation; slowly Walter Lee peeks around the boy to catch the violent rays from his wife's eyes and draws his head back as if shot*)
WALTER. You better get down now — and get to school, man.
TRAVIS. (*At the door*) O.K. Good-bye.
  (*He exits*)
WALTER. (*After him, pointing with pride*) That's *my* boy. (*She looks at him in disgust and turns back to her work*) You know what I was thinking 'bout in the bathroom this morning?
RUTH. No.
WALTER. How come you always try to be so pleasant!
RUTH. What is there to be pleasant 'bout!
WALTER. You want to know what I was thinking 'bout in the bathroom or not!
RUTH. I know what you thinking 'bout.
WALTER. (*Ignoring her*) 'Bout what me and Willy Harris was talking about last night.
RUTH. (*Immediately — a refrain*) Willy Harris is a good-for-nothing loud mouth.
WALTER. Anybody who talks to me has got to be a good-for-nothing loud mouth, ain't he? And what you know about who is just a good-for-nothing loud mouth? Charlie Atkins was just a "good-for-nothing loud mouth" too, wasn't he! When he wanted me to go in the dry-cleaning business with him. And now — he's grossing a hundred thousand a year. A hundred thousand dollars a year! You still call *him* a loud mouth!
RUTH. (*Bitterly*) Oh, Walter Lee . . .
  (*She folds her head on her arms over the table*)
WALTER. (*Rising and coming to her and standing over her*) You tired, ain't you? Tired of everything. Me, the boy, the way we live — this

beat-up hole — everything. Ain't you? (*She doesn't look up, doesn't answer*) So tired — moaning and groaning all the time, but you wouldn't do nothing to help, would you? You couldn't be on my side that long for nothing, could you?

RUTH. Walter, please leave me alone.

WALTER. A man needs for a woman to back him up . . .

RUTH. Walter —

WALTER. Mama would listen to you. You know she listen to you more than she do me and Bennie. She think more of you. All you have to do is just sit down with her when you drinking your coffee one morning and talking 'bout things like you do and — (*He sits down beside her and demonstrates graphically what he thinks her methods and tone should be*) — you just sip your coffee, see, and say easy like that you been thinking 'bout that deal Walter Lee is so interested in, 'bout the store and all, and sip some more coffee, like what you saying ain't really that important to you — And the next thing you know, she be listening good and asking you questions and when I come home — I can tell her the details. This ain't no fly-by-night proposition, baby. I mean we figured it out, me and Willy and Bobo.

RUTH. (*With a frown*) Bobo?

WALTER. Yeah. You see, this little liquor store we got in mind cost seventy-five thousand and we figured the initial investment on the place be 'bout thirty thousand, see. That be ten thousand each. Course, there's a couple of hundred you got to pay so's you don't spend your life just waiting for them clowns to let your license get approved —

RUTH. You mean graft?

WALTER. (*Frowning impatiently*) Don't call it that. See there, that just goes to show you what women understand about the world. Baby, don't *nothing* happen for you in this world 'less you pay *somebody* off!

RUTH. Walter, leave me alone! (*She raises her head and stares at him vigorously — then says, more quietly*) Eat your eggs, they gonna be cold.

WALTER. (*Straightening up from her and looking off*) That's it. There you are. Man say to his woman: I got me a dream. His woman say: Eat your eggs. (*Sadly, but gaining in power*) Man say: I got to take hold of this here world, baby! And a woman will say: Eat your eggs and go to work. (*Passionately now*) Man say: I got to change my life, I'm choking to death, baby! And his woman say — (*In utter anguish as he brings his fists down on his thighs*) — Your eggs is getting cold!

RUTH. (*Softly*) Walter, that ain't none of our money.

WALTER. (*Not listening at all or even looking at her*) This morning, I was lookin' in the mirror and thinking about it . . . I'm thirty-five years old; I been married eleven years and I got a boy who sleeps in the living room — (*Very, very quietly*) — and all I got to give him is stories about how rich white people live . . .

RUTH. Eat your eggs, Walter.

WALTER. *Damn my eggs . . . damn all the eggs that ever was!*

RUTH. Then go to work.

WALTER. (*Looking up at her*) See — I'm trying to talk to you 'bout myself — (*Shaking his head with the repetition*) — and all you can say is eat them eggs and go to work.

RUTH. (*Wearily*) Honey, you never say nothing new. I listen to you every day, every night and every morning, and you never say nothing new. (*Shrugging*) So you would rather *be* Mr. Arnold than be his chauffeur. So — I would *rather* be living in Buckingham Palace.

WALTER. That is just what is wrong with the colored woman in this world . . . Don't understand about building their men up and making 'em feel like they somebody. Like they can do something.

RUTH. (*Drily, but to hurt*) There *are* colored men who do things.

WALTER. No thanks to the colored woman.

RUTH. Well, being a colored woman, I guess I can't help myself none.

(*She rises and gets the ironing board and sets it up and attacks a huge pile of rough-dried clothes, sprinkling them in preparation for the ironing and then rolling them into tight fat balls*)

WALTER. (*Mumbling*) We one group of men tied to a race of women with small minds.

(*His sister Beneatha enters. She is about twenty, as slim and intense as her brother. She is not as pretty as her sister-in-law, but her lean, almost intellectual face has a handsomeness of its own. She wears a bright-red flannel nightie, and her thick hair stands wildly about her head. Her speech is a mixture of many things; it is different from the rest of the family's insofar as education has permeated her sense of English — and perhaps the Midwest rather than the South has finally — at last — won out in her inflection; but not altogether, because over all of it is a soft slurring and transformed use of vowels which is the decided influence of the Southside. She passes through the room without looking at either Ruth or Walter and goes to the outside door and looks, a little blindly, out to the bathroom. She sees that it has been lost to the Johnsons. She closes the door with a sleepy vengeance and crosses to the table and sits down a little defeated*)

BENEATHA. I am going to start timing those people.

WALTER. You should get up earlier.

BENEATHA. (*Her face in her hands. She is still fighting the urge to go back to bed*) Really — would you suggest dawn? Where's the paper?

WALTER. (*Pushing the paper across the table to her as he studies her almost clinically, as though he has never seen her before*) You a horrible-looking chick at this hour.

BENEATHA. (*Drily*) Good morning, everybody.

WALTER. (*Senselessly*) How is school coming?

BENEATHA. (*In the same spirit*) Lovely. Lovely. And you know, biology is the greatest. (*Looking up at him*) I dissected something that looked just like you yesterday.

WALTER. I just wondered if you've made up your mind and everything.

BENEATHA. (*Gaining in sharpness and impatience*) And what did I answer yesterday morning — and the day before that?

RUTH. (*From the ironing board, like someone disinterested and old*) Don't be so nasty, Bennie.

BENEATHA. (*Still to her brother*) And the day before that and the day before that!

WALTER. (*Defensively*) I'm interested in you. Something wrong with that? Ain't many girls who decide —

WALTER *and* BENEATHA. (*In unison*) — "to be a doctor." (*Silence*)

WALTER. Have we figured out yet just exactly how much medical school is going to cost?

RUTH. Walter Lee, why don't you leave that girl alone and get out of here to work?

BENEATHA. (*Exits to the bathroom and bangs on the door*) Come on out of there, please!

(*She comes back into the room*)

WALTER. (*Looking at his sister intently*) You know the check is coming tomorrow.

BENEATHA. (*Turning on him with a sharpness all her own*) That money belongs to Mama, Walter, and it's for her to decide how she wants to use it. I don't care if she wants to buy a house or a rocket ship or just nail it up somewhere and look at it. It's hers. Not ours — hers.

WALTER. (*Bitterly*) Now ain't that fine! You just got your mother's interest at heart, ain't you, girl? You such a nice girl — but if Mama got that money she can always take a few thousand and help you through school too — can't she?

BENEATHA. I have never asked anyone around here to do anything for me!

WALTER. No! And the line between asking and just accepting when the time comes is big and wide — ain't it!

BENEATHA. (*With fury*) What do you want from me, Brother — that I quit school or just drop dead, which!

WALTER. I don't want nothing but for you to stop acting holy 'round here. Me and Ruth done made some sacrifices for you — why can't you do something for the family?

RUTH. Walter, don't be dragging me in it.

WALTER. You are in it — Don't you get up and go to work in somebody's kitchen for the last three years to help put clothes on her back?

RUTH. Oh, Walter — that's not fair . . .

WALTER. It ain't that nobody expects you to get on your knees and say thank you, Brother; thank you, Ruth; thank you, Mama — and thank you, Travis, for wearing the same pair of shoes for two semesters —

BENEATHA. (*Dropping to her knees*) Well — I *do* — all right? — thank everybody . . . and forgive me for ever wanting to be anything at all . . . forgive me, forgive me!

RUTH. Please stop it! Your mama'll hear you.

WALTER. Who the hell told you you had to be a doctor? If you so crazy 'bout messing 'round with sick people — then go be a nurse like other women — or just get married and be quiet . . .

BENEATHA. Well — you finally got it said . . . It took you three years but you finally got it said. Walter, give up; leave me alone — it's Mama's money.

WALTER. *He was my father, too!*

BENEATHA. So what? He was mine, too — and Travis' grandfather — but the insurance money belongs to Mama. Picking on me is not going to make her give it to you to invest in any liquor stores — (*Under breath, dropping into a chair*) — and I for one say, God bless Mama for that!

WALTER. (*To Ruth*) See — did you hear? Did you hear!

RUTH. Honey, please go to work.

WALTER. Nobody in this house is ever going to understand me.

BENEATHA. Because you're a nut.

WALTER. Who's a nut?

BENEATHA. You — you are a nut. Thee is mad, boy.

WALTER. (*Looking at his wife and his sister from the door, very sadly*) The world's most backward race of people, and that's a fact.

BENEATHA. (*Turning slowly in her chair*) And then there are all those prophets who would lead us out of the wilderness — (*Walter slams out of the house*) — into the swamps!

RUTH. Bennie, why you always gotta be pickin' on your brother? Can't you be a little sweeter sometimes? (*Door opens. Walter walks in*)

WALTER. (*To Ruth*) I need some money for carfare.

RUTH. (*Looks at him, then warms; teasing, but tenderly*) Fifty cents? (*She goes to her bag and gets money*) Here, take a taxi.

(*Walter exits. Mama enters. She is a woman in her early sixties, full-bodied and strong. She is one of those women of a certain grace and beauty who wear it so unobtrusively that it takes a while to notice. Her dark-brown face is surrounded by the total whiteness of her hair, and, being a woman who has adjusted to many things in life and overcome many more, her face is full of strength. She has, we can see, wit and faith of a kind that keep her eyes lit and full of interest and expectancy. She is, in a word, a beautiful woman. Her bearing is perhaps most like the noble bearing of the women of the Hereros of Southwest Africa — rather as if she imagines that as she walks she still bears a basket or a vessel upon her head. Her speech, on the other hand, is as careless as her carriage is precise — she is inclined to slur everything — but her voice is perhaps not so much quiet as simply soft*)

MAMA. Who that 'round here slamming doors at this hour?

(*She crosses through the room, goes to the window, opens it, and brings in a feeble little plant growing doggedly in a small pot on the window sill. She feels the dirt and puts it back out*)

RUTH. That was Walter Lee. He and Bennie was at it again.

MAMA. My children and they tempers. Lord, if this little old plant don't get more sun than it's been getting it ain't never going to see spring again. (*She turns from the window*) What's the matter with you this morning, Ruth? You looks right peaked. You aiming to iron all them things? Leave some for me. I'll get to 'em this afternoon. Bennie honey, it's too drafty for you to be sitting 'round half dressed. Where's your robe?

BENEATHA. In the cleaners.

MAMA. Well, go get mine and put it on.

BENEATHA. I'm not cold, Mama, honest.

MAMA. I know — but you so thin . . .

BENEATHA. (*Irritably*) Mama, I'm not cold.

MAMA. (*Seeing the make-down bed as Travis has left it*) Lord have mercy, look at that poor bed. Bless his heart — he tries, don't he?

(*She moves to the bed Travis has sloppily made up*)

RUTH. No — he don't half try at all 'cause he knows you going to come along behind him and fix everything. That's just how come he don't know how to do nothing right now — you done spoiled that boy so.

MAMA. Well — he's a little boy. Ain't supposed to know 'bout housekeeping. My baby, that's what he is. What you fix for his breakfast this morning?

RUTH. (*Angrily*) I feed my son, Lena!

MAMA. I ain't meddling — (*Underbreath; busy-bodyish*) I just noticed all last week he had cold cereal, and when it starts getting this chilly in the fall a child ought to have some hot grits or something when he goes out in the cold —

RUTH. (*Furious*) I gave him hot oats — is that all right!

MAMA. I ain't meddling. (*Pause*) Put a lot of nice butter on it? (*Ruth shoots her an angry look and does not reply*) He likes lots of butter.

RUTH. (*Exasperated*) Lena —
MAMA. (*To Beneatha. Mama is inclined to wander conversationally sometimes*) What was you and your brother fussing 'bout this morning?
BENEATHA. It's not important, Mama.
   (*She gets up and goes to look out at the bathroom, which is apparently free, and she picks up her towels and rushes out*)
MAMA. What was they fighting about?
RUTH. Now you know as well as I do.
MAMA. (*Shaking her head*) Brother still worrying hisself sick about that money?
RUTH. You know he is.
MAMA. You had breakfast?
RUTH. Some coffee.
MAMA. Girl, you better start eating and looking after yourself better. You almost thin as Travis.
RUTH. Lena —
MAMA. Un-hunh?
RUTH. What are you going to do with it?
MAMA. Now don't you start, child. It's too early in the morning to be talking about money. It ain't Christian.
RUTH. It's just that he got his heart set on that store —
MAMA. You mean that liquor store that Willy Harris want him to invest in?
RUTH. Yes —
MAMA. We ain't no business people, Ruth. We just plain working folks.
RUTH. Ain't nobody business people till they go into business. Walter Lee say colored people ain't never going to start getting ahead till they start gambling on some different kinds of things in the world — investments and things.
MAMA. What done got into you, girl? Walter Lee done finally sold you on investing.
RUTH. No. Mama, something is happening between Walter and me. I don't know what it is — but he needs something — something I can't give him any more. He needs this chance, Lena.
MAMA. (*Frowning deeply*) But liquor, honey —
RUTH. Well — like Walter say — I spec people going to always be drinking themselves some liquor.
MAMA. Well — whether they drinks it or not ain't none of my business. But whether I go into business selling it to 'em *is,* and I don't want that on my ledger this late in life. (*Stopping suddenly and studying her daughter-in-law*) Ruth Younger, what's the matter with you today? You look like you could fall over right there.
RUTH. I'm tired.
MAMA. Then you better stay home from work today.

RUTH. I can't stay home. She'd be calling up the agency and screaming at them, "My girl didn't come in today — send me somebody! My girl didn't come in!" Oh, she just have a fit . . .

MAMA. Well, let her have it. I'll just call her up and say you got the flu —

RUTH. (*Laughing*) Why the flu?

MAMA. 'Cause it sounds respectable to 'em. Something white people get, too. They know 'bout the flu. Otherwise they think you been cut up or something when you tell 'em you sick.

RUTH. I got to go in. We need the money.

MAMA. Somebody would of thought my children done all but starved to death the way they talk about money here late. Child, we got a great big old check coming tomorrow.

RUTH. (*Sincerely, but also self-righteously*) Now that's your money. It ain't got nothing to do with me. We all feel like that — Walter and Bennie and me — even Travis.

MAMA. (*Thoughtfully, and suddenly very far away*) Ten thousand dollars —

RUTH. Sure is wonderful.

MAMA. Ten thousand dollars.

RUTH. You know what you should do, Miss Lena? You should take yourself a trip somewhere. To Europe or South America or someplace —

MAMA. (*Throwing up her hands at the thought*) Oh, child!

RUTH. I'm serious, Just pack up and leave! Go on away and enjoy yourself some. Forget about the family and have yourself a ball for once in your life —

MAMA. (*Drily*) You sound like I'm just about ready to die. Who'd go with me? What I look like wandering 'round Europe by myself?

RUTH. Shoot — these here rich white women do it all the time. They don't think nothing of packing up they suitcases and piling on one of them big steamships and — swoosh! — they gone, child.

MAMA. Something always told me I wasn't no rich white woman.

RUTH. Well — what are you going to do with it then?

MAMA. I ain't rightly decided. (*Thinking. She speaks now with emphasis*) Some of it got to be put away for Beneatha and her schoolin' — and ain't nothing going to touch that part of it. Nothing. (*She waits several seconds, trying to make up her mind about something, and looks at Ruth a little tentatively before going on*) Been thinking that we maybe could meet the notes on a little old two-story somewhere, with a yard where Travis could play in the summertime, if we use part of the insurance for a down payment and everybody kind of pitch in. I could maybe take on a little day work again, few days a week —

RUTH. (*Studying her mother-in-law furtively and concentrating on her ironing, anxious to encourage without seeming to*) Well, Lord knows, we've put enough rent into this here rat trap to pay for four houses by now . . .

MAMA. (*Looking up at the words "rat trap" and then looking around and leaning back and sighing — in a suddenly reflective mood —*) "Rat trap" — yes, that's all it is. (*Smiling*) I remember just as well the day me and Big Walter moved in here. Hadn't been married but two weeks and wasn't planning on living here no more than a year. (*She shakes her head at the dissolved dream*) We was going to set away, little by little, don't you know, and buy a little place out in Morgan Park. We had even picked out the house. (*Chuckling a little*) Looks right dumpy today. But Lord, child, you should know all the dreams I had 'bout buying that house and fixing it up and making me a little garden in the back — (*She waits and stops smiling*) And didn't none of it happen.

(*Dropping her hands in a futile gesture*)

RUTH. (*Keeps her head down, ironing*) Yes, life can be a barrel of disappointments, sometimes.

MAMA. Honey, Big Walter would come in here some nights back then and slump down on that couch there and just look at the rug, and look at me and look at the rug and then back at me — and I'd know he was down then . . . really down. (*After a second very long and thoughtful pause; she is seeing back to times that only she can see*) And then, Lord, when I lost that baby — little Claude — I almost thought I was going to lose Big Walter too. Oh, that man grieved hisself! He was one man to love his children.

RUTH. Ain't nothin' can tear at you like losin' your baby.

MAMA. I guess that's how come that man finally worked hisself to death like he done. Like he was fighting his own war with this here world that took his baby from him.

RUTH. He sure was a fine man, all right. I always liked Mr. Younger.

MAMA. Crazy 'bout his children! God knows there was plenty wrong with Walter Younger — hard-headed, mean, kind of wild with women — plenty wrong with him. But he sure loved his children. Always wanted them to have something — be something. That's where Brother gets all these notions, I reckon. Big Walter used to say, he'd get right wet in the eye sometimes, lean his head back with the water standing in his eyes and say, "Seem like God didn't see fit to give the black man nothing but dreams — but He did give us children to make them dreams seem worth while." (*She smiles*) He could talk like that, don't you know.

RUTH. Yes, he sure could. He was a good man, Mr. Younger.

MAMA. Yes, a fine man — just couldn't never catch up with his dreams, that's all.

(*Beneatha comes in, brushing her hair and looking up to the ceiling, where the sound of a vacuum cleaner has started up*)

BENEATHA. What could be so dirty on that woman's rugs that she has to vacuum them every single day?

RUTH. I wish certain young women 'round here who I could name would take inspiration about certain rugs in a certain apartment I could also mention.

BENEATHA. (*Shrugging*) How much cleaning can a house need, for Christ's sakes.

MAMA. (*Not liking the Lord's name used thus*) Bennie!

RUTH. Just listen to her — just listen!

BENEATHA. Oh, God!

MAMA. If you use the Lord's name just one more time —

BENEATHA. (*A bit of a whine*) Oh, Mama —

RUTH. Fresh — just fresh as salt, this girl!

BENEATHA. (*Drily*) Well — if the salt loses its savor —

MAMA. Now that will do. I just ain't going to have you 'round here reciting the scriptures in vain — you hear me?

BENEATHA. How did I manage to get on everybody's wrong side by just walking into a room?

RUTH. If you weren't so fresh —

BENEATHA. Ruth, I'm twenty years old.

MAMA. What time you be home from school today?

BENEATHA. Kind of late. (*With enthusiasm*) Madeline is going to start my guitar lessons today.

(*Mama and Ruth look up with the same expression*)

MAMA. Your *what* kind of lessons?

BENEATHA. Guitar.

RUTH. Oh, Father!

MAMA. How come you done taken it in your mind to learn to play the guitar?

BENEATHA. I just want to, that's all.

MAMA. (*Smiling*) Lord, child, don't you know what to do with yourself? How long it going to be before you get tired of this now — like you got tired of that little play-acting group you joined last year? (*Looking at Ruth*) And what was it the year before that?

RUTH. The horseback-riding club for which she bought that fifty-five-dollar riding habit that's been hanging in the closet ever since!

MAMA. (*To Beneatha*) Why you got to flit so from one thing to another, baby?

BENEATHA. (*Sharply*) I just want to learn to play the guitar. Is there anything wrong with that?

MAMA. Ain't nobody trying to stop you. I just wonders sometimes why you has to flit so from one thing to another all the time. You ain't never done nothing with all that camera equipment you brought home —

BENEATHA. I don't flit! I — I experiment with different forms of expression —

RUTH. Like riding a horse?

BENEATHA. — People have to express themselves one way or another.

MAMA. What is it you want to express?

BENEATHA. (*Angrily*) Me! (*Mama and Ruth look at each other and burst into raucous laughter*) Don't worry — I don't expect you to understand.

MAMA. (*To change the subject*) Who you going out with tomorrow night?

BENEATHA. (*With displeasure*) George Murchison again.

MAMA. (*Pleased*) Oh — you getting a little sweet on him?

RUTH. You ask me, this child ain't sweet on nobody but herself — (*Underbreath*) Express herself!

(*They laugh*)

BENEATHA. Oh — I like George all right, Mama. I mean I like him enough to go out with him and stuff, but —

RUTH. (*For devilment*) What does *and stuff* mean?

BENEATHA. Mind your own business.

MAMA. Stop picking at her now, Ruth. (*A thoughtful pause, and then a suspicious sudden look at her daughter as she turns in her chair for emphasis*) What *does* it mean?

BENEATHA. (*Wearily*) Oh, I just mean I couldn't ever really be serious about George. He's — he's so shallow.

RUTH. Shallow — what do you mean he's shallow? He's *rich!*

MAMA. Hush, Ruth.

BENEATHA. I know he's rich. He knows he's rich, too.

RUTH. Well — what other qualities a man got to have to satisfy you, little girl?

BENEATHA. You wouldn't even begin to understand. Anybody who married Walter could not possibly understand.

MAMA. (*Outraged*) What kind of way is that to talk about your brother?

BENEATHA. Brother is a flip — let's face it.

MAMA. (*To Ruth, helplessly*) What's a flip?

RUTH. (*Glad to add kindling*) She's saying he's crazy.

BENEATHA. Not crazy. Brother isn't really crazy yet — he — he's an elaborate neurotic.

MAMA. Hush your mouth!

BENEATHA. As for George. Well. George looks good — he's got a beautiful car and he takes me to nice places and, as my sister-in-law says, he is probably the richest boy I will ever get to know and I even like him sometimes — but if the Youngers are sitting around waiting to see if their little Bennie is going to tie up the family with the Murchisons, they are wasting their time.

RUTH. You mean you wouldn't marry George Murchison if he asked you someday? That pretty, rich thing? Honey, I knew you was odd —

BENEATHA. No I would not marry him if all I felt for him was what I feel now. Besides, George's family wouldn't really like it.

MAMA. Why not?

BENEATHA. Oh, Mama — The Murchisons are honest-to-God-real-*live*-rich colored people, and the only people in the world who are more snobbish than rich white people are rich colored people. I thought everybody knew that. I've met Mrs. Murchison. She's a scene!

MAMA. You must not dislike people 'cause they well off, honey.

BENEATHA. Why not? It makes just as much sense as disliking people 'cause they are poor, and lots of people do that.

RUTH. (*A wisdom-of-the-ages manner. To Mama*) Well, she'll get over some of this —

BENEATHA. Get over it? What are you talking about, Ruth? Listen, I'm going to be a doctor. I'm not worried about who I'm going to marry yet — if I ever get married.

MAMA *and* RUTH. *If!*

MAMA. Now, Bennie —

BENEATHA. Oh, I probably will . . . but first I'm going to be a doctor, and George, for one, still thinks that's pretty funny. I couldn't be bothered with that. I am going to be a doctor and everybody around here better understand that!

MAMA. (*Kindly*) 'Course you going to be a doctor, honey, God willing.

BENEATHA. (*Drily*) God hasn't got a thing to do with it.

MAMA. Beneatha — that just wasn't necessary.

BENEATHA. Well — neither is God. I get sick of hearing about God.

MAMA. Beneatha!

BENEATHA. I mean it! I'm just tired of hearing about God all the time. What has He got to do with anything? Does he pay tuition?

MAMA. You 'bout to get your fresh little jaw slapped!

RUTH. That's just what she needs, all right!

BENEATHA. Why? Why can't I say what I want to around here, like everybody else?

MAMA. It don't sound nice for a young girl to say things like that — you wasn't brought up that way. Me and your father went to trouble to get you and Brother to church every Sunday.

BENEATHA. Mama, you don't understand. It's all a matter of ideas, and God is just one idea I don't accept. It's not important. I am not going out and be immoral or commit crimes because I don't believe in God. I don't even think about it. It's just that I get tired of Him getting credit for all the things the human race achieves through its own stubborn effort. There simply is no blasted God — there is only man and it is he who makes miracles!

(*Mama absorbs this speech, studies her daughter and rises slowly and crosses to Beneatha and slaps her powerfully across the face. After, there is only silence and the daughter drops her eyes from her mother's face, and Mama is very tall before her*)

MAMA. Now — you say after me, in my mother's house there is still God. (*There is a long pause and Beneatha stares at the floor wordlessly. Mama repeats the phrase with precision and cool emotion*) In my mother's house there is still God.

BENEATHA. In my mother's house there is still God.

(*A long pause*)

MAMA. (*Walking away from Beneatha, too disturbed for triumphant posture. Stopping and turning back to her daughter*) There are some ideas we ain't going to have in this house. Not long as I am at the head of this family.

BENEATHA. Yes, ma'am.

(*Mama walks out of the room*)

RUTH. (*Almost gently, with profound understanding*) You think you a woman, Bennie — but you still a little girl. What you did was childish — so you got treated like a child.

BENEATHA. I see. (*Quietly*) I also see that everybody thinks it's all right for Mama to be a tyrant. But all the tyranny in the world will never put a God in the heavens!

(*She picks up her books and goes out*)

RUTH. (*Goes to Mama's door*) She said she was sorry.

MAMA. (*Coming out, going to her plant*) They frightens me, Ruth. My children.

RUTH. You got good children, Lena. They just a little off sometimes — but they're good.

MAMA. No — there's something come down between me and them that don't let us understand each other and I don't know what it is. One done almost lost his mind thinking 'bout money all the time and the other done commence to talk about things I can't seem to understand in no form or fashion. What is it that's changing, Ruth?

RUTH. (*Soothingly, older than her years*) Now . . . you taking it all too seriously. You just got strong-willed children and it takes a strong woman like you to keep 'em in hand.

MAMA. (*Looking at her plant and sprinkling a little water on it*) They spirited all right, my children. Got to admit they got spirit —

Bennie and Walter. Like this little old plant that ain't never had enough sunshine or nothing — and look at it . . .

*(She has her back to Ruth, who has had to stop ironing and lean against something and put the back of her hand to her forehead)*

RUTH. *(Trying to keep Mama from noticing)* You . . . sure . . . loves that little old thing, don't you? . . .

MAMA. Well, I always wanted me a garden like I used to see sometimes at the back of the houses down home. This plant is close as I ever got to having one. *(She looks out of the window as she replaces the plant)* Lord, ain't nothing as dreary as the view from this window on a dreary day, is there? Why ain't you singing this morning, Ruth? Sing that "No Ways Tired." That song always lifts me up so — *(She turns at last to see that Ruth has slipped quietly into a chair, in a state of semiconsciousness)* Ruth! Ruth honey — what's the matter with you . . . Ruth!

*Curtain*

SCENE TWO

It is the following morning; a Saturday morning, and house cleaning is in progress at the Youngers. Furniture has been shoved hither and yon and Mama is giving the kitchen-area walls a washing down. Beneatha, in dungarees, with a handkerchief tied around her face, is spraying insecticide into the cracks in the walls. As they work, the radio is on and a Southside disk-jockey program is inappropriately filling the house with a rather exotic saxophone blues. Travis, the sole idle one, is leaning on his arms, looking out of the window.

TRAVIS. Grandmama, that stuff Bennie is using smells awful. Can I go downstairs, please?

MAMA. Did you get all them chores done already? I ain't seen you doing much.

TRAVIS. Yes'm — finished early. Where did Mama go this morning?

MAMA. *(Looking at Beneatha)* She had to go on a little errand.

TRAVIS. Where?

MAMA. To tend to her business.

TRAVIS. Can I go outside then?

MAMA. Oh, I guess so. You better stay right in front of the house, though . . . and keep a good lookout for the postman.

TRAVIS. Yes'm. *(He starts out and decides to give his Aunt Beneatha a good swat on the legs as he passes her)* Leave them poor little old cockroaches alone, they ain't bothering you none.

*(He runs as she swings the spray gun at him both viciously and playfully. Walter enters from the bedroom and goes to the phone)*

MAMA. Look out there, girl, before you be spilling some of that stuff on that child!

TRAVIS. *(Teasing)* That's right — look out now!

*(He exits)*

BENEATHA. *(Drily)* I can't imagine that it would hurt him — it has never hurt the roaches.

MAMA. Well, little boys' hides ain't as tough as Southside roaches.

WALTER. *(Into phone)* Hello — Let me talk to Willy Harris.

MAMA. You better get over there behind the bureau. I seen one marching out of there like Napoleon yesterday.

WALTER. Hello, Willy? It ain't come yet. It'll be here in a few minutes. Did the lawyer give you the papers?

BENEATHA. There's really only one way to get rid of them, Mama —

MAMA. How?

BENEATHA. Set fire to this building.

WALTER. Good. Good. I'll be right over.

BENEATHA. Where did Ruth go, Walter!

WALTER. I don't know.

*(He exits abruptly)*

BENEATHA. Mama, where did Ruth go?

MAMA. *(Looking at her with meaning)* To the doctor, I think.

BENEATHA. The doctor? What's the matter? *(They exchange glances)* You don't think —

MAMA. *(With her sense of drama)* Now I ain't saying what I think. But I ain't never been wrong 'bout a woman neither.

*(The phone rings)*

BENEATHA. *(At the phone)* Hay-lo . . . *(Pause, and a moment of recognition)* Well — when did you get back! . . . And how was it? . . . Of course I've missed you — in my way . . . This morning? No . . . house cleaning and all that and Mama hates it if I let people come over when the house is like this . . . You *have*? Well, that's different . . . What is it — Oh, what the hell, come on over . . . Right, see you then.

*(She hangs up)*

MAMA. *(Who has listened vigorously, as is her habit)* Who is that you inviting over here with this house looking like this? You ain't got the pride you was born with!

BENEATHA. Asagai doesn't care how houses look, Mama — he's an intellectual.

MAMA. *Who?*

BENEATHA. Asagai — Joseph Asagai. He's an African boy I met on campus. He's been studying in Canada all summer.

MAMA. What's his name?

BENEATHA. Asagai, Joseph. Ah-sah-guy . . . He's from Nigeria.

MAMA. Oh, that's the little country that was founded by slaves way back . . .
BENEATHA. No, Mama — that's Liberia.
MAMA. I don't think I never met no African before.
BENEATHA. Well, do me a favor and don't ask him a whole lot of ignorant questions about Africans. I mean, do they wear clothes and all that —
MAMA. Well, now, I guess if you think we so ignorant 'round here maybe you shouldn't bring your friends here —
BENEATHA. It's just that people ask such crazy things. All anyone seems to know about when it comes to Africa is Tarzan —
MAMA. (*Indignantly*) Why should I know anything about Africa?
BENEATHA. Why do you give money at church for the missionary work?
MAMA. Well, that's to help save people.
BENEATHA. You mean save them from *heathenism* —
MAMA. (*Innocently*) Yes.
BENEATHA. I'm afraid they need more salvation from the British and the French.
    (*Ruth comes in forlornly and pulls off her coat with dejection. They both turn to look at her*)
RUTH. (*Dispiritedly*) Well, I guess from all the happy faces — everybody knows.
BENEATHA. You pregnant?
MAMA. Lord have mercy, I sure hope it's a little old girl. Travis ought to have a sister.
    (*Beneatha and Ruth give her a hopeless look for this grandmotherly enthusiasm*)
BENEATHA. How far along are you?
RUTH. Two months.
BENEATHA. Did you mean to? I mean did you plan it or was it an accident?
MAMA. What do you know about planning or not planning?
BENEATHA. Oh, Mama.
RUTH. (*Wearily*) She's twenty years old, Lena.
BENEATHA. Did you plan it, Ruth?
RUTH. Mind your own business.
BENEATHA. It is my business — where is he going to live, on the *roof*? (*There is silence following the remark as the three women react to the sense of it*) Gee — I didn't mean that, Ruth, honest. Gee, I don't feel like that at all. I — I think it is wonderful.
RUTH. (*Dully*) Wonderful.
BENEATHA. Yes — really.
MAMA. (*Looking at Ruth, worried*) Doctor say everything going to be all right?

RUTH. (*Far away*) Yes — she says everything is going to be fine . . .
MAMA. (*Immediately suspicious*) "She" — What doctor you went to?
(*Ruth folds over, near hysteria*)
MAMA. (*Worriedly hovering over Ruth*) Ruth honey — what's the matter with you — you sick?
(*Ruth has her fists clenched on her thighs and is fighting hard to suppress a scream that seems to be rising in her*)
BENEATHA. What's the matter with her, Mama?
MAMA. (*Working her fingers in Ruth's shoulder to relax her*) She be all right. Women gets right depressed sometimes when they get her way. (*Speaking softly, expertly, rapidly*) Now you just relax. That's right . . . just lean back, don't think 'bout nothing at all . . . nothing at all —
RUTH. I'm all right . . .
(*The glassy-eyed look melts and then she collapses into a fit of heavy sobbing. The bell rings*)
BENEATHA. Oh, my God — that must be Asagai.
MAMA. (*To Ruth*) Come on now, honey. You need to lie down and rest awhile . . . then have some nice hot food.
(*They exit, Ruth's weight on her mother-in-law. Beneatha, herself profoundly disturbed, opens the door to admit a rather dramatic-looking young man with a large package*)
ASAGAI. Hello, Alaiyo —
BENEATHA. (*Holding the door open and regarding him with pleasure*) Hello . . . (*Long pause*) Well — come in. And please excuse everything. My mother was very upset about my letting anyone come here with the place like this.
ASAGAI. (*Coming into the room*) You look disturbed too . . . Is something wrong?
BENEATHA. (*Still at the door, absently*) Yes . . . we've all got acute ghetto-itus. (*She smiles and comes toward him, finding a cigarette and sitting*) So — sit down! How was Canada?
ASAGAI. (*A sophisticate*) Canadian.
BENEATHA. (*Looking at him*) I'm very glad you are back.
ASAGAI. (*Looking back at her in turn*) Are you really?
BENEATHA. Yes — very.
ASAGAI. Why — you were quite glad when I went away. What happened?
BENEATHA. You went away.
ASAGAI. Ahhhhhhhh.
BENEATHA. Before — you wanted to be so serious before there was time.
ASAGAI. How much time must there be before one knows what one feels?

BENEATHA. (*Stalling this particular conversation. Her hands pressed together, in a deliberately childish gesture*) What did you bring me?
ASAGAI. (*Handing her the package*) Open it and see.
BENEATHA. (*Eagerly opening the package and drawing out some records and the colorful robes of a Nigerian woman*) Oh, Asagai! . . . You got them for me! . . . How beautiful . . . and the records too! (*She lifts out the robes and runs to the mirror with them and holds the drapery up in front of herself*)
ASAGAI. (*Coming to her at the mirror*) I shall have to teach you how to drape it properly. (*He flings the material about her for the moment and stands back to look at her*) Ah — Oh-pay-gay-day, oh-gbah-mu-shay. (*A Yoruba exclamation for admiration*) You wear it well . . . very well . . . mutilated hair and all.
BENEATHA. (*Turning suddenly*) My hair — what's wrong with my hair?
ASAGAI. (*Shrugging*) Were you born with it like that?
BENEATHA. (*Reaching up to touch it*) No . . . of course not.
   (*She looks back to the mirror, disturbed*)
ASAGAI. (*Smiling*) How then?
BENEATHA. You know perfectly well how . . . as crinkly as yours . . . that's how.
ASAGAI. And it is ugly to you that way?
BENEATHA. (*Quickly*) Oh, no — not ugly . . . (*More slowly, apologetically*) But it's so hard to manage when it's, well — raw.
ASAGAI. And so to accommodate that — you mutilate it every week?
BENEATHA. It's not mutilation!
ASAGAI. (*Laughing aloud at her seriousness*) Oh . . . please! I am only teasing you because you are so very serious about these things. (*He stands back from her and folds his arms across his chest as he watches her pulling at her hair and frowning in the mirror*) Do you remember the first time you met me at school? . . . (*He laughs*) You came up to me and you said — and I thought you were the most serious little thing I had ever seen — you said: (*He imitates her*) "Mr. Asagai — I want very much to talk with you. About Africa. You see, Mr. Asagai, I am looking for my *identity!*"
   (*He laughs*)
BENEATHA. (*Turning to him, not laughing*) Yes — (*Her face is quizzical, profoundly disturbed*)
ASAGAI. (*Still teasing and reaching out and taking her face in his hands and turning her profile to him*) Well . . . it is true that this is not so much a profile of a Hollywood queen as perhaps a queen of the Nile — (*A mock dismissal of the importance of the question*) But what does it matter? Assimilationism is so popular in your country.
BENEATHA. (*Wheeling, passionately, sharply*) I am not an assimilationist!
ASAGAI. (*The protest hangs in the room for a moment and Asagai studies her, his laughter fading*) Such a serious one. (*There is a pause*)

So — you like the robes? You must take excellent care of them — they are from my sister's personal wardrobe.

BENEATHA. (*With incredulity*) You — you sent all the way home — for me?

ASAGAI. (*With charm*) For you — I would do much more . . . Well, that is what I came for. I must go.

BENEATHA. Will you call me Monday?

ASAGAI. Yes . . . We have a great deal to talk about. I mean about identity and time and all that.

BENEATHA. Time?

ASAGAI. Yes. About how much time one needs to know what one feels.

BENEATHA. You never understood that there is more than one kind of feeling which can exist between a man and a woman — or, at least, there should be.

ASAGAI. (*Shaking his head negatively but gently*) No. Between a man and a woman there need be only one kind of feeling. I have that for you . . . Now even . . . right this moment . . .

BENEATHA. I know — and by itself — it won't do. I can find that anywhere.

ASAGAI. For a woman it should be enough.

BENEATHA. I know — because that's what it says in all the novels that men write. But it isn't. Go ahead and laugh — but I'm not interested in being someone's little episode in America or — (*With feminine vengeance*) — one of them! (*Asagai has burst into laughter again*) That's funny as hell, huh!

ASAGAI. It's just that every American girl I have known has said that to me. White — black — in this you are all the same. And the same speech, too!

BENEATHA. (*Angrily*) Yuk, yuk, yuk!

ASAGAI. It's how you can be sure that the world's most liberated women are not liberated at all. You all talk about it too much!

(*Mama enters and is immediately all social charm because of the presence of a guest*)

BENEATHA. Oh — Mama — this is Mr. Asagai.

MAMA. How do you do?

ASAGAI. (*Total politeness to an elder*) How do you do, Mrs. Younger. Please forgive me for coming at such an outrageous hour on a Saturday.

MAMA. Well, you are quite welcome. I just hope you understand that our house don't always look like this. (*Chatterish*) You must come again. I would love to hear all about — (*Not sure of the name*) — your country. I think it's so sad the way our American Negroes don't know nothing about Africa 'cept Tarzan and all that. And all that money they pour into these churches when they ought to be helping you people over there drive out them French and Englishmen done taken away your land.

*(The mother flashes a slightly superior look at her daughter upon completion of the recitation)*

ASAGAI. *(Taken aback by this sudden and acutely unrelated expression of sympathy)* Yes . . . yes . . .

MAMA. *(Smiling at him suddenly and relaxing and looking him over)* How many miles is it from here to where you come from?

ASAGAI. Many thousands.

MAMA. *(Looking at him as she would Walter)* I bet you don't half look after yourself, being away from your mama either. I spec you better come 'round here from time to time and get yourself some decent home-cooked meals . . .

ASAGAI. *(Moved)* Thank you. Thank you very much. *(They are all quiet, then —)* Well . . . I must go. I will call you Monday, Alaiyo.

MAMA. What's that he call you?

ASAGAI. Oh — "Alaiyo." I hope you don't mind. It is what you would call a nickname, I think. It is a Yoruba word. I am a Yoruba.

MAMA. *(Looking at Beneatha)* I — I thought he was from —

ASAGAI. *(Understanding)* Nigeria is my country. Yoruba is my tribal origin —

BENEATHA. You didn't tell us what Alaiyo means . . . for all I know, you might be calling me Little Idiot or something . . .

ASAGAI. Well . . . let me see . . . I do not know how just to explain it . . . The sense of a thing can be so different when it changes languages.

BENEATHA. You're evading.

ASAGAI. No — really it is difficult . . . *(Thinking)* It means . . . it means One for Whom Bread — Food — Is Not Enough. *(He looks at her)* Is that all right?

BENEATHA. *(Understanding, softly)* Thank you.

MAMA. *(Looking from one to the other and not understanding any of it)* Well . . . that's nice . . . You must come see us again — Mr. —

ASAGAI. Ah-sah-guy . . .

MAMA. Yes . . . Do come again.

ASAGAI. Good-bye.

*(He exits)*

MAMA. *(After him)* Lord, that's a pretty thing just went out here! *(Insinuatingly, to her daughter)* Yes, I guess I see why we done commence to get so interested in Africa 'round here. Missionaries my aunt Jenny!

*(She exits)*

BENEATHA. Oh, Mama! . . .

*(She picks up the Nigerian dress and holds it up to her in front of the mirror again. She sets the headdress on haphazardly and then notices her*

*hair again and clutches at it and then replaces the headdress and frowns at herself. Then she starts to wriggle in front of the mirror as she thinks a Nigerian woman might. Travis enters and regards her*)

TRAVIS. You cracking up?

BENEATHA. Shut up.

(*She pulls the headdress off and looks at herself in the mirror and clutches at her hair again and squinches her eyes as if trying to imagine something. Then, suddenly she gets her raincoat and kerchief and hurriedly prepares for going out*)

MAMA. (*Coming back into the room*) She's resting now. Travis, baby, run next door and ask Miss Johnson to please let me have a little kitchen cleanser. This here can is empty as Jacob's kettle.

TRAVIS. I just came in.

MAMA. Do as you told. (*He exits and she looks at her daughter*) Where you going?

BENEATHA. (*Halting at the door*) To become a queen of the Nile!

(*She exits in a breathless blaze of glory. Ruth appears in the bedroom doorway*)

MAMA. Who told you to get up?

RUTH. Ain't nothing wrong with me to be lying in no bed for. Where did Bennie go?

MAMA. (*Drumming her fingers*) Far as I could make out — to Egypt. (*Ruth just looks at her*) What time is it getting to?

RUTH. Ten twenty. And the mailman going to ring that bell this morning just like he done every morning for the last umpteen years.

(*Travis comes in with the cleanser can*)

TRAVIS. She say to tell you that she don't have much.

MAMA. (*Angrily*) Lord, some people I could name sure is tight-fisted! (*Directing her grandson*) Mark two cans of cleanser down on the list there. If she that hard up for kitchen cleanser, I sure don't want to forget to get her none!

RUTH. Lena — maybe the woman is just short on cleanser —

MAMA. (*Not listening*) — Much baking powder as she done borrowed from me all these years, she could of done gone into the baking business!

(*The bell sounds suddenly and sharply and all three are stunned — serious and silent — mid-speech. In spite of all the other conversations and distractions of the morning, this is what they have been waiting for, even Travis, who looks helplessly from his mother to his grandmother. Ruth is the first to come to life again*)

RUTH. (*To Travis*) Get down them steps, boy!

(*Travis snaps to life and flies out to get the mail*)

MAMA. (*Her eyes wide, her hand to her breast*) You mean it done really come?

RUTH. (*Excited*) Oh, Miss Lena!
MAMA. (*Collecting herself*) Well . . . I don't know what we all so excited about 'round here for. We known it was coming for months.
RUTH. That's a whole lot different from having it come and being able to hold it in your hands . . . a piece of paper worth ten thousand dollars . . . (*Travis bursts back into the room. He holds the envelope high above his head, like a little dancer, his face is radiant and he is breathless. He moves to his grandmother with sudden slow ceremony and puts the envelope into her hands. She accepts it, and then merely holds it and looks at it*) Come on! Open it . . . Lord have mercy, I wish Walter Lee was here!
TRAVIS. Open it, Grandmama!
MAMA. (*Staring at it*) Now you all be quiet. It's just a check.
RUTH. Open it . . .
MAMA. (*Still staring at it*) Now don't act silly . . . We ain't never been no people to act silly 'bout no money —
RUTH. (*Swiftly*) We ain't never had none before — *open it!*
   (*Mama finally makes a good strong tear and pulls out the thin blue slice of paper and inspects it closely. The boy and his mother study it raptly over Mama's shoulders*)
MAMA. *Travis!* (*She is counting off with doubt*) Is that the right number of zeros.
TRAVIS. Yes'm . . . ten thousand dollars. Gaalee, Grandmama, you rich.
MAMA. (*She holds the check away from her, still looking at it. Slowly her face sobers into a mask of unhappiness*) Ten thousand dollars. (*She hands it to Ruth*) Put it away somewhere, Ruth. (*She does not look at Ruth; her eyes seem to be seeing something somewhere very far off*) Ten thousand dollars they give you. Ten thousand dollars.
TRAVIS. (*To his mother, sincerely*) What's the matter with Grandmama — don't she want to be rich?
RUTH. (*Distractedly*) You go on out and play now, baby. (*Travis exits. Mama starts wiping dishes absently, humming intently to herself. Ruth turns to her, with kind exasperation*) You've gone and got yourself upset.
MAMA. (*Not looking at her*) I spec if it wasn't for you all . . . I would just put that money away or give it to the church or something.
RUTH. Now what kind of talk is that. Mr. Younger would just be plain mad if he could hear you talking foolish like that.
MAMA. (*Stopping and staring off*) Yes . . . he sure would. (*Sighing*) We got enough to do with that money, all right. (*She halts then, and turns and looks at her daughter-in-law hard; Ruth avoids her eyes and Mama wipes her hands with finality and starts to speak firmly to Ruth*) Where did you go today, girl?
RUTH. To the doctor.

MAMA. (*Impatiently*) Now, Ruth . . . you know better than that. Old Doctor Jones is strange enough in his way but there ain't nothing 'bout him make somebody slip and call him "she" — like you done this morning.

RUTH. Well, that's what happened — my tongue slipped.

MAMA. You went to see that woman, didn't you?

RUTH. (*Defensively, giving herself away*) What woman you talking about?

MAMA. (*Angrily*) That woman who —

(*Walter enters in great excitement*)

WALTER. Did it come?

MAMA. (*Quietly*) Can't you give people a Christian greeting before you start asking about money?

WALTER. (*To Ruth*) Did it come? (*Ruth unfolds the check and lays it quietly before him, watching him intently with thoughts of her own. Walter sits down and grasps it close and counts off the zeros*) Ten thousand dollars — (*He turns suddenly, frantically to his mother and draws some papers out of his breast pocket*) Mama — look. Old Willy Harris put everything on paper —

MAMA. Son — I think you ought to talk to your wife . . . I'll go on out and leave you alone if you want —

WALTER. I can talk to her later — Mama, look —

MAMA. Son —

WALTER. WILL SOMEBODY PLEASE LISTEN TO ME TODAY!

MAMA. (*Quietly*) I don't 'low no yellin' in this house, Walter Lee, and you know it — (*Walter stares at them in frustration and starts to speak several times*) And there ain't going to be no investing in no liquor stores. I don't aim to have to speak on that again.

(*A long pause*)

WALTER. Oh — so you don't aim to have to speak on that again? So *you* have decided . . . (*Crumpling his papers*) Well, *you* tell that to my boy tonight when you put him to sleep on the living-room couch . . . (*Turning to Mama and speaking directly to her*) Yeah — and tell it to my wife, Mama, tomorrow when she has to go out of here to look after somebody else's kids. And tell it to *me*, Mama, every time we need a new pair of curtains and I have to watch *you* go out and work in somebody's kitchen. Yeah, you tell me then!

(*Walter starts out*)

RUTH. Where you going?

WALTER. I'm going out!

RUTH. Where?

WALTER. Just out of this house somewhere —

RUTH. (*Getting her coat*) I'll come too.

WALTER. I don't want you to come!

RUTH. I got something to talk to you about, Walter.

WALTER. That's too bad.

MAMA. (*Still quietly*) Walter Lee — (*She waits and he finally turns and looks at her*) Sit down.

WALTER. I'm a grown man, Mama.

MAMA. Ain't nobody said you wasn't grown. But you still in my house and my presence. And as long as you are — you'll talk to your wife civil. Now sit down.

RUTH. (*Suddenly*) Oh, let him go on out and drink himself to death! He makes me sick to my stomach! (*She flings her coat against him*)

WALTER. (*Violently*) And you turn mine too, baby! (*Ruth goes into their bedroom and slams the door behind her*) That was my greatest mistake —

MAMA. (*Still quietly*) Walter, what is the matter with you?

WALTER. Matter with me? Ain't nothing the matter with *me!*

MAMA. Yes there is. Something eating you up like a crazy man. Something more than me not giving you this money. The past few years I been watching it happen to you. You get all nervous acting and kind of wild in the eyes — (*Walter jumps up impatiently at her words*) I said sit there now, I'm talking to you!

WALTER. Mama — I don't need no nagging at me today.

MAMA. Seem like you getting to a place where you always tied up in some kind of knot about something. But if anybody ask you 'bout it you just yell at 'em and bust out the house and go out and drink somewheres. Walter Lee, people can't live with that. Ruth's a good, patient girl in her way — but you getting to be too much. Boy, don't make the mistake of driving that girl away from you.

WALTER. Why — what she do for me?

MAMA. She loves you.

WALTER. Mama — I'm going out. I want to go off somewhere and be by myself for a while.

MAMA. I'm sorry 'bout your liquor store, son. It just wasn't the thing for us to do. That's what I want to tell you about —

WALTER. I got to go out, Mama —
(*He rises*)

MAMA. It's dangerous, son.

WALTER. What's dangerous?

MAMA. When a man goes outside his home to look for peace.

WALTER. (*Beseechingly*) Then why can't there never be no peace in this house then?

MAMA. You done found it in some other house?

WALTER. No — there ain't no woman! Why do women always think there's a woman somewhere when a man gets restless. (*Coming to her*) Mama — Mama — I want so many things . . .

MAMA. Yes, son —

WALTER. I want so many things that they are driving me kind of crazy . . . Mama — look at me.

MAMA. I'm looking at you. You a good-looking boy. You got a job, a nice wife, a fine boy and —

WALTER. A job. (*Looks at her*) Mama, a job? I open and close car doors all day long. I drive a man around in his limousine and I say, "Yes, sir; no, sir; very good, sir; shall I take the Drive, sir?" Mama, that ain't no kind of job . . . that ain't nothing at all. (*Very quietly*) Mama, I don't know if I can make you understand.

MAMA. Understand what, baby?

WALTER. (*Quietly*) Sometimes it's like I can see the future stretched out in front of me — just plain as day. The future, Mama. Hanging over there at the edge of my days. Just waiting for me — a big, looming blank space — full of *nothing*. Just waiting for *me*. (*Pause*) Mama — sometimes when I'm downtown and I pass them cool, quiet-looking restaurants where them white boys are sitting back and talking 'bout things . . . sitting there turning deals worth millions of dollars . . . sometimes I see guys don't look much older than me —

MAMA. Son — how come you talk so much 'bout money?

WALTER. (*With immense passion*) Because it is life, Mama!

MAMA. (*Quietly*) Oh — (*Very quietly*) So now it's life. Money is life. Once upon a time freedom used to be life — now it's money. I guess the world really do change . . .

WALTER. No — it was always money, Mama. We just didn't know about it.

MAMA. No . . . something has changed. (*She looks at him*) You something new, boy. In my time we was worried about not being lynched and getting to the North if we could and how to stay alive and still have a pinch of dignity too . . . Now here come you and Bemeatha — talking 'bout things we ain't never even thought about hardly, me and your daddy. You ain't satisfied or proud of nothing we done. I mean that you had a home; that we kept you out of trouble till you was grown; that you don't have to ride to work on the back of nobody's streetcar — You my children — but how different we done become.

WALTER. You just don't understand, Mama, you just don't understand.

MAMA. Son — do you know your wife is expecting another baby? (*Walter stands, stunned, and absorbs what his mother has said*) That's what she wanted to talk to you about. (*Walter sinks down into a chair*) This ain't for me to be telling — but you ought to know. (*She waits*) I think Ruth is thinking 'bout getting rid of that child.

WALTER. (*Slowly understanding*) No — no — Ruth wouldn't do that.

MAMA. When the world gets ugly enough — a woman will do anything for her family. *The part that's already living.*
WALTER. You don't know Ruth, Mama, if you think she would do that.
(*Ruth opens the bedroom door and stands there a little limp*)
RUTH. (*Beaten*) Yes I would too, Walter. (*Pause*) I gave her a five-dollar down payment.
(*There is total silence as the man stares at his wife and the mother stares at her son*)
MAMA. (*Presently*) Well — (*Tightly*) Well — son, I'm waiting to hear you say something . . . I'm waiting to hear how you be your father's son. Be the man he was . . . (*Pause*) Your wife say she going to destroy your child. And I'm waiting to hear you talk like him and say we a people who give children life, not who destroys them — (*She rises*) I'm waiting to see you stand up and look like your daddy and say we done give up one baby to poverty and that we ain't going to give up nary another one . . . I'm waiting.
WALTER. Ruth —
MAMA. If you a son of mine, tell her! (*Walter turns, looks at her and can say nothing. She continues, bitterly*) You . . . you are a disgrace to your father's memory. Somebody get me my hat.

*Curtain*

*Act II*

SCENE I

*Time: Later the same day.*
*At rise: Ruth is ironing again. She has the radio going. Presently Beneatha's bedroom door opens and Ruth's mouth falls and she puts down the iron in fascination.*
RUTH. What have we got on tonight!
BENEATHA. (*Emerging grandly from the doorway so that we can see her thoroughly robed in the costume Asagai brought*) You are looking at what a well-dressed Nigerian woman wears — (*She parades for Ruth, her hair completely hidden by the headdress; she is coquettishly fanning herself with an ornate oriental fan, mistakenly more like Butterfly than any Nigerian that ever was*) Isn't it beautiful? (*She promenades to the radio and, with an arrogant flourish, turns off the good loud blues that is playing*) Enough of this assimilationist junk! (*Ruth follows her with her eyes as she goes to the phonograph and puts on a record and turns and waits ceremoniously for the music to come up. Then, with a shout —*) OCOMOGOSIAY!
(*Ruth jumps. The music comes up, a lovely Nigerian melody. Beneatha*

listens, enraptured, her eyes far away — "back to the past." She begins to dance. Ruth is dumfounded)
RUTH. What kind of dance is that?
BENEATHA. A folk dance.
RUTH. (Pearl Bailey) What kind of folks do that, honey?
BENEATHA. It's from Nigeria. It's a dance of welcome.
RUTH. Who you welcoming?
BENEATHA. The men back to the village.
RUTH. Where they been?
BENEATHA. How should I know — out hunting or something. Anyway, they are coming back now . . .
RUTH. Well, that's good.
BENEATHA. (With the record)
Alundi, alundi
Alundi alunya
Jop pu a jeepua
Ang gu sooooooooooo

Ai yai yae . . .
Ayehaye — alundi . . .

(Walter comes in during this performance; he has obviously been drinking. He leans against the door heavily and watches his sister, at first with distaste. Then his eyes look off — "back to the past" — as he lifts both his fists to the roof, screaming)
WALTER. YEAH . . . AND ETHIOPIA STRETCH FORTH HER HANDS AGAIN! . . .
RUTH. (Drily, looking at him) Yes — and Africa sure is claiming her own tonight. (She gives them both up and starts ironing again)
WALTER. (All in a drunken, dramatic shout) Shut up! . . . I'm digging them drums . . . them drums move me! . . . (He makes his weaving way to his wife's face and leans in close to her) In my heart of hearts — (He thumps his chest) — I am much warrior!
RUTH. (Without even looking up) In your heart of hearts you are much drunkard.
WALTER. (Coming away from her and starting to wander around the room, shouting) Me and Jomo . . . (Intently, in his sister's face. She has stopped dancing to watch him in this unknown mood) That's my man, Kenyatta. (Shouting and thumping his chest) FLAMING SPEAR! HOT DAMN! (He is suddenly in possession of an imaginary spear and actively spearing enemies all over the room) OCOMOGOSIAY . . . THE LION IS WAKING . . . OWIMOWEH! (He pulls his shirt open and leaps up on a table and gestures with his spear. The bell rings. Ruth goes to answer)
BENEATHA. (To encourage Walter, thoroughly caught up with this side of him) OCOMOGOSIAY, FLAMING SPEAR!
WALTER. (On the table, very far gone, his eyes pure glass sheets. He sees

what we cannot, that he is a leader of his people, a great chief, a descendant of Chaka, and that the hour to march has come) Listen, my black brothers —

BENEATHA. OCOMOGOSIAY!

WALTER. — Do you hear the waters rushing against the shores of the coastlands —

BENEATHA. OCOMOGOSIAY!

WALTER. — Do you hear the screeching of the cocks in yonder hills beyond where the chiefs meet in council for the coming of the mighty war —

BENEATHA. OCOMOGOSIAY!

WALTER. — Do you hear the beating of the wings of the birds flying low over the mountains and the low places of our land —

(*Ruth opens the door. George Murchison enters*)

BENEATHA. OCOMOGOSIAY!

WALTER. — Do you hear the singing of the women, singing the war songs of our fathers to the babies in the great houses . . . singing the sweet war songs? OH, DO YOU HEAR, MY BLACK BROTHERS!

BENEATHA. (*Completely gone*) We hear you, Flaming Spear —

WALTER. Telling us to prepare for the greatness of the time — (*To George*) Black Brother!

(*He extends his hand for the fraternal clasp*)

GEORGE. Black Brother, hell!

RUTH. (*Having had enough, and embarrassed for the family*) Beneatha, you got company — what's the matter with you? Walter Lee Younger, get down off that table and stop acting like a fool . . .

(*Walter comes down off the table suddenly and makes a quick exit to the bathroom*)

RUTH. He's had a little to drink . . . I don't know what her excuse is.

GEORGE. (*To Beneatha*) Look honey, we're going *to* the theatre — we're not going to be *in* it . . . so go change, huh?

RUTH. You expect this boy to go out with you looking like that?

BENEATHA. (*Looking at George*) That's up to George. If he's ashamed of his heritage —

GEORGE. Oh, don't be so proud of yourself, Bennie — just because you look eccentric.

BENEATHA. How can something that's natural be eccentric?

GEORGE. That's what being eccentric means — being natural. Get dressed.

BENEATHA. I don't like that, George.

RUTH. Why must you and your brother make an argument out of everything people say?

BENEATHA. Because I hate assimilationist Negroes!

RUTH. Will somebody please tell me what assimila-whoever means!

GEORGE. Oh, it's just a college girl's way of calling people Uncle Toms — but that isn't what it means at all.

RUTH. Well, what does it mean?

BENEATHA. (*Cutting George off and staring at him as she replies to Ruth*) It means someone who is willing to give up his own culture and submerge himself completely in the dominant, and in this case, *oppressive* culture!

GEORGE. Oh, dear, dear, dear! Here we go! A lecture on the African past! On our Great West African Heritage! In one second we will hear all about the great Ashanti empires; the great Songhay civilizations; and the great sculpture of Bénin — and then some poetry in the Bantu — and the whole monologue will end with the word *heritage!* (*Nastily*) Let's face it, baby, your heritage is nothing but a bunch of raggedy-assed spirituals and some grass huts!

BENEATHA. Grass huts! (*Ruth crosses to her and forcibly pushes her toward the bedroom*) See there . . . you are standing there in your splendid ignorance talking about people who were the first to smelt iron on the face of the earth! (*Ruth is pushing her through the door*) The Ashanti were performing surgical operations when the English — (*Ruth pulls the door to, with Beneatha on the other side, and smiles graciously at George. Beneatha opens the door and shouts the end of the sentence defiantly at George*) — were still tatooing themselves with blue dragons . . . (*She goes back inside*)

RUTH. Have a seat, George. (*They both sit. Ruth folds her hands rather primly on her lap, determined to demonstrate the civilization of the family*) Warm, ain't it? I mean for September. (*Pause*) Just like they always say about Chicago weather: If it's too hot or cold for you, just wait a minute and it'll change. (*She smiles happily at this cliché of clichés*) Everybody say it's got to do with them bombs and things they keep setting off. (*Pause*) Would you like a nice cold beer?

GEORGE. No, thank you. I don't care for beer. (*He looks at his watch*) I hope she hurries up.

RUTH. What time is the show?

GEORGE. It's an eight-thirty curtain. That's just Chicago, though. In New York standard curtain time is eight-forty.

(*He is rather proud of this knowledge*)

RUTH. (*Properly appreciating it*) You get to New York a lot?

GEORGE. (*Offhand*) Few times a year.

RUTH. Oh — that's nice. I've never been to New York. (*Walter enters. We feel he has relieved himself, but the edge of unreality is still with him*)

WALTER. New York ain't got nothing Chicago ain't. Just a bunch of hustling people all squeezed up together — being "Eastern."

(*He turns his face into a screw of displeasure*)

GEORGE. Oh — you've been?

WALTER. *Plenty* of times.

RUTH. (*Shocked at the lie*) Walter Lee Younger!
WALTER. (*Staring her down*) Plenty! (*Pause*) What we got to drink in this house? Why don't you offer this man some refreshment. (*To George*) They don't know how to entertain people in this house, man.
GEORGE. Thank you — I don't really care for anything.
WALTER. (*Feeling his head; sobriety coming*) Where's Mama?
RUTH. She ain't come back yet.
WALTER. (*Looking Murchison over from head to toe, scrutinizing his carefully casual tweed sports jacket over cashmere V-neck sweater over soft eyelet shirt and tie, and soft slacks, finished off with white buckskin shoes*) Why all you college boys wear them fairyish-looking white shoes?
RUTH. Walter Lee!
 (*George Murchison ignores the remark*)
WALTER. (*To Ruth*) Well, they look crazy as hell — white shoes, cold as it is.
RUTH. (*Crushed*) You have to excuse him —
WALTER. No he don't! Excuse me for what? What you always excusing me for! I'll excuse myself when I needs to be excused! (*A pause*) They look as funny as them black knee socks Beneatha wears out of here all the time.
RUTH. It's the college *style*, Walter.
WALTER. Style, hell. She looks like she got burnt legs or something!
RUTH. Oh, Walter —
WALTER. (*An irritable mimic*) Oh, Walter! Oh, Walter! (*To Murchison*) How's your old man making out? I understand you all going to buy that big hotel on the Drive? (*He finds a beer in the refrigerator, wanders over to Murchison, sipping and wiping his lips with the back of his hand, and straddling a chair backwards to talk to the other man*) Shrewd move. Your old man is all right, man. (*Tapping his head and half winking for emphasis*) I mean he knows how to operate. I mean he thinks *big*, you know what I mean, I mean for a *home*, you know? But I think he's kind of running out of ideas now. I'd like to talk to him. Listen, man, I got some plans that could turn this city upside down. I mean I think like he does. *Big*. Invest big, gamble big, hell, lose *big* if you have to, you know what I mean. It's hard to find a man on this whole Southside who understands my kind of thinking — you dig? (*He scrutinizes Murchison again, drinks his beer, squints his eyes and leans in close, confidential, man to man*) Me and you ought to sit down and talk sometimes, man. Man, I got me some ideas . . .
MURCHISON. (*With boredom*) Yeah — sometimes we'll have to do that, Walter.
WALTER. (*Understanding the indifference, and offended*) Yeah — well, when you get the time, man. I know you a busy little boy.

RUTH. Walter, please —

WALTER. (*Bitterly, hurt*) I know ain't nothing in this world as busy as you colored college boys with your fraternity pins and white shoes . . .

RUTH. (*Covering her face with humiliation*) Oh, Walter Lee —

WALTER. I see you all all the time — with the books tucked under your arms — going to your (*British A – a mimic*) "clahsses." And for what! What the hell you learning over there? Filling up your heads — (*Counting off on his fingers*) — with the sociology and the psychology — but they teaching you how to be a man? How to take over and run the world? They teaching you how to run a rubber plantation or a steel mill? Naw — just to talk proper and read books and wear white shoes . . .

GEORGE. (*Looking at him with distaste, a little above it all*) You're all wacked up with bitterness, man.

WALTER. (*Intently, almost quietly, between the teeth, glaring at the boy*) And you — ain't you bitter, man? Ain't you just about had it yet? Don't you see no stars gleaming that you can't reach out and grab? You happy? — You contented son-of-a-bitch — you happy? You got it made? Bitter? Man, I'm a volcano. Bitter? Here I am a giant — surrounded by ants! Ants who can't even understand what it is the giant is talking about.

RUTH. (*Passionately and suddenly*) Oh, Walter — ain't you with nobody!

WALTER. (*Violently*) No! 'Cause ain't nobody with me! Not even my own mother!

RUTH. Walter, that's a terrible thing to say!

(*Beneatha enters, dressed for the evening in a cocktail dress and earrings*)

GEORGE. Well — hey, you look great.

BENEATHA. Let's go, George. See you all later.

RUTH. Have a nice time.

GEORGE. Thanks. Good night. (*To Walter, sarcastically*) Good night, Prometheus.

(*Beneatha and George exit*)

WALTER. (*To Ruth*) Who is Prometheus?

RUTH. I don't know. Don't worry about it.

WALTER. (*In fury, pointing after George*) See there — they get to a point where they can't insult you man to man — they got to go talk about something ain't nobody never heard of!

RUTH. How do you know it was an insult? (*To humor him*) Maybe Prometheus is a nice fellow.

WALTER. Prometheus! I bet there ain't even no such thing! I bet that simple-minded clown —

RUTH. Walter —

(*She stops what she is doing and looks at him*)

WALTER. *(Yelling)* Don't start!

RUTH. Start what?

WALTER. Your nagging! Where was I? Who was I with? How much money did I spend?

RUTH. *(Plaintively)* Walter Lee — why don't we just try to talk about it . . .

WALTER. *(Not listening)* I been out talking with people who understand me. People who care about the things I got on my mind.

RUTH. *(Wearily)* I guess that means people like Willy Harris.

WALTER. Yes, people like Willy Harris.

RUTH. *(With a sudden flash of impatience)* Why don't you all just hurry up and go into the banking business and stop talking about it!

WALTER. Why? You want to know why? 'Cause we all tied up in a race of people that don't know how to do nothing but moan, pray and have babies!

(*The line is too bitter even for him and he looks at her and sits down*)

RUTH. Oh, Walter . . . *(Softly)* Honey, why can't you stop fighting me?

WALTER. *(Without thinking)* Who's fighting you? Who even cares about you?

(*This line begins the retardation of his mood*)

RUTH. Well — (*She waits a long time, and then with resignation starts to put away her things*) I guess I might as well go on to bed . . . (*More or less to herself*) I don't know where we lost it . . . but we have . . . (*Then, to him*) I — I'm sorry about this new baby, Walter. I guess maybe I better go on and do what I started . . . I guess I just didn't realize how bad things was with us . . . I guess I just didn't really realize — (*She starts out to the bedroom and stops*) You want some hot milk?

WALTER. Hot milk?

RUTH. Yes — hot milk.

WALTER. Why hot milk?

RUTH. 'Cause after all that liquor you come home with you ought to have something hot in your stomach.

WALTER. I don't want no milk.

RUTH. You want some coffee then?

WALTER. No, I don't want no coffee. I don't want nothing hot to drink. (*Almost plaintively*) Why you always trying to give me something to eat?

RUTH. (*Standing and looking at him helplessly*) What else can I give you, Walter Lee Younger?

(*She stands and looks at him and presently turns to go out again. He lifts his head and watches her going away from him in a new mood which began to emerge when he asked her "Who cares about you?"*)

WALTER. It's been rough, ain't it, baby? (*She hears and stops but does not turn around and he continues to her back*) I guess between two people there ain't never as much understood as folks generally thinks there is. I mean like between me and you — (*She turns to face him*) How we gets to the place where we scared to talk softness to each other. (*He waits, thinking hard himself*) Why you think it got to be like that? (*He is thoughtful, almost as a child would be*) Ruth, what is it gets into people ought to be close?

RUTH. I don't know, honey. I think about it a lot.

WALTER. On account of you and me, you mean? The way things are with us. The way something done come down between us.

RUTH. There ain't so much between us, Walter . . . Not when you come to me and try to talk to me. Try to be with me . . . a little even.

WALTER. (*Total honesty*) Sometimes . . . sometimes . . . I don't even know how to try.

RUTH. Walter —

WALTER. Yes?

RUTH. (*Coming to him, gently and with misgiving, but coming to him*) Honey . . . life don't have to be like this. I mean sometimes people can do things so that things are better . . . You remember how we used to talk when Travis was born . . . about the way we were going to live . . . the kind of house . . . (*She is stroking his head*) Well, it's all starting to slip away from us . . .

(*Mama enters, and Walter jumps up and shouts at her*)

WALTER. Mama, where have you been?

MAMA. My — them steps is longer than they used to be. Whew! (*She sits down and ignores him*) How you feeling this evening, Ruth?

(*Ruth shrugs, disturbed some at having been prematurely interrupted and watching her husband knowingly*)

WALTER. Mama, where have you been all day?

MAMA. (*Still ignoring him and leaning on the table and changing to more comfortable shoes*) Where's Travis?

RUTH. I let him go out earlier and he ain't come back yet. Boy, is he going to get it!

WALTER. Mama!

MAMA. (*As if she has heard him for the first time*) Yes, son?

WALTER. Where did you go this afternoon?

MAMA. I went downtown to tend to some business that I had to tend to.

WALTER. What kind of business?

MAMA. You know better than to question me like a child, Brother.

WALTER. (*Rising and bending over the table*) Where were you, Mama? (*Bringing his fists down and shouting*) Mama, you didn't go do something with that insurance money, something crazy?

*A RAISIN IN THE SUN*    177

(*The front door opens slowly, interrupting him, and Travis peeks his head in, less than hopefully*)

TRAVIS. (*To his mother*) Mama, I —

RUTH. "Mama I" nothing! You're going to get it, boy! Get on in that bedroom and get yourself ready!

TRAVIS. But I —

MAMA. Why don't you all never let the child explain hisself.

RUTH. Keep out of it now, Lena.

(*Mama clamps her lips together, and Ruth advances toward her son menacingly*)

RUTH. A thousand times I have told you not to go off like that —

MAMA. (*Holding out her arms to her grandson*) Well — at least let me tell him something. I want him to be the first one to hear . . . Come here, Travis. (*The boy obeys, gladly*) Travis — (*She takes him by the shoulder and looks into his face*) — you know that money we got in the mail this morning?

TRAVIS. Yes'm —

MAMA. Well — what you think your grandmama gone and done with that money?

TRAVIS. I don't know, Grandmama.

MAMA. (*Putting her finger on his nose for emphasis*) She went out and she bought you a house! (*The explosion comes from Walter at the end of the revelation and he jumps up and turns away from all of them in a fury. Mama continues, to Travis*) You glad about the house? It's going to be yours when you get to be a man.

TRAVIS. Yeah — I always wanted to live in a house.

MAMA. All right, gimme some sugar then — (*Travis puts his arms around her neck as she watches her son over the boy's shoulder. Then, to Travis, after the embrace*) Now when you say your prayers tonight, you thank God and your grandfather — 'cause it was him who give you the house — in his way.

RUTH. (*Taking the boy from Mama and pushing him toward the bedroom*) Now you get out of here and get ready for your beating.

TRAVIS. Aw, Mama —

RUTH. Get on in there — (*Closing the door behind him and turning radiantly to her mother-in-law*) So you went and did it!

MAMA. (*Quietly, looking at her son with pain*) Yes, I did.

RUTH. (*Raising both arms classically*) *Praise God!* (*Looks at Walter a moment, who says nothing. She crosses rapidly to her husband*) Please, honey — let me be glad . . . you be glad too. (*She has laid her hands on his shoulders, but he shakes himself free of her roughly, without turning to face her*) Oh, Walter . . . a home . . . a home. (*She comes back to Mama*) Well — where is it? How big is it? How much it going to cost?

MAMA. Well —

RUTH. When we moving?

MAMA. (*Smiling at her*) First of the month.

RUTH. (*Throwing back her head with jubilance*) Praise God!

MAMA. (*Tentatively, still looking at her son's back turned against her and Ruth*) It's — it's a nice house too . . . (*She cannot help speaking directly to him. An imploring quality in her voice, her manner, makes her almost like a girl now*) Three bedrooms — nice big one for you and Ruth. . . . Me and Beneatha still have to share our room, but Travis have one of his own — and (*With difficulty*) I figure if the — new baby — is a boy, we could get one of them double-decker outfits . . . And there's a yard with a little patch of dirt where I could maybe get to grow me a few flowers . . . And a nice big basement . . .

RUTH. Walter honey, be glad —

MAMA. (*Still to his back, fingering things on the table*) 'Course I don't want to make it sound fancier than it is . . . It's just a plain little old house — but it's made good and solid — and it will be *ours*. Walter Lee — it makes a difference in a man when he can walk on floors that belong to *him* . . .

RUTH. Where is it?

MAMA. (*Frightened at this telling*) Well — well — it's out there in Clybourne Park —

(*Ruth's radiance fades abruptly, and Walter finally turns slowly to face his mother with incredulity and hostility*)

RUTH. Where?

MAMA. (*Matter-of-factly*) Four o six Clybourne Street, Clybourne Park.

RUTH. Clybourne Park? Mama, there ain't no colored people living in Clybourne Park.

MAMA. (*Almost idiotically*) Well, I guess there's going to be some now.

WALTER. (*Bitterly*) So that's the peace and comfort you went out and bought for us today!

MAMA. (*Raising her eyes to meet his finally*) Son — I just tried to find the nicest place for the least amount of money for my family.

RUTH. (*Trying to recover from the shock*) Well — well — 'course I ain't one never been 'fraid of no crackers, mind you — but — well, wasn't there no other houses nowhere?

MAMA. Them houses they put up for colored in them areas way out all seem to cost twice as much as other houses. I did the best I could.

RUTH. (*Struck senseless with the news, in its various degrees of goodness and trouble, she sits a moment, her fists propping her chin in thought, and then she starts to rise, bringing her fists down with vigor, the radiance spreading from cheek to cheek again*) Well — well! — All I can say is — if this is my time in life — *my time* — to say good-bye — (*And she builds with momentum as she starts to circle the room with an exuberant, almost tearfully happy release*) — to these Goddamned cracking walls! — (*She pounds the walls*) — and these marching roaches! — (*She wipes at an imaginary army of marching roaches*) — and this cramped little closet which ain't now or never was no kitchen! . . . then I say it loud and good, *Hallelujah! and good-bye misery . . . I don't never want to see your ugly face again!* (*She laughs joyously, having practically destroyed the apartment, and flings her arms up and lets them come down happily, slowly, reflectively, over her abdomen, aware for the first time perhaps that the life therein pulses with happiness and not despair*) Lena?

MAMA. (*Moved, watching her happiness*) Yes, honey?

RUTH. (*Looking off*) Is there — is there a whole lot of sunlight?

MAMA. (*Understanding*) Yes, child, there's a whole lot of sunlight.

(*Long pause*)

RUTH. (*Collecting herself and going to the door of the room Travis is in*) Well — I guess I better see 'bout Travis. (*To Mama*) Lord, I sure don't feel like whipping nobody today!

(*She exits*)

MAMA. (*The mother and son are left alone now and the mother waits a long time, considering deeply, before she speaks*) Son — you — you understand what I done, don't you? (*Walter is silent and sullen*) I — I just seen my family falling apart today . . . just falling to pieces in front of my eyes . . . We couldn't of gone on like we was today. We was going backwards 'stead of forwards — talking 'bout killing babies and wishing each other was dead . . . When it gets like that in life — you just got to do something different, push on out and do something bigger . . . (*She waits*) I wish you say something, son . . . I wish you'd say how deep inside you you think I done the right thing —

WALTER. (*Crossing slowly to his bedroom door and finally turning there and speaking measuredly*) What you need me to say you done right for? *You* the head of this family. You run our lives like you want to. It was your money and you did what you wanted with it. So what you need for me to say it was all right for? (*Bitterly, to hurt her as deeply as he knows is possible*) So you butchered up a dream of mine — you — who always talking 'bout your children's dreams . . .

MAMA. Walter Lee —

(*He just closes the door behind him. Mama sits alone, thinking heavily*)

*Curtain*

SCENE II

*Time:* Friday night. A few weeks later.

*At rise:* Packing crates mark the intention of the family to move. Beneatha and George come in, presumably from an evening out again.

GEORGE. O.K. . . . O.K., whatever you say . . . (*They both sit on the couch. He tries to kiss her. She moves away*) Look, we've had a nice evening; let's not spoil it, huh? . . .

(*He again turns her head and tries to nuzzle in and she turns away from him, not with distaste but with momentary lack of interest; in a mood to pursue what they were talking about*)

BENEATHA. I'm *trying* to talk to you.

GEORGE. We always talk.

BENEATHA. Yes — and I love to talk.

GEORGE. (*Exasperated; rising*) I know it and I don't mind it sometimes . . . I want you to cut it out, see — The moody stuff, I mean. I don't like it. You're a nice-looking girl . . . all over. That's all you need, honey, forget the atmosphere. Guys aren't going to go for the atmosphere — they're going to go for what they see. Be glad for that. Drop the Garbo routine. It doesn't go with you. As for myself, I want a nice — (*Groping*) — simple (*Thoughtfully*) — sophisticated girl . . . not a poet — O.K.?

(*She rebuffs him again and he starts to leave*)

BENEATHA. Why are you angry?

GEORGE. Because this is stupid! I don't go out with you to discuss the nature of "quiet desperation" or to hear all about your thoughts — because the world will go on thinking what it thinks regardless —

BENEATHA. Then why read books? Why go to school?

GEORGE. (*With artificial patience, counting on his fingers*) It's simple. You read books — to learn facts — to get grades — to pass the course — to get a degree. That's all — it has nothing to do with thoughts.

(*A long pause*)

BENEATHA. I see. (*A longer pause as she looks at him*) Good night, George.

(*George looks at her a little oddly, and starts to exit. He meets Mama coming in*)

GEORGE. Oh — hello, Mrs. Younger.

MAMA. Hello, George, how you feeling?

GEORGE. Fine — fine, how are you?

MAMA. Oh, a little tired. You know them steps can get you after a day's work. You all have a nice time tonight?

GEORGE. Yes — a fine time. Well, good night.

MAMA. Good night. (*He exits. Mama closes the door behind her*) Hello, honey. What you sitting like that for?

BENEATHA. I'm just sitting.

MAMA. Didn't you have a nice time?

BENEATHA. No.

MAMA. No? What's the matter?

BENEATHA. Mama, George is a fool — honest. (*She rises*)

MAMA. (*Hustling around unloading the packages she has entered with. She stops*) Is he, baby?

BENEATHA. Yes.

(*Beneatha makes up Travis' bed as she talks*)

MAMA. You sure?

BENEATHA. Yes.

MAMA. Well — I guess you better not waste your time with no fools.

(*Beneatha looks up at her mother, watching her put groceries in the refrigerator. Finally she gathers up her things and starts into the bedroom. At the door she stops and looks back at her mother*)

BENEATHA. Mama —

MAMA. Yes, baby —

BENEATHA. Thank you.

MAMA. For what?

BENEATHA. For understanding me this time.

(*She exits quickly and the mother stands, smiling a little, looking at the place where Beneatha just stood. Ruth enters*)

RUTH. Now don't you fool with any of this stuff, Lena —

MAMA. Oh, I just thought I'd sort a few things out.

(*The phone rings. Ruth answers*)

RUTH. (*At the phone*) Hello — Just a minute. (*Goes to door*) Walter, It's Mrs. Arnold. (*Waits. Goes back to the phone. Tense*) Hello. Yes, this is his wife speaking . . . He's lying down now. Yes . . . well, he'll be in tomorrow. He's been very sick. Yes — I know we should have called, but we were so sure he'd be able to come in today. Yes — yes, I'm very sorry. Yes . . . Thank you very much. (*She hangs up. Walter is standing in the doorway of the bedroom behind her*) That was Mrs. Arnold.

WALTER. (*Indifferently*) Was it?

RUTH. She said if you don't come in tomorrow that they are getting a new man . . .

WALTER. Ain't that sad — ain't that crying sad.

RUTH. She said Mr. Arnold has had to take a cab for three days . . . Walter, you ain't been to work for three days! (*This is a revelation to her*) Where you been, Walter Lee Younger? (*Walter looks at her and starts to laugh*) You're going to lose your job.

WALTER. That's right . . .

RUTH. Oh, Walter, and with your mother working like a dog every day —

WALTER. That's sad too — Everything is sad.

MAMA. What you been doing for these three days, son?

WALTER. Mama — you don't know all the things a man what got leisure can find to do in this city . . . What's this — Friday night?

Well — Wednesday I borrowed Willy Harris' car and I went for a drive . . . just me and myself and I drove and drove . . . Way out . . . way past South Chicago, and I parked the car and I sat and looked at the steel mills all day long. I just sat in the car and looked at them big black chimneys for hours. Then I drove back and I went to the Green Hat. (*Pause*) And Thursday — Thursday I borrowed the car again and I got in it and I pointed it the other way and I drove the other way — for hours — way, way up to Wisconsin, and I looked at the farms. I just drove and looked at the farms. Then I drove back and I went to the Green Hat. (*Pause*) And today — today I didn't get the car. Today I just walked. All over the Southside. And I looked at the Negroes and they looked at me and finally I just sat down on the curb at Thirty-ninth and South Parkway and I just sat there and watched the Negroes go by. And then I went to the Green Hat. You all sad? You all depressed? And you know where I am going right now —

(*Ruth goes out quietly*)

MAMA. Oh, Big Walter, is this the harvest of our days?

WALTER. You know what I like about the Green Hat? (*He turns the radio on and a steamy, deep blues pours into the room*) I like this little cat they got there who blows a sax . . . He blows. He talks to me. He ain't but 'bout five feet tall and he's got a conked head and his eyes is always closed and he's all music —

MAMA. (*Rising and getting some papers out of her handbag*) Walter —

WALTER. And there's this other guy who plays the piano . . . and they got a sound. I mean they can work on some music . . . They got the best little combo in the world in the Green Hat . . . You can just sit there and drink and listen to them three men play and you realize that don't nothing matter worth a damn, but just being there —

MAMA. I've helped do it to you, haven't I, son? Walter, I been wrong.

WALTER. Naw — you ain't never been wrong about nothing, Mama.

MAMA. Listen to me, now. I say I been wrong, son. That I been doing to you what the rest of the world been doing to you. (*She stops and he looks up slowly at her and she meets his eyes pleadingly*) Walter — what you ain't never understood is that I ain't got nothing, don't own nothing, ain't never really wanted nothing that wasn't for you. There ain't nothing as precious to me . . . There ain't nothing worth holding on to, money, dreams, nothing else — if it means — if it means it's going to destroy my boy. (*She puts her papers in front of him and he watches her without speaking or moving*) I paid the man thirty-five hundred dollars down on the house. That leaves sixty-five hundred dollars. Monday morning I want you to take this money and take three thousand dollars and put it in a savings account for Beneatha's medical schooling. The rest you put in a checking account — with your name on it. And from now on any penny that come out of it or that go in it is for you to look after. For you to decide. (*She drops her hands a little helplessly*) It ain't much, but it's all I got in the world and I'm putting it in your hands. I'm telling you to be the head of this family from now on like you supposed to be.

WALTER. (*Stares at the money*) You trust me like that, Mama?

MAMA. I ain't never stop trusting you. Like I ain't never stop loving you.

(*She goes out, and Walter sits looking at the money on the table as the music continues in its idiom, pulsing in the room. Finally, in a decisive gesture, he gets up, and, in mingled joy and desperation, picks up the money. At the same moment, Travis enters for bed*)

TRAVIS. What's the matter, Daddy? You drunk?

WALTER. (*Sweetly, more sweetly than we have ever known him*) No, Daddy ain't drunk. Daddy ain't going to never be drunk again. . . .

TRAVIS. Well, good night, Daddy.

(*The Father has come from behind the couch and leans over, embracing his son*)

WALTER. Son, I feel like talking to you tonight.

TRAVIS. About what?

WALTER. Oh, about a lot of things. About you and what kind of man you going to be when you grow up. . . . Son — son, what do you want to be when you grow up?

TRAVIS. A bus driver.

WALTER. (*Laughing a little*) A what? Man, that ain't nothing to want to be!

TRAVIS. Why not?

WALTER. 'Cause, man — it ain't big enough — you know what I mean.

TRAVIS. I don't know then. I can't make up my mind. Sometimes Mama asks me that too. And sometimes when I tell you I just want to be like you — she says she don't want me to be like that and sometimes she says she does. . . .

WALTER. (*Gathering him up in his arms*) You know what, Travis? In seven years you going to be seventeen years old. And things is going to be very different with us in seven years, Travis. . . . One day when you are seventeen I'll come home — home from my office downtown somewhere —

TRAVIS. You don't work in no office, Daddy.

WALTER. No — but after tonight. After what your daddy gonna do tonight, there's going to be offices — a whole lot of offices. . . .

TRAVIS. What you gonna to tonight, Daddy?

WALTER. You wouldn't understand yet, son, but your daddy's gonna make a transaction . . . a business transaction that's going to change our lives. . . . That's how come one day when you 'bout seventeen years old I'll come home and I'll be pretty tired, you know what I mean, after a day of conferences and secretaries getting things wrong the way they do . . . 'cause an executive's life is hell, man — (*The more he talks the farther away he gets*) And I'll pull the car up on the driveway . . . just a plain black Chrysler, I think, with white walls — no — black tires. More elegant. Rich people don't have to be flashy . . . though I'll have to get something a little sportier for Ruth — maybe a Cadillac convertible to do her shopping in. . . . And I'll come up the steps to the house and the gardener will be clipping away at the hedges and he'll say, "Good evening, Mr. Younger." And I'll say, "Hello, Jefferson, how are you this evening?" And I'll go inside and Ruth will come downstairs and meet me at the door and we'll kiss each other and she'll take my arm and we'll go up to your room to see you sitting on the floor with the catalogues of all the great schools in America around you. . . . All the great schools in the world! And — and I'll say, all right son — it's your seventeenth birthday, what is it you've decided? . . . Just tell me where you want to go to school and you'll go. Just tell me, what it is you want to be — and you'll *be* it. . . . Whatever you want to be — Yessir! (*He holds his arms open for Travis*) You just name it, son . . . (*Travis leaps into them*) and I hand you the world!

(*Walter's voice has risen in pitch and hysterical promise and on the last line he lifts Travis high*)

(*Blackout*)

SCENE III

*Time: Saturday, moving day, one week later.*

*Before the curtain rises, Ruth's voice, a strident, dramatic church alto, cuts through the silence.*

*It is, in the darkness, a triumphant surge, a penetrating statement of expectation:* "Oh, Lord, I don't feel no ways tired! Children, oh, glory hallelujah!"

*As the curtain rises we see that Ruth is alone in the living room, finishing up the family's packing. Beneatha enters, carrying a guitar case, and watches her exuberant sister-in-law.*

RUTH. Hey!
BENEATHA. (*Putting away the case*) Hi.
RUTH. (*Pointing at a package*) Honey — look in that package there and see what I found on sale this morning at the South Center. (*Ruth gets up and moves to the package and draws out some curtains*) Lookahere — hand-turned hems!

BENEATHA. How do you know the window size out there?

RUTH. (*Who hadn't thought of that*) Oh — Well, they bound to fit something in the whole house. Anyhow, they was too good a bargain to pass up. (*Ruth slaps her head, suddenly remembering something*) Oh, Bennie — I meant to put a special note on that carton over there. That's your mama's good china and she wants 'em to be very careful with it.

BENEATHA. I'll do it.

(*Beneatha finds a piece of paper and starts to draw large letters on it*)

RUTH. You know what I'm going to do soon as I get in that new house?

BENEATHA. What?

RUTH. Honey — I'm going to run me a tub of water up to here . . . (*With her fingers practically up to her nostrils*) And I'm going to get in it — and I am going to sit . . . and sit . . . and sit in that hot water and the first person who knocks to tell *me* to hurry up and come out —

BENEATHA. Gets shot at sunrise.

RUTH. (*Laughing happily*) You said it, sister! (*Noticing how large Beneatha is absent-mindedly making the note*) Honey, they ain't going to read that from no airplane.

BENEATHA. (*Laughing herself*) I guess I always think things have more emphasis if they are big, somehow.

RUTH. (*Looking up at her and smiling*) You and your brother seem to have that as a philosophy of life. Lord, that man — done changed so 'round here. You know — you know what we did last night? Me and Walter Lee?

BENEATHA. What?

RUTH. (*Smiling to herself*) We went to the movies. (*Looking at Beneatha to see if she understands*) We went to the movies. You know the last time me and Walter went to the movies together?

BENEATHA. No.

RUTH. Me neither. That's how long it been. (*Smiling again*) But we went last night. The picture wasn't much good, but that didn't seem to matter. We went — and we held hands.

BENEATHA. Oh, Lord!

RUTH. We held hands — and you know what?

BENEATHA. What?

RUTH. When we come out of the show it was late and dark and all the stores and things was closed up . . . and it was kind of chilly and there wasn't many people on the streets . . . and we was still holding hands, me and Walter.

BENEATHA. You're killing me.

(*Walter enters with a large package. His happiness is deep in him; he cannot keep still with his new-found exuberance. He is singing and wiggling and snapping his fingers. He puts his package in a corner and puts a phonograph record, which he has brought in with him, on the record player. As the music comes up he dances over to Ruth and tries to get her to dance with him. She gives in at last to his raunchiness and in a fit of giggling allows herself to be drawn into his mood and together they deliberately burlesque an old social dance of their youth)*

BENEATHA. (*Regarding them a long time as they dance, then drawing in her breath for a deeply exaggerated comment which she does not particularly mean*) Talk about — olddddddddddd-fashionedddddddd — Negroes!

WALTER. (*Stopping momentarily*) What kind of Negroes?

(*He says this in fun. He is not angry with her today, nor with anyone. He starts to dance with his wife again*)

BENEATHA. Old-fashioned.

WALTER. (*As he dances with Ruth*) You know, when these *New Negroes* have their convention — (*Pointing at his sister*) — that is going to be the chairman of the Committee on Unending Agitation. (*He goes on dancing, then stops*) Race, race, race! . . . Girl, I do believe you are the first person in the history of the entire human race to successfully brainwash yourself. (*Beneatha breaks up and he goes on dancing. He stops again, enjoying his tease*) Damn, even the N double A C P takes a holiday sometimes! (*Beneatha and Ruth laugh. He dances with Ruth some more and starts to laugh and stops and pantomimes someone over an operating table*) I can just see that chick someday looking down at some poor cat on an operating table before she starts to slice him, saying . . . (*Pulling his sleeves back maliciously*) "By the way, what are your views on civil rights down there? . . ."

(*He laughs at her again and starts to dance happily. The bell sounds*)

BENEATHA. Sticks and stones may break my bones but . . . words will never hurt me!

(*Beneatha goes to the door and opens it as Walter and Ruth go on with the clowning. Beneatha is somewhat surprised to see a quiet-looking middle-aged white man in a business suit holding his hat and a briefcase in his hand and consulting a small piece of paper*)

MAN. Uh — how do you do, miss. I am looking for a Mrs. — (*He looks at the slip of paper*) Mrs. Lena Younger?

BENEATHA. (*Smoothing her hair with slight embarrassment*) Oh — yes, that's my mother. Excuse me (*She closes the door and turns to quiet the other two*) Ruth! Brother! Somebody's here. (*Then she opens the door. The man casts a curious quick glance at all of them*) Uh — come in please.

MAN. (*Coming in*) Thank you.

BENEATHA. My mother isn't here just now. Is it business?

MAN. Yes . . . well, of a sort.
WALTER. (*Freely, the Man of the House*) Have a seat. I'm Mrs. Younger's son. I look after most of her business matters.
(*Ruth and Beneatha exchange amused glances*)
MAN. (*Regarding Walter, and sitting*) Well — My name is Karl Lindner . . .

WALTER. (*Stretching out his hand*) Walter Younger. This is my wife — (*Ruth nods politely*) — and my sister.
LINDNER. How do you do.
WALTER. (*Amiably, as he sits himself easily on a chair, leaning with interest forward on his knees and looking expectantly into the newcomer's face*) What can we do for you, Mr. Lindner!
LINDNER. (*Some minor shuffling of the hat and briefcase on his knees*) Well — I am a representative of the Clybourne Park Improvement Association —
WALTER. (*Pointing*) Why don't you sit your things on the floor?
LINDNER. Oh — yes. Thank you. (*He slides the briefcase and hat under the chair*) And as I was saying — I am from the Clybourne Park Improvement Association and we have had it brought to our attention at the last meeting that you people — or at least your mother — has bought a piece of residential property at — (*He digs for the slip of paper again*) — four o six Clybourne Street . . .
WALTER. That's right. Care for something to drink? Ruth, get Mr. Lindner a beer.
LINDNER. (*Upset for some reason*) Oh — no, really. I mean thank you very much, but no thank you.
RUTH. (*Innocently*) Some coffee?
LINDNER. Thank you, nothing at all.
(*Beneatha is watching the man carefully*)
LINDNER. Well, I don't know how much you folks know about our organization. (*He is a gentle man; thoughtful and somewhat labored in his manner*) It is one of these community organizations set up to look after — oh, you know, things like block upkeep and special projects and we also have what we call our New Neighbors Orientation Committee . . .
BENEATHA. (*Drily*) Yes — and what do they do?
LINDNER. (*Turning a little to her and then returning the main force to Walter*) Well — it's what you might call a sort of welcoming committee, I guess. I mean they, we, I'm the chairman of the committee — go around and see the new people who move into the neighborhood and sort of give them the lowdown on the way we do things out in Clybourne Park.
BENEATHA. (*With appreciation of the two meanings, which escape Ruth and Walter*) Uh-huh.

LINDNER. And we also have the category of what the association calls — (*He looks elsewhere*) — uh — special community problems . . .
BENEATHA. Yes — and what are some of those?
WALTER. Girl, let the man talk.
LINDNER. (*With understated relief*) Thank you. I would sort of like to explain this thing in my own way. I mean I want to explain to you in a certain way.
WALTER. Go ahead.
LINDNER. Yes. Well. I'm going to try to get right to the point. I'm sure we'll all appreciate that in the long run.
BENEATHA. Yes.
WALTER: Be still now!
LINDNER. Well —
RUTH. (*Still innocently*) Would you like another chair — you don't look comfortable.
LINDNER. (*More frustrated than annoyed*) No, thank you very much. Please. Well — to get right to the point I — (*A great breath, and he is off at last*) I am sure you people must be aware of some of the incidents which have happened in various parts of the city when colored people have moved into certain areas — (*Beneatha exhales heavily and starts tossing a piece of fruit up and down in the air*) Well — because we have what I think is going to be a unique type of organization in American community life — not only do we deplore that kind of thing — but we are trying to do something about it. (*Beneatha stops tossing and turns with a new and quizzical interest to the man*) We feel — (*gaining confidence in his mission because of the interest in the faces of the people he is talking to*) — we feel that most of the trouble in this world, when you come right down to it — (*He hits his knee for emphasis*) — most of the trouble exists because people just don't sit down and talk to each other.
RUTH. (*Nodding as she might in church, pleased with the remark*) You can say that again, mister.
LINDNER. (*More encouraged by such affirmation*) That we don't try hard enough in this world to understand the other fellow's problem. The other guy's point of view.
RUTH. Now that's right.
(*Beneatha and Walter merely watch and listen with genuine interest*)
LINDNER. Yes — and that's the way we feel out in Clybourne Park. And that's why I was elected to come here this afternoon and talk to you people. Friendly like, you know, the way people should talk to each other and see if we couldn't find some way to work this thing out. As I say, the whole business is a matter of *caring* about the other fellow. Anybody can see that you are a nice family of folks, hard working and honest I'm sure. (*Beneatha frowns*

*slightly, quizzically, her head tilted regarding him*) Today everybody knows what it means to be on the outside of *something.* And of course, there is always somebody who is out to take the advantage of people who don't always understand.

WALTER. What do you mean?

LINDNER. Well — you see our community is made up of people who've worked hard as the dickens for years to build up that little community. They're not rich and fancy people; just hard-working, honest people who don't really have much but those little homes and a dream of the kind of community they want to raise their children in. Now, I don't say we are perfect and there is a lot wrong in some of the things they want. But you've got to admit that a man, right or wrong, has the right to have the neighborhood he lives in a certain kind of way. And at the moment the overwhelming majority of our people out there feel that people get along better, take more of a common interest in the life of the community, when they share a common background. I want you to believe me when I tell you that race prejudice simply doesn't enter into it. It is a matter of the people of Clybourne Park believing, rightly or wrongly, as I say, that for the happiness of all concerned that our Negro families are happier when they live in their *own* communities.

BENEATHA. (*With a grand and bitter gesture*) This, friends, is the Welcoming Committee!

WALTER. (*Dumfounded, looking at Lindner*) Is this what you came marching all the way over here to tell us?

LINDNER. Well, now we've been having a fine conversation. I hope you'll hear me all the way through.

WALTER. (*Tightly*) Go ahead, man.

LINDNER. You see — in the face of all things I have said, we are prepared to make your family a very generous offer . . .

BENEATHA. Thirty pieces and not a coin less!

WALTER. Yeah?

LINDNER. (*Putting on his glasses and drawing a form out of the briefcase*) Our association is prepared, through the collective effort of our people, to buy the house from you at a financial gain to your family.

RUTH. Lord have mercy, ain't this the living gall!

WALTER. All right, you through?

LINDNER. Well, I want to give you the exact terms of the financial arrangement —

WALTER. We don't want to hear no exact terms of no arrangements. I want to know if you got any more to tell us 'bout getting together?

LINDNER. (*Taking off his glasses*) Well — I don't suppose that you feel . . .

WALTER. Never mind how I feel — you got any more to say 'bout how people ought to sit down and talk to each other? . . . Get out of my house, man.

(*He turns his back and walks to the door*)

LINDNER. (*Looking around at the hostile faces and reaching and assembling his hat and briefcase*) Well — I don't understand why you people are reacting this way. What do you think you are going to gain by moving into a neighborhood where you just aren't wanted and where some elements — well — people can get awful worked up when they feel that their whole way of life and everything they've ever worked for is threatened.

WALTER. Get out.

LINDNER. (*At the door, holding a small card*) Well — I'm sorry it went like this.

WALTER. Get out.

LINDNER. (*Almost sadly regarding Walter*) You just can't force people to change their hearts, son.

(*He turns and puts his card on a table and exits. Walter pushes the door to with stinging hatred, and stands looking at it. Ruth just sits and Beneatha just stands. They say nothing. Mama and Travis enter*)

MAMA. Well — this all the packing got done since I left out of here this morning. I testify before God that my children got all the energy of the dead. What time the moving men due?

BENEATHA. Four o'clock. You had a caller, Mama.

(*She is smiling, teasingly*)

MAMA. Sure enough — who?

BENEATHA. (*Her arms folded saucily*) The Welcoming Committee.

(*Walter and Ruth giggle*)

MAMA. (*Innocently*) Who?

BENEATHA. The Welcoming Committee. They said they're sure going to be glad to see you when you get there.

WALTER. (*Devilishly*) Yeah, they said they can't hardly wait to see your face.

(*Laughter*)

MAMA. (*Sensing their facetiousness*) What's the matter with you all?

WALTER. Ain't nothing the matter with us. We just telling you 'bout the gentleman who came to see you this afternoon. From the Clybourne Park Improvement Association.

MAMA. What he want?

RUTH. (*In the same mood as Beneatha and Walter*) To welcome you, honey.

WALTER. He said they can't hardly wait. He said the one thing they don't have, that they just *dying* to have out there is a fine family of colored people! (*To Ruth and Beneatha*) Ain't that right!

RUTH and BENEATHA. (*Mockingly*) Yeah! He left his card in case —

(*They indicate the card, and Mama picks it up and throws it on the floor — understanding and looking off as she draws her chair up to the table on which she has put her plant and some sticks and some cord*)

MAMA. Father, give us strength. (*Knowingly — and without fun*) Did he threaten us?

BENEATHA. Oh — Mama — they don't do it like that any more. He talked Brotherhood. He said everybody ought to learn how to sit down and hate each other with good Christian fellowship.

(*She and Walter shake hands to ridicule the remark*)

MAMA. (*Sadly*) Lord, protect us . . .

RUTH. You should hear the money those folks raised to buy the house from us. All we paid and then some.

BENEATHA. What do they think we going to do — eat 'em?

RUTH. No, honey, marry 'em.

MAMA. (*Shaking her head*) Lord, Lord, Lord . . .

RUTH. Well — that's the way the crackers crumble. Joke.

BENEATHA. (*Laughingly noticing what her mother is doing*) Mama, what are you doing?

MAMA. Fixing my plant so it won't get hurt none on the way . . .

BENEATHA. Mama, you going to take *that* to the new house?

MAMA. Un-huh —

BENEATHA. That raggedy-looking old thing?

MAMA. (*Stopping and looking at her*) It expresses *me*.

RUTH. (*With delight, to Beneatha*) So there, Miss Thing!

(*Walter comes to Mama suddenly and bends down behind her and squeezes her in his arms with all his strength. She is overwhelmed by the suddenness of it and, though delighted, her manner is like that of Ruth with Travis*)

MAMA. Look out now, boy! You make me mess up my thing here!

WALTER. (*His face lit, he slips down on his knees beside her, his arms still about her*) Mama . . . you know what it means to climb up in the chariot?

MAMA. (*Gruffly, very happy*) Get on away from me now . . .

RUTH. (*Near the gift-wrapped package, trying to catch Walter's eye*) Psst —

WALTER. What the old song say, Mama . . .

RUTH. Walter — Now?

(*She is pointing at the package.*)

WALTER. (*Speaking the lines, sweetly, playfully, in his mother's face*)
I got wings . . . you got wings . . .
All God's Children got wings . . .

MAMA. Boy — get out of my face and do some work . . .

WALTER.
> *When I get to heaven gonna put on my wings,*
> *Gonna fly all over God's heaven . . .*

BENEATHA. (*Teasingly, from across the room*) Everybody talking 'bout heaven ain't going there!

WALTER. (*To Ruth, who is carrying the box across to them*) I don't know, you think we ought to give her that . . . Seems to me she ain't been very appreciative around here.

MAMA. (*Eying the box, which is obviously a gift*) What is that?

WALTER. (*Taking it from Ruth and putting it on the table in front of Mama*) Well — what you all think? Should we give it to her?

RUTH. Oh — she was pretty good today.

MAMA. I'll good you —

(*She turns her eyes to the box again*)

BENEATHA. Open it, Mama.

(*She stands up, looks at it, turns and looks at all of them, and then presses her hands together and does not open the package*)

WALTER. (*Sweetly*) Open it, Mama. It's for you. (*Mama looks in his eyes. It is the first present in her life without its being Christmas. Slowly she opens her package and lifts out, one by one, a brand-new sparkling set of gardening tools. Walter continues, prodding*) Ruth made up the note — read it . . .

MAMA. (*Picking up the card and adjusting her glasses*) "To our own Mrs. Miniver — Love from Brother, Ruth and Beneatha." Ain't that lovely . . .

TRAVIS. (*Tugging at his father's sleeve*) Daddy, can I give her mine now?

WALTER. All right, son. (*Travis flies to get his gift*) Travis didn't want to go in with the rest of us, Mama. He got his own. (*Somewhat amused*) We don't know what it is . . .

TRAVIS. (*Racing back in the room with a large hatbox and putting it in front of his grandmother*) Here!

MAMA. Lord have mercy, baby. You done gone and bought your grandmother a hat?

TRAVIS. (*Very proud*) Open it!

(*She does and lifts out an elaborate, but very elaborate, wide gardening hat, and all the adults break up at the sight of it*)

RUTH. Travis, honey, what is that?

TRAVIS. (*Who thinks it is beautiful and appropriate*) It's a gardening hat! Like the ladies always have on in the magazines when they work in their gardens.

BENEATHA. (*Giggling fiercely*) Travis — we were trying to make Mama Mrs. Miniver — not Scarlett O'Hara!

MAMA. (*Indignantly*) What's the matter with you all! This here is a beautiful hat! (*Absurdly*) I always wanted me one just like it!

(*She pops it on her head to prove it to her grandson, and the hat is ludicrous and considerably oversized*)

RUTH. Hot dog! Go, Mama!

WALTER. (*Doubled over with laughter*) I'm sorry, Mama — but you look like you ready to go out and chop you some cotton sure enough!
(*They all laugh except Mama, out of deference to Travis' feelings*)

MAMA. (*Gathering the boy up to her*) Bless your heart — this is the prettiest hat I ever owned — (*Walter, Ruth and Beneatha chime in — noisily, festively and insincerely congratulating Travis on his gift*) What are we all standing around here for? We ain't finished packin' yet. Bennie, you ain't packed one book.
(*The bell rings*)

BENEATHA. That couldn't be the movers . . . it's not hardly two good yet —
(*Beneatha goes into her room. Mama starts for door*)

WALTER. (*Turning, stiffening*) Wait — wait — I'll get it.
(*He stands and looks at the door*)

MAMA. You expecting company, son?

WALTER. (*Just looking at the door*) Yeah — yeah . . .
(*Mama looks at Ruth, and they exchange innocent and unfrightened glances*)

MAMA. (*Not understanding*) Well, let them in, son.

BENEATHA. (*From her room*) We need some more string.

MAMA. Travis — you run to the hardware and get me some string cord.
(*Mama goes out and Walter turns and looks at Ruth. Travis goes to a dish for money*)

RUTH. Why don't you answer the door, man?

WALTER. (*Suddenly bounding across the floor to her*) 'Cause sometimes it hard to let the future begin! (*Stooping down in her face*)

I got wings! You got wings!
All God's children got wings!

(*He crosses to the door and throws it open. Standing there is a very slight little man in a not too prosperous business suit and with haunted frightened eyes and a hat pulled down tightly, brim up, around his forehead. Travis passes between the men and exits. Walter leans deep in the man's face, still in his jubilance*)

When I get to heaven gonna put on my wings,
Gonna fly all over God's heaven . . .
(*The little man just stares at him*)
Heaven —
(*Suddenly he stops and looks past the little man into the empty hallway*)
Where's Willy, man?

BOBO. He ain't with me.

WALTER. (*Not disturbed*) Oh — come on in. You know my wife.

BOBO. (*Dumbly, taking off his hat*) Yes — h'you, Miss Ruth.
RUTH. (*Quietly, a mood apart from her husband already, seeing Bobo*) Hello, Bobo.
WALTER. You right on time today . . . Right on time. That's the way! (*He slaps Bobo on his back*) Sit down . . . lemme hear.
   (*Ruth stands stiffly and quietly in back of them, as though somehow she senses death, her eyes fixed on her husband*)
BOBO. (*His frightened eyes on the floor, his hat in his hands*) Could I please get a drink of water, before I tell you about it, Walter Lee?
   (*Walter does not take his eyes off the man. Ruth goes blindly to the tap and gets a glass of water and brings it to Bobo*)
WALTER. There ain't nothing wrong, is there?
BOBO. Lemme tell you —
WALTER. Man — didn't nothing go wrong?
BOBO. Lemme tell you — Walter Lee. (*Looking at Ruth and talking to her more than to Walter*) You know how it was. I got to tell you how it was. I mean first I got to tell you how it was all the way . . . I mean about the money I put in, Walter Lee . . .
WALTER. (*With taut agitation now*) What about the money you put in?
BOBO. Well — it wasn't much as we told you — me and Willy — (*He stops*) I'm sorry, Walter. I got a bad feeling about it. I got a real bad feeling about it . . .
WALTER. Man, what you telling me about all this for? . . . Tell me what happened in Springfield . . .
BOBO. Springfield.
RUTH. (*Like a dead woman*) What was supposed to happen in Springfield?
BOBO. (*To her*) This deal that me and Walter went into with Willy — Me and Willy was going to go down to Springfield and spread some money 'round so's we wouldn't have to wait so long for the liquor license . . . That's what we were going to do. Everybody said that was the way you had to do, you understand, Miss Ruth?
WALTER. Man — what happened down there?
BOBO. (*A pitiful man, near tears*) I'm trying to tell you, Walter.
WALTER. (*Screaming at him suddenly*) THEN TELL ME, GODDAMMIT . . . WHAT'S THE MATTER WITH YOU?
BOBO. Man . . . I didn't go to no Springfield, yesterday.
WALTER. (*Halted, life hanging in the moment*) Why not?
BOBO. (*The long way, the hard way to tell*) 'Cause I didn't have no reasons to . . .
WALTER. Man, what are you talking about!
BOBO. I'm talking about the fact that when I got to the train station yesterday morning — eight o'clock like we planned . . . Man — *Willy didn't never show up.*

WALTER. Why . . . where was he . . . where is he?
BOBO. That's what I'm trying to tell you . . . I don't know . . . I waited six hours . . . I called his house . . . and I waited . . . six hours . . . I waited in that train station six hours . . . (*Breaking into tears*) That was all the extra money I had in the world . . . (*Looking up at Walter with the tears running down his face*) Man, Willy is gone.
WALTER. Gone, what you mean Willy is gone? Gone where? You mean he went by himself. You mean he went off to Springfield by himself — to take care of getting the license — (*Turns and looks anxiously at Ruth*) You mean maybe he didn't want too many people in on the business down there? (*Looks to Ruth again, as before*) You know Willy got his own ways. (*Looks back to Bobo*) Maybe you was late yesterday and he just went on down there without you. Maybe — maybe — he's been callin' you at home tryin' to tell you what happened or something. Maybe — maybe — he just got sick. He's somewhere — he's got to be somewhere. We just got to find him — me and you got to find him. (*Grabs Bobo senselessly by the collar and starts to shake him*) We got to!
BOBO. (*In sudden angry, frightened agony*) What's the matter with you, Walter! *When a cat take off with your money he don't leave you no maps!*
WALTER. (*Turning madly, as though he is looking for Willy in the very room*) Willy! . . . Willy . . . don't do it . . . Please don't do it . . . Man, not with that money . . . Man, please, not with that money . . . Oh, God . . . Don't let it be true . . . (*He is wandering around, crying out for Willy and looking for him or perhaps for help from God*) Man . . . I trusted you . . . Man, I put my life in your hands . . . (*He starts to crumple down on the floor as Ruth just covers her face in horror. Mama opens the door and comes into the room, with Beneatha behind her*) Man . . . (*He starts to pound the floor with his fists, sobbing wildly*) That money is made out of my father's flesh . . .
BOBO. (*Standing over him helplessly*) I'm sorry, Walter . . . (*Only Walter's sobs reply. Bobo puts on his hat*) I had my life staked on this deal, too . . .
   (*He exits*)
MAMA. (*To Walter*) Son — (*She goes to him, bends down to him, talks to his bent head*) Son . . . Is it gone? Son, I gave you sixty-five hundred dollars. Is it gone? All of it? Beneatha's money too?
WALTER. (*Lifting his head slowly*) Mama . . . I never . . . went to the bank at all . . .
MAMA. (*Not wanting to believe him*) You mean . . . your sister's school money . . . you used that too . . . Walter? . . .
WALTER. Yessss! . . . All of it . . . It's all gone . . .
   (*There is total silence. Ruth stands with her face covered with her hands; Beneatha leans forlornly against a wall, fingering a piece of red ribbon from the mother's gift. Mama stops and looks at her son without recogni-*

*tion and then, quite without thinking about it, starts to beat him senselessly in the face. Beneatha goes to them and stops it)*
BENEATHA. Mama!
   *(Mama stops and looks at both of her children and rises slowly and wanders vaguely, aimlessly away from them)*
MAMA. I seen . . . him . . . night after night . . . come in . . . and look at that rug . . . and then look at me . . . the red showing in his eyes . . . the veins moving in his head . . . I seen him grow thin and old before he was forty . . . working and working and working like somebody's old horse . . . killing himself . . . and you — you give it all away in a day . . .
BENEATHA. Mama —
MAMA. Oh, God . . . *(She looks up to Him)* Look down here — and show me the strength.
BENEATHA. Mama —
MAMA. *(Folding over)* Strength . . .
BENEATHA. *(Plaintively)* Mama . . .
MAMA. Strength!

*Curtain*


## Act III

*An hour later.*
   *At curtain, there is a sullen light of gloom in the living room, gray light not unlike that which began the first scene of Act One. At left we can see Walter within his room, alone with himself. He is stretched out on the bed, his shirt out and open, his arms under his head. He does not smoke, he does not cry out, he merely lies there, looking up at the ceiling, much as if he were alone in the world.*
   *In the living room Beneatha sits at the table, still surrounded by the now almost ominous packing crates. She sits looking off. We feel that this is a mood struck perhaps an hour before, and it lingers now, full of the empty sound of profound disappointment. We see on a line from her brother's bedroom the sameness of their attitudes. Presently the bell rings and Beneatha rises without ambition or interest in answering. It is Asagai, smiling broadly, striding into the room with energy and happy expectation and conversation.*

ASAGAI. I came over . . . I had some free time. I thought I might help with the packing. Ah, I like the look of packing crates! A household in preparation for a journey! It depresses some people . . . but for me . . . it is another feeling. Something full of the flow of life, do you understand? Movement, progress . . . It makes me think of Africa.
BENEATHA. Africa!

ASAGAI. What kind of a mood is this? Have I told you how deeply you move me?

BENEATHA. He gave away the money, Asagai . . .

ASAGAI. Who gave away what money?

BENEATHA. The insurance money. My brother gave it away.

ASAGAI. Gave it away?

BENEATHA. He made an investment! With a man even Travis wouldn't have trusted.

ASAGAI. And it's gone?

BENEATHA. Gone!

ASAGAI. I'm very sorry . . . And you, now?

BENEATHA. Me? . . . Me? . . . Me I'm nothing . . . Me. When I was very small . . . we used to take our sleds out in the wintertime and the only hills we had were the ice-covered stone steps of some houses down the street. And we used to fill them in with snow and make them smooth and slide down them all day . . . and it was very dangerous you know . . . far too steep . . . and sure enough one day a kid named Rufus came down too fast and hit the sidewalk . . . and we saw his face just split open right there in front of us . . . And I remember standing there looking at his bloody open face thinking that was the end of Rufus. But the ambulance came and they took him to the hospital and they fixed the broken bones and they sewed it all up . . . and the next time I saw Rufus he just had a little line down the middle of his face . . . I never got over that . . .

*(Walter sits up, listening on the bed. Throughout this scene it is important that we feel his reaction at all times, that he visibly respond to the words of his sister and Asagai)*

ASAGAI. What?

BENEATHA. That that was what one person could do for another, fix him up — sew up the problem, make him all right again. That was the most marvelous thing in the world . . . I wanted to do that. I always thought it was the one concrete thing in the world that a human being could do. Fix up the sick, you know — and make them whole again. This was truly being God . . .

ASAGAI. You wanted to be God?

BENEATHA. No — I wanted to cure. It used to be so important to me. I wanted to cure. It used to matter. I used to care. I mean about people and how their bodies hurt . . .

ASAGAI. And you've stopped caring?

BENEATHA. Yes — I think so.

ASAGAI. Why?

*(Walter rises, goes to the door of his room and is about to open it, then stops and stands listening, leaning on the door jamb)*

BENEATHA. Because it doesn't seem deep enough, close enough to what ails mankind — I mean this thing of sewing up bodies or administering drugs. Don't you understand? It was a child's reaction to the world. I thought that doctors had the secret to all the hurts. . . . That's the way a child sees things — or an idealist.

ASAGAI. Children see things very well sometimes — and idealists even better.

BENEATHA. I know that's what you think. Because you are still where I left off — you still care. This is what you see for the world, for Africa. You with the dreams of the future will patch up Africa — you are going to cure the Great Sore of colonialism with Independence —

ASAGAI. Yes!

BENEATHA. Yes — and you think that one word is the penicillin of the human spirit: "Independence!" But then what?

ASAGAI. That will be the problem for another time. First we must get there.

BENEATHA. And where does it end?

ASAGAI. End? Who even spoke of an end? To life? To living?

BENEATHA. An end to misery!

ASAGAI. (*Smiling*) You sound like a French intellectual.

BENEATHA. No! I sound like a human being who just had her future taken right out of her hands! While I was sleeping in my bed in there, things were happening in this world that directly concerned me — and nobody asked me, consulted me — they just went out and did things — and changed my life. Don't you see there isn't any real progress, Asagai, there is only one large circle that we march in, around and around, each of us with our own little picture — in front of us — our own little mirage that we think is the future.

ASAGAI. That is the mistake.

BENEATHA. What?

ASAGAI. What you just said — about the circle. It isn't a circle — it is simply a long line — as in geometry, you know, one that reaches into infinity. And because we cannot see the end — we also cannot see how it changes. And it is very odd but those who see the changes are called "idealists" — and those who cannot, or refuse to think, they are the "realists." It is very strange, and amusing too, I think.

BENEATHA. You — you are almost religious.

ASAGAI. Yes . . . I think I have the religion of doing what is necessary in the world — and of worshipping man — because he is so marvelous, you see.

BENEATHA. Man is foul! And the human race deserves its misery!

ASAGAI. You see: *you* have become the religious one in the old sense. Already, and after such a small defeat, you are worshipping despair.

BENEATHA. From now on, I worship the truth — and the truth is that people are puny, small and selfish. . . .

ASAGAI. Truth? Why is it that you despairing ones always think that only you have the truth? I never thought to see *you* like that. You! Your brother made a stupid, childish mistake — and you are grateful to him. So that now you can give up the ailing human race on account of it. You talk about what good is struggle; what good is anything? Where are we all going? And why are we bothering?

BENEATHA. *And you cannot answer it!* All your talk and dreams about Africa and Independence. Independence and then what? What about all the crooks and petty thieves and just plain idiots who will come into power to steal and plunder the same as before — only now they will be black and do it in the name of the new Independence — You cannot answer that.

ASAGAI. (*Shouting over her*) *I live the answer!* (*Pause*) In my village at home it is the exceptional man who can even read a newspaper . . . or who ever *sees* a book at all. I will go home and much of what I will have to say will seem strange to the people of my village . . . But I will teach and work and things will happen, slowly and swiftly. At times it will seem that nothing changes at all . . . and then again . . . the sudden dramatic events which make history leap into the future. And then quiet again. Retrogression even. Guns, murder, revolution. And I even will have moments when I wonder if the quiet was not better than all that death and hatred. But I will look about my village at the illiteracy and disease and ignorance and I will not wonder long. And perhaps . . . perhaps I will be a great man . . . I mean perhaps I will hold on to the substance of truth and find my way always with the right course . . . and perhaps for it I will be butchered in my bed some night by the servants of empire . . .

BENEATHA. *The martyr!*

ASAGAI. . . . or perhaps I shall live to be a very old man, respected and esteemed in my new nation . . . And perhaps I shall hold office and this is what I'm trying to tell you, Alaiyo, perhaps the things I believe now for my country will be wrong and outmoded, and I will not understand and do terrible things to have things my way or merely to keep my power. Don't you see that there will be young men and women, not British soldiers then, but my own black countrymen . . . to step out of the shadows some evening and slit my then useless throat? Don't you see they have always been there . . . that they always will be. And that such a thing as

my own death will be an advance? They who might kill me even
. . . actually replenish me!

BENEATHA. Oh, Asagai, I know all that.

ASAGAI. Good! Then stop moaning and groaning and tell me what
you plan to do.

BENEATHA. Do?

ASAGAI. I have a bit of a suggestion.

BENEATHA. What?

ASAGAI. (*Rather quietly for him*) That when it is all over — that you
come home with me —

BENEATHA. (*Slapping herself on the forehead with exasperation born of
misunderstanding*) Oh — Asagai — at this moment you decide to be
romantic!

ASAGAI. (*Quickly understanding the misunderstanding*) My dear, young
creature of the New World — I do not mean across the city — I
mean across the ocean; home — to Africa.

BENEATHA. (*Slowly understanding and turning to him with murmured
amazement*) To — to Nigeria?

ASAGAI. Yes! . . . (*Smiling and lifting his arms playfully*) Three hundred
years later the African Prince rose up out of the seas and swept
the maiden back across the middle passage over which her ances-
tors had come —

BENEATHA. (*Unable to play*) Nigeria?

ASAGAI. Nigeria. Home. (*Coming to her with genuine romantic flippancy*)
I will show you our mountains and our stars; and give you cool
drinks from gourds and teach you the old songs and the ways of
our people — and, in time, we will pretend that — (*Very
softly*) — you have only been away for a day —

(*She turns her back to him, thinking. He swings her around and takes
her full in his arms in a long embrace which proceeds to passion*)

BENEATHA. (*Pulling away*) You're getting me all mixed up —

ASAGAI. Why?

BENEATHA. Too many things — too many things have happened
today. I must sit down and think. I don't know what I feel about
anything right this minute.

(*She promptly sits down and props her chin on her fist*)

ASAGAI. (*Charmed*) All right, I shall leave you. No — don't get up.
(*Touching her, gently, sweetly*) Just sit awhile and think . . . Never be
afraid to sit awhile and think. (*He goes to door and looks at her*) How
often I have looked at you and said, "Ah — so this is what the New
World hath finally wrought . . ."

(*He exits. Beneatha sits on alone. Presently Walter enters from his room
and starts to rummage through things, feverishly looking for something.
She looks up and turns in her seat*)

BENEATHA. (*Hissingly*) Yes — just look at what the New World hath wrought! . . . Just look! (*She gestures with bitter disgust*) There he is! *Monsieur le petit bourgeois noir* — himself! There he is — Symbol of a Rising Class! Entrepreneur! Titan of the system! (*Walter ignores her completely and continues frantically and destructively looking for something and hurling things to floor and tearing things out of their place in his search. Beneatha ignores the eccentricity of his actions and goes on with the monologue of insult*) Did you dream of yachts on Lake Michigan, Brother? Did you see yourself on that Great Day sitting down at the Conference Table, surrounded by all the mighty bald-headed men in America? All halted, waiting, breathless, waiting for your pronouncements on industry? Waiting for you — Chairman of the Board? (*Walter finds what he is looking for — a small piece of white paper — and pushes it in his pocket and puts on his coat and rushes out without ever having looked at her. She shouts after him*) I look at you and I see the final triumph of stupidity in the world!

(*The door slams and she returns to just sitting again. Ruth comes quickly out of Mama's room*)

RUTH. Who was that?

BENEATHA. Your husband.

RUTH. Where did he go?

BENEATHA. Who knows — maybe he has an appointment at U.S. Steel.

RUTH. (*Anxiously, with frightened eyes*) You didn't say nothing bad to him, did you?

BENEATHA. Bad? Say anything bad to him? No — I told him he was a sweet boy and full of dreams and everything is strictly peachy keen, as the ofay kids say!

(*Mama enters from her bedroom. She is lost, vague, trying to catch hold, to make some sense of her former command of the world, but it still eludes her. A sense of waste overwhelms her gait; a measure of apology rides on her shoulders. She goes to her plant, which has remained on the table, looks at it, picks it up and takes it to the window sill and sits it outside, and she stands and looks at it a long moment. Then she closes the window, straightens her body with effort and turns around to her children*)

MAMA. Well — ain't it a mess in here, though? (*A false cheerfulness, a beginning of something*) I guess we all better stop moping around and get some work done. All this unpacking and everything we got to do. (*Ruth raises her head slowly in response to the sense of the line; and Beneatha in similar manner turns very slowly to look at her mother*) One of you all better call the moving people and tell 'em not to come.

RUTH. Tell 'em not to come?

MAMA. Of course, baby. Ain't no need in 'em coming all the way here and having to go back. They charges for that too. (*She sits down, fingers to her brow, thinking*) Lord, ever since I was a little girl, I always remembers people saying, "Lena — Lena Eggleston, you aims too high all the time. You needs to slow down and see life a little more like it is. Just slow down some." That's what they always used to say down home — "Lord, that Lena Eggleston is a high-minded thing. She'll get her due one day!"

RUTH. No, Lena . . .

MAMA. Me and Big Walter just didn't never learn right.

RUTH. Lena, no! We gotta go. Bennie — tell her . . . (*She rises and crosses to Beneatha with her arms outstretched. Beneatha doesn't respond*) Tell her we can still move . . . the notes ain't but a hundred and twenty-five a month. We got four grown people in this house — we can work . . .

MAMA. (*To herself*) Just aimed too high all the time —

RUTH. (*Turning and going to Mama fast — the words pouring out with urgency and desperation*) Lena — I'll work . . . I'll work twenty hours a day in all the kitchens in Chicago . . . I'll strap my baby on my back if I have to and scrub all the floors in America and wash all the sheets in America if I have to — but we got to move . . . We got to get out of here . . .

(*Mama reaches out absently and pats Ruth's hand*)

MAMA. No — I sees things differently now. Been thinking 'bout some of the things we could do to fix this place up some. I seen a second-hand bureau over on Maxwell Street just the other day that could fit right there. (*She points to where the new furniture might go. Ruth wanders away from her*) Would need some new handles on it and then a little varnish and then it look like something brand-new. And — we can put up them new curtains in the kitchen . . . Why this place be looking fine. Cheer us all up so that we forget trouble ever came . . . (*To Ruth*) And you could get some nice screens to put up in your room round the baby's bassinet . . . (*She looks at both of them, pleadingly*) Sometimes you just got to know when to give up some things . . . and hold on to what you got.

(*Walter enters from the outside, looking spent and leaning against the door, his coat hanging from him*)

MAMA. Where you been, son?

WALTER. (*Breathing hard*) Made a call.

MAMA. To who, son?

WALTER. To The Man.

MAMA. What man, baby?

WALTER. The Man, Mama. Don't you know who The Man is?

RUTH. Walter Lee?

WALTER. *The Man.* Like the guys in the streets say — The Man. Captain Boss — Mistuh Charley . . . Old Captain Please Mr. Bossman . . .

BENEATHA. (*Suddenly*) Lindner!
WALTER. That's right! That's good. I told him to come right over.
BENEATHA. (*Fiercely, understanding*) For what? What do you want to see him for!
WALTER. (*Looking at his sister*) We going to do business with him.
MAMA. What you talking 'bout son?
WALTER. Talking 'bout life, Mama. You all always telling me to see life like it is. Well — I laid in there on my back today . . . and I figured it out. Life just like it is. Who gets and who don't get. (*He sits down with his coat on and laughs*) Mama, you know it's all divided up. Life is. Sure enough. Between the takers and the "tooken." (*He laughs*) I've figured it out finally. (*He looks around at them*) Yeah. Some of us always getting "tooken." (*He laughs*) People like Willy Harris, they don't never get "tooken." And you know why the rest of us do? 'Cause we all mixed up. Mixed up bad. We get to looking 'round for the right and the wrong; and we worry about it and cry about it and stay up nights trying to figure out 'bout the wrong and the right of things all the time . . . And all the time, man, them takers is out there operating, just taking and taking. Willy Harris? Shoot — Willy Harris don't even count. He don't even count in the big scheme of things. But I'll say one thing for old Willy Harris . . . he's taught me something. He's taught me to keep my eye on what counts in this world. Yeah — (*Shouting out a little*) Thanks, Willy!
RUTH. What did you call that man for, Walter Lee?
WALTER. Called him to tell him to come on over to the show. Gonna put on a show for the man. Just what he wants to see. You see, Mama, the man came here today and he told us that them people out there where you want us to move — well they so upset they willing to pay us not to move out there. (*He laughs again*) And — and oh, Mama — you would of been proud of the way me and Ruth and Bennie acted. We told him to get out . . . Lord have mercy! We told the man to get out. Oh, we was some proud folks this afternoon, yeah. (*He lights a cigarette*) We were still full of that old-time stuff . . .
RUTH. (*Coming toward him slowly*) You talking 'bout taking them people's money to keep us from moving in that house?
WALTER. I ain't just talking 'bout it, baby — I'm telling you that's what's going to happen.
BENEATHA. Oh, God! Where is the bottom! Where is the real honest-to-God bottom so he can't go any farther!
WALTER. See — that's the old stuff. You and that boy that was here today. You all want everybody to carry a flag and a spear and sing some marching songs, huh? You wanna spend your life looking

into things and trying to find the right and the wrong part, huh? Yeah. You know what's going to happen to that boy someday — he'll find himself sitting in a dungeon, locked in forever — and the takers will have the key! Forget it, baby! There ain't no causes — there ain't nothing but taking in this world, and he who takes most is smartest — and it don't make a damn bit of difference *how*.

MAMA. You making something inside me cry, son. Some awful pain inside me.

WALTER. Don't cry, Mama. Understand. That white man is going to walk in that door able to write checks for more money than we ever had. It's important to him and I'm going to help him . . . I'm going to put on the show, Mama.

MAMA. Son — I come from five generations of people who was slaves and sharecroppers — but ain't nobody in my family never let nobody pay 'em no money that was a way of telling us we wasn't fit to walk the earth. We ain't never been that poor. (*Raising her eyes and looking at him*) We ain't never been that dead inside.

BENEATHA. Well — we are dead now. All the talk about dreams and sunlight that goes on in this house. All dead.

WALTER. What's the matter with you all! I didn't make this world! It was give to me this way! Hell, yes, I want me some yachts someday! Yes, I want to hang some real pearls 'round my wife's neck. Ain't she supposed to wear no pearls? Somebody tell me — tell me, who decides which women is suppose to wear pearls in this world. I tell you I am a *man* — and I think my wife should wear some pearls in this world!

(*This last line hangs a good while and Walter begins to move about the room. The word "Man" has penetrated his consciousness; he mumbles it to himself repeatedly between strange agitated pauses as he moves about*)

MAMA. Baby, how you going to feel on the inside?

WALTER. Fine! . . . Going to feel fine . . . a man . . .

MAMA. You won't have nothing left then, Walter Lee.

WALTER. (*Coming to her*) I'm going to feel fine, Mama. I'm going to look that son-of-a-bitch in the eyes and say — (*He falters*) — and say, "All right, Mr. Lindner — (*He falters even more*) — that's your neighborhood out there. You got the right to keep it like you want. You got the right to have it like you want. Just write the check and — the house is yours." And, and I am going to say — (*His voice almost breaks*) And you — you people just put the money in my hand and you won't have to live next to this bunch of stinking niggers! . . . (*He straightens up and moves away from his mother, walking around the room*) Maybe — maybe I'll just get down on my black knees . . . (*He does so; Ruth and Bennie and Mama watch him in frozen horror*) Captain, Mistuh, Bossman. (*He starts crying*) A-hee-hee-hee! (*Wringing his hands in profoundly anguished imitation*) Yasssssuh! Great White Father, just gi' ussen de money, fo' God's sake, and we's ain't gwine come out deh and dirty up yo' white folks neighborhood . . .

(*He breaks down completely, then gets up and goes into the bedroom*)

BENEATHA. That is not a man. That is nothing but a toothless rat.

MAMA. Yes — death done come in this here house. (*She is nodding, slowly, reflectively*) Done come walking in my house. On the lips of my children. You what supposed to be my beginning again. You — what supposed to be my harvest. (*To Beneatha*) You — you mourning your brother?

BENEATHA. He's no brother of mine.

MAMA. What you say?

BENEATHA. I said that that individual in that room is no brother of mine.

MAMA. That's what I thought you said. You feeling like you better than he is today? (*Beneatha does not answer*) Yes? What you tell him a minute ago? That he wasn't a man? Yes? You give him up for me? You done wrote his epitaph too — like the rest of the world? Well, who give you the privilege?

BENEATHA. Be on my side for once! You saw what he just did, Mama! You saw him — down on his knees. Wasn't it you who taught me — to despise any man who would do that. Do what he's going to do.

MAMA. Yes — I taught you that. Me and your daddy. But I thought I taught you something else too . . . I thought I taught you to love him.

BENEATHA. Love him? There is nothing left to love.

MAMA. There is always something left to love. And if you ain't learned that, you ain't learned nothing. (*Looking at her*) Have you cried for that boy today? I don't mean for yourself and for the family 'cause we lost the money. I mean for him; what he been through and what it done to him. Child, when do you think is the time to love somebody the most; when they done good and made things easy for everybody? Well then, you ain't through learning — because that ain't the time at all. It's when he's at his lowest and can't believe in hisself 'cause the world done whipped him so. When you starts measuring somebody, measure him right, child, measure him right. Make sure you done taken into account what hills and valleys he come through before he got to wherever he is.

(*Travis bursts into the room at the end of the speech, leaving the door open*)

TRAVIS. Grandmama — the moving men are downstairs! The truck just pulled up.

MAMA. (*Turning and looking at him*) Are they, baby? They downstairs?

(*She sighs and sits. Lindner appears in the doorway. He peers in and knocks lightly, to gain attention, and comes in. All turn to look at him*)

LINDNER. (*Hat and briefcase in hand*) Uh — hello . . . (*Ruth crosses mechanically to the bedroom door and opens it and lets it swing open freely and slowly as the lights come up on Walter within, still in his coat, sitting at the far corner of the room. He looks up and out through the room to Lindner*)

RUTH. He's here.

(*A long minute passes and Walter slowly gets up*)

LINDNER. (*Coming to the table with efficiency, putting his briefcase on the table and starting to unfold papers and unscrew fountain pens*) Well, I certainly was glad to hear from you people. (*Walter has begun the trek out of the room, slowly and awkwardly, rather like a small boy, passing the back of his sleeve across his mouth from time to time*) Life can really be so much simpler than people let it be most of the time. Well — with whom do I negotiate? You, Mrs. Younger, or your son here? (*Mama sits with her hands folded on her lap and her eyes closed as Walter advances. Travis goes close to Lindner and looks at the papers curiously*) Just some official papers, sonny.

RUTH. Travis, you go downstairs.

MAMA. (*Opening her eyes and looking into Walter's*) No. Travis, you stay right here. And you make him understand what you doing, Walter Lee. You teach him good. Like Willy Harris taught you. You show where our five generations done come to. Go ahead, son —

WALTER. (*Looks down into his boy's eyes. Travis grins at him merrily and Walter draws him beside him with his arm lightly around his shoulders*) Well, Mr. Lindner. (*Beneatha turns away*) We called you — (*There is a profound, simple groping quality in his speech*) — because, well, me and my family (*He looks around and shifts from one foot to the other*) Well — we are very plain people . . .

LINDNER. Yes —

WALTER. I mean — I have worked as a chauffeur most of my life — and my wife here, she does domestic work in people's kitchens. So does my mother. I mean — we are plain people . . .

LINDNER. Yes, Mr. Younger —

WALTER. (*Really like a small boy, looking down at his shoes and then up at the man*) And — uh — well, my father, well, he was a laborer most of his life.

LINDNER. (*Absolutely confused*) Uh, yes —

WALTER. (*Looking down at his toes once again*) My father almost beat a man to death once because this man called him a bad name or something, you know what I mean?

LINDNER. No, I'm afraid I don't.

WALTER. (*Finally straightening up*) Well, what I mean is that we come from people who had a lot of pride. I mean — we are very proud people. And that's my sister over there and she's going to be a doctor — and we are very proud —

LINDNER. Well — I am sure that is very nice, but —

WALTER. (*Starting to cry and facing the man eye to eye*) What I am telling you is that we called you over here to tell you that we are very proud and that this is — this is my son, who makes the sixth generation of our family in this country, and that we have all thought about your offer and we have decided to move into our house because my father — my father — he earned it. (*Mama has her eyes closed and is rocking back and forth as though she were in church, with her head nodding the amen yes*) We don't want to make no trouble for nobody or fight no causes — but we will try to be good neighbors. That's all we got to say. (*He looks the man absolutely in the eyes*) We don't want your money.

(*He turns and walks away from the man*)

LINDNER. (*Looking around at all of them*) I take it then that you have decided to occupy.

BENEATHA. That's what the man said.

LINDNER. (*To Mama in her reverie*) Then I would like to appeal to you, Mrs. Younger. You are older and wiser and understand things better I am sure . . .

MAMA. (*Rising*) I am afraid you don't understand. My son said we was going to move and there ain't nothing left for me to say. (*Shaking her head with double meaning*) You know how these young folks is nowadays, mister. Can't do a thing with 'em. Good-bye.

LINDNER. (*Folding up his materials*) Well — if you are that final about it . . . There is nothing left for me to say. (*He finishes. He is almost ignored by the family, who are concentrating on Walter Lee. At the door Lindner halts and looks around*) I sure hope you people know what you're doing.

(*He shakes his head and exits*)

RUTH. (*Looking around and coming to life*) Well, for God's sake — if the moving men are here — LET'S GET THE HELL OUT OF HERE!

MAMA. (*Into action*) Ain't it the truth! Look at all this here mess. Ruth, put Travis' good jacket on him . . . Walter Lee, fix your tie and tuck your shirt in, you look just like somebody's hoodlum. Lord have mercy, where is my plant? (*She flies to get it amid the general bustling of the family, who are deliberately trying to ignore the nobility of the past moment*) You all start on down . . . Travis child, don't go empty-handed . . . Ruth, where did I put that box with my skillets in it? I want to be in charge of it myself . . . I'm going to make us the biggest dinner we ever ate tonight . . . Beneatha, what's the matter with them stockings? Pull them things up, girl . . .

(*The family starts to file out as two moving men appear and begin to carry out the heavier pieces of furniture, bumping into the family as they move about*)

BENEATHA. Mama, Asagai — asked me to marry him today and go to Africa —

MAMA. (*In the middle of her getting-ready activity*) He did? You ain't old enough to marry nobody — (*Seeing the moving men lifting one of her chairs precariously*) Darling, that ain't no bale of cotton, please handle it so we can sit in it again. I had that chair twenty-five years . . .

(*The movers sigh with exasperation and go on with their work*)

BENEATHA. (*Girlishly and unreasonably trying to pursue the conversation*) To go to Africa, Mama — be a doctor in Africa . . .

MAMA. (*Distracted*) Yes, baby —

WALTER. Africa! What he want you to go to Africa for?

BENEATHA. To practice there . . .

WALTER. Girl, if you don't get all them silly ideas out your head! You had better marry yourself a man with some loot . . .

BENEATHA. (*Angrily, precisely as in the first scene of the play*) What have you got to do with who I marry!

WALTER. Plenty. Now I think George Murchison —

(*He and Beneatha go out yelling at each other vigorously; Beneatha is heard saying that she would not marry George Murchison if he were Adam and she were Eve, etc. The anger is loud and real till their voices diminish. Ruth stands at the door and turns to Mama and smiles knowingly*)

MAMA. (*Fixing her hat at last*) Yeah — they something all right, my children . . .

RUTH. Yeah — they're something. Let's go, Lena.

MAMA. (*Stalling, starting to look around at the house*) Yes — I'm coming. Ruth —

RUTH. Yes?

MAMA. (*Quietly, woman to woman*) He finally come into his manhood today, didn't he? Kind of like a rainbow after the rain . . .

RUTH. (*Biting her lip lest her own pride explode in front of Mama*) Yes, Lena.

(*Walter's voice calls for them raucously*)

MAMA. (*Waving Ruth out vaguely*) All right, honey — go on down. I be down directly.

(*Ruth hesitates, then exits. Mama stands, at last alone in the living room, her plant on the table before her as the lights start to come down. She looks around at all the walls and ceilings and suddenly, despite herself, while the children call below, a great heaving thing rises in her and she puts her fist to her mouth, takes a final desperate look, pulls her coat about her, pats her hat and goes out. The lights dim down. The door opens and she comes back in, grabs her plant, and goes out for the last time)*

*Curtain*

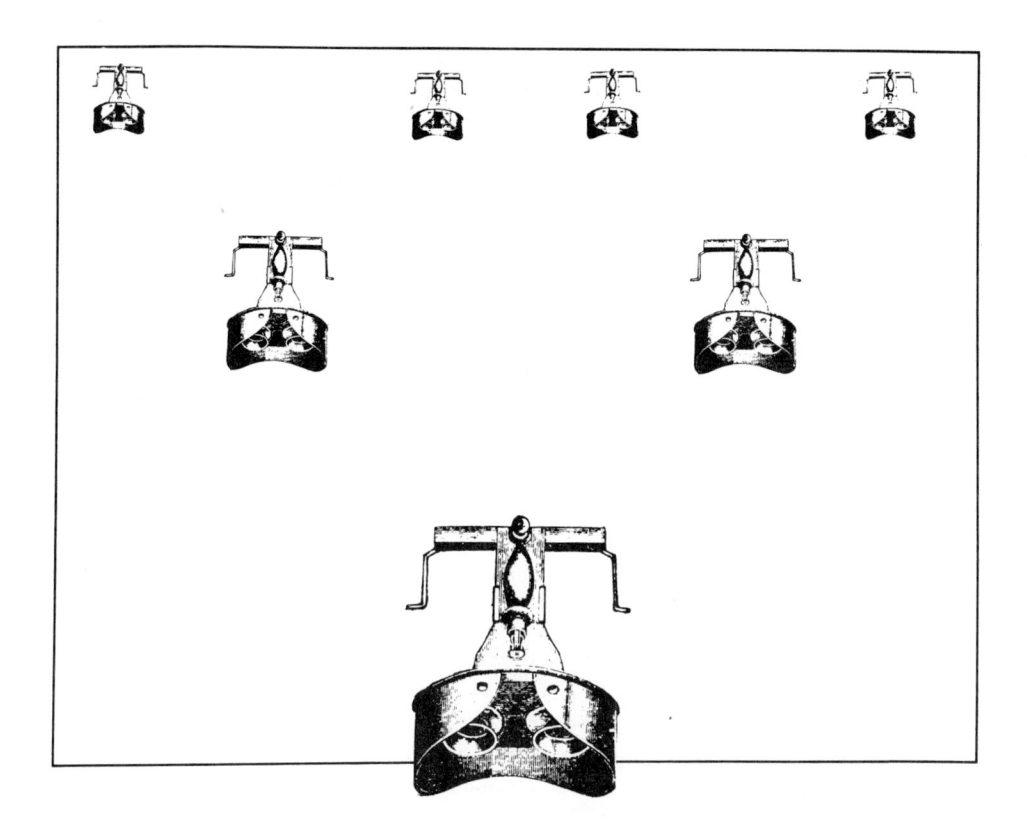

# FICTION

In this third section, you study and write about fiction. First, you examine pieces of your own writing for the features they share with short stories and novels. Once you have these features in mind, you then go on to write a long critical essay comparing two fictional works.

The writing assignments in this part differ from those in the two earlier sections. Instead of writing several short critical papers, you spend the first four chapters prewriting on various aspects of fiction in preparation for a longer paper. The paper itself is not assigned until the last chapter. The prewriting allows you to generate a great deal of evidence before you sit down to write your paper.

The paper also calls for documentation, that is, the use of other people's opinions as counters and balances to your own ideas. But you do not look at outside opinions until you have analyzed the stories thoroughly yourself. Stress is laid upon the techniques of documentation, upon how to blend in outside judgments, but not upon comprehensive research into the critical statements made about the stories.

As the organization of this part implies, you are invited to study fiction thoroughly first before you read other people's opinions about it. You are asked to trust your perceptions and the text's system of prewriting before you consider others' judgments. It is so easy to get overwhelmed by the judgment of professional critics that it is sometimes necessary to remind yourself of the worth of your ideas and the ability of your voice to express them. The purpose of bringing in outside criticism is to bring fresh perspectives to a work worth writing about; the purpose is not to intimidate those who haven't yet had their say about the work.

Don't worry about duplicating the insights of professional critics. The fact that you agree with a published person should give you confidence. If you should disagree with a critic after having carefully studied the fiction before setting out to write yourself, don't doubt your own method of research or your own judgments.

Even the writing from your experience differs a bit in the third part from similar assignments in earlier sections. For in this part, once you have a basic narrative written, you return to analyze it several times, each time from a new perspective that corresponds to the aspect of fiction you are about to study. You begin with a survival story and take it through several transformations. Each transformation corresponds to the technique of fiction under study — plot, character, point of view, language, and theme.

# 12

# Plot in Fiction

## 22 · DISCOVERING PLOT IN SURVIVAL STORIES

*WRITING* Tell your best survival story, the one where you survived some physical, mental, or moral crisis to become the person you are. Tell about the time you flew the neighbor's cat in a rocket in your backyard — and you and the cat both lived. Or the time you rode in a child's baby carriage down a busy street in St. Louis. Or the time you answered an ad and left town with a sleazy employer to become a magazine salesman. Or endured questions about your motorcycle at a painful family reunion. Or survived the loneliness of being lost in a strange city. Or talked a policeman out of a ticket.

Think of a single incident to relate: "How I whipped my brother in a fishing contest, earned my father's esteem as an outdoor person, and defeated the stereotype of a soft girl who could be trusted with a curtain rod, not a fishing rod."

*DISCUSSION* Bring your survival stories to class. Discuss them in light of these questions. (Before you begin the discussion, read about concepts of plot in the Comments and Examples section.)

1. Does each narrative center on a single act of survival? Could you describe a few other narratives from your experience where this would be one among a series of survival episodes?
2. What traits in the people telling the survival stories caused them to be in difficult situations, such as stranded in a foreign city, in the first place? What traits enabled them to survive?

## COMMENTS AND EXAMPLES

If you were to imagine an autobiography, let's say one based on just your survival experiences, the one you have just written about would be only one action in a series. This single incident corresponds to one action in the series of actions that makes up a plot in fiction. *Plot,* then, is the term used to designate the entire series of actions, but the series itself can be broken down into small, subordinate units of action. For example, suppose that you describe the plot of a short story as: "a young, hopeful man gets his first glimpses of evil in the world, can't cope with the new insights that damage his optimism, and it doesn't survive so that he becomes a hopeless cynic for the rest of his life." That would be the plot, the main action of the story, but each incident would be a smaller, subordinate unit of action. Suppose we describe the subordinate units: (1) an episode when we see him doubting his wife's fidelity; (2) another where his new vision of evil so stuns him that he can't reach out to a person like his former teacher, who has been close to him; (3) finally, a look at him in some incident when he is old, has never gained a balanced view that life is a mixture of good and evil, and dies leaving a gloomy epitaph on his gravestone.

We tend to discuss plot in terms of what causes a unit of action or an entire plot to happen. And we also tend to prefer, because they are more believable, individual actions and larger plots that emerge out of character. That way we seem to be able to connect them with ourselves or with people we know. Optimistic friends, for example, leave themselves open for pain when they find good or put trust in people the rest of us distrust. We have ourselves had favorite illusions stripped away by the world. Thus we can identify with optimistic friends or characters who appear to be riding for the same fall.

An optimist, especially one with illusions about how basically good all people are, is a natural for a narrative where the subordinate series of actions points to the main plot of how those illusions are ripped away. Let's say the optimist is a woman, who trusts even obvious con artists like rural Bible salesmen. That is, her trust, as a character trait, leads her into situations some people might avoid. When in Flannery O'Conner's *Good Country People,* a Bible salesman runs off with Joy's wooden leg, the breaking of her trust results in disillusionment, the major action in the story.[1]

Let's examine briefly two student papers that demonstrate the similarities shared by your survival stories and the plots of pieces of

---

1. This discussion is indebted to E. M. Forster, *Aspects of the Novel* (New York: Harcourt, Brace, and World, 1954), pp. 83–103.

fiction. Look first at a less complex story, one by Paul Faber on his feelings crossing the ocean from Holland as a twentieth-century emigrant to the United States.

THE CROSSING

He was four years old, small, skinny, and very scared. Around him teemed hundreds of kids, big kids, little kids, black kids, white kids, all kinds of kids.

His parents were two decks below him. They were enjoying a good breakfast with three other couples. It was about 9:00 A.M. Outside the sun was shining, and the seagulls were flying in the breeze, sweeping low against the water, picking up garbage that was thrown overboard from the large ocean liner.

He knew no one in the large nursery. A sixteen-year-old girl came to where he was sitting in a corner, next to the big door, and asked if he wanted to join some children in a game. He shrank back in his corner and started to cry. He could not understand her English. She took his hand and led him to a table. He continued to cry and ran back to his corner.

The boy was on his way to America from the Netherlands with his mother and father and his two-year-old sister. He did not know a word of English. Oh, how he wanted to be with his parents, or at least with his sister, who was in the baby nursery, which was on the other side of the deck.

He sat there for two hours, waiting and crying for his parents to come and claim him. At last the big door opened and there stood his dad.

*Paul Faber*

Notice that Paul focuses on a single incident: out of all those that happened during his family's crossing, he tells us about the memorable one, the one where he was most lonely and isolated. In this sense, Paul's "plot" is one action out of a series of possible stories about his crossing. You also see that Paul's dependency and inability to understand English causes the action of his shrinking from the other kids, his crying, and his fearing even a girl who tries to help him.

In a more complex survival story, Susan Quick talks about an abortion. Her paper demonstrates that survival narratives, like plots in fiction, have a unity made up of a series of smaller actions and that action emerges out of character.

THE ABORTION

Zimansky had just finished his explanation of Crane's suicide when the minute hand hit the one and he realized he had kept us five minutes past the hour. He muttered apologies and received bashful forgiveness from the class as they shuffled out the door. Usually I enjoyed Zimansky's diversions, but not today. Today of all days he kept us late; today, when I felt such a throbbing, dulling, incessant pain as though I had a hot knife embedded in my side. It was the kind of pain that gets behind your eyes, draining pigment so that all you see are shades of white.

It was snowing as I walked across campus, and laughing children scooted by dragging their sleds. That force behind my eyes imagined the children sliding down the hill into the path of passing trucks which reduced them to red pulp and splinters. "Only a few more blocks home," I thought to myself, "and then I can lie down." It seemed like days by the time I had climbed the stairs laden with books and heavy winter clothes and reached my dorm room.

"I'm sorry, Susan," the nurse on the other end of the line squawked, "the doctor is seeing a patient now; he can call you back at 5:30 tonight if you'd like."

"Listen," I said calmly, "I think this is an emergency."

"Yes, hello, Susan," Dr. Peterson's voice had an anesthetizing effect, "now, how do you feel?"

"Like I wish I had a bullet to bite on, or better yet, a truck to run over me and get it over with."

"Sounds like we've got some complications. Better get down here to St. Luke's by this evening, and we'll see if we can't clear everything up. Don't worry, these things happen all the time. And take some of the medication I gave you to ease the pain. We wouldn't want you running in front of any truck, now, would we?" he chuckled nervously. "See you this evening." Click. Buzz.

I fell back on the bed and the room swirled; white circles superimposed on shades of grey spun opposite one another. I felt a gentle touch on my shoulder which brought with it a resurrection of the pain, and I realized I had dozed off. But this was a new pain, muted, due to the medication. John stood over me, his face tight and pale. John, who I'd only known a few weeks, had managed to touch a place deep within my being; a place I had thought beyond reach. When we met, it was as though in another incarnation we had been the same person, but in this one we were forced into our separate male/female roles.

"Hey, you look terrible" his voice so quiet as not to break my sleepy numbness.

"Dr. Peterson says to meet him at the hospital at 6:00. Can you drive me into the city?" my voice cut the foggy air as I spoke. The air began to bleed.

"Of course . . . I'd better get Tony to go along; you and I will be in no shape to handle this alone." As he spoke he noticed a drop of air-blood touch his sleeve.

Outside, the sky was like a pause in the pain, leaden with snow; ready to break at any second, yet hesitating slightly. As we got on the freeway, the clouds spewed out their contents with such force we had to crawl along to see the road in between the rhythm of the windshield wipers. Tony leaned up from the back seat to be near us. He knew how we needed his strength — his calm, rational, light-witted strength — just to keep a lid on sanity. He put one arm around me and one around John and smiled, "How're you feelin', kid?"

"Oh, OK. The dope they gave me is like eating 20 reds, man, like I'm melting into the seat," I drawled in that drug-fiend sarcasm we used only among the three of us.

"Yeah? Maybe we ought to go to the hill and sell 'em to make some bucks. And when we get the hang of it, we'll start pushin' to make next year's tuition."

"Hey yeah, then we could join the Mafia and sell heroin to grade school kids," John said, keeping up the level of absurdity and relief.

"Sure," I said, "then we wouldn't have to worry about GRE's or CPA's or BA's or BSA's . . ."

"Or RCA or LTD or BLT or LSD or TWA or ITT or DDT or GMC . . ."

Tony was cut off suddenly as the car seemed to lose all sense of gravity; all sense of any logical direction. I realized we were spinning helplessly around and around on the icy road. In an instant we were stopped, facing the traffic as it burst toward us. The cars eddied around us, crashing against the guard rails and embankments. The sound of crashing metal ran up my spine. Then came the silence. I saw a man jump out of his truck, holding his head, his mouth open as an outlet for his pain. The scream pierced the silence, and for the first time I noticed the red color, flowing out onto the snow. A blue woman stumbled out of her station wagon; a jaundiced man scraped himself off his windshield. I sat immobile, horrified at the colorful bodies amongst all that virgin white. Tony and John had long since leapt out of the car. John ran to call an ambulance. Tony had ripped up his shirt and was applying tourniquets. He moved swiftly from body to body; his bare back against the falling snow.

In the midst of this red-stained confusion I heard a wail higher and more sustained than the others. I opened the car door and felt the wet snow slap my face as I stumbled over to the station wagon. On the floor lay an infant, half unwrapped in blankets. His face was crimson from screaming and squirming and having lost his station wagon security. Gently, I lifted him and wrapped the blankets around his exposed arms and toes. Slowly I rocked him in time with the approaching siren, as he screamed louder and louder. The snow continued to fall, harder now, muffling the red stains. But the child did not stop screaming; and I marveled at how one so new to the world could know so much about it.

*Susan Quick*

If you were to state the plot of Susan's survival story, you might say, "A young woman, pregnant, sick, and self-centered, survives not only a preabortion illness and fears, but also a car wreck on the way to the hospital to find out that her personal pain is just a fragment of the hurt in the world." There are a large number of identifiable, smaller, subordinate actions that make up this central plot. For example, when the students joke in the car, they show how people in tough situations avoid pain by becoming flippant and pretending to be more callous and self-centered than they really are. One minute they are joking about selling dope to children, the next minute performing rescues at a freeway wreck. The rescuing incident supports the basic change in the narrator in the course of the survival experience — she is not as self-centered or callous as she thought. In this sense, then, both the callous talk and the kind actions emerge from the same source: in the complex and confusing ways these people react to their own and other people's pain.

## 23 · PREWRITING: PLOT IN FICTION

As mentioned in the introduction to the fiction section, the critical writing exercises in this part lead you step by step toward the development of a documented paper, that is, one where you use critical essays by professional writers as well as short stories as evidence in your papers. This assignment differs from the traditional research paper in that it is much more limited in scope. It doesn't ask you to research a topic exhaustively. Instead it asks you to draw from a few sources so you learn to handle the problems that writers face incorporating opinions other than their own into papers.

Using this step-by-step process, you develop your paper in four prewriting stages. Each helps you focus on the extended paper you will be writing. You begin this section by selecting two pieces of fiction, and by continually comparing and contrasting them each time with a new topic and a fresh set of prewriting questions, so that you will have generated considerable evidence before you sit down to write.

Chapters 12 through 15 have prewriting exercises. It isn't until chapter 16 that the essay itself is assigned. And that essay will ask you to compare and contrast two pieces of fiction, and to show how aspects of plot, character, point of view, language, and theme not only shape the meaning of the individual stories but also illuminate what they share or how they differ as pieces of fiction.

Student writing illustrates chapters 12 through 15 in the way it has in the earlier sections of the text. Exercises 23, 25, 27, and 29 center on the two short stories printed in Fiction Readings: Nathaniel Hawthorne's *Young Goodman Brown* and James Alan McPherson's *Gold Coast*. Before you do your own prewriting, you would do well to examine how other students have approached the two pieces of fiction in their prewriting. Then turn to the stories in Fiction Readings or to novels assigned by your instructor.

*PREWRITING* The main purpose of this exercise is to identify and then to compare and contrast the plots of two pieces of fiction. Do this prewriting exercise in two stages:

1 Describe in brief paragraphs the primary actions of the two stories that you are working with:
   a What happens to the main character or characters in the stories — any developments or discoveries or changes?
   b What traits in these main characters caused the actions in the first place? Do the plots emerge out of the characters?
2 Identify a smaller, subordinate action in each story and relate it to the central action; that is, where does this unit fit into the series of actions that make up the plot?
   a What light does the subordinate action shed on the main character or main action?
   b Does the smaller action anticipate the main one, or does it define a trait in one of the main characters?

*DISCUSSION* In class, discuss your prewriting exercises. Read the description of each story that you are comparing and contrasting. Focus on these questions:

1 What are the stories' central similarities or differences? In terms of complexity? In terms of development, change, or revelation of the major characters?
2 Does the central action in each story emerge from a central character? That is, do the traits of these characters get them into certain situations or do they make certain things happen? Do special traits emerge under the stress of action? Compare and contrast the two stories.
3 Examine a subordinate action in each story: something that happens to a minor character or a little incident that happens to a major character. How does it fit into the main action — does it present a preview of the eventual outcome of the story? Does it give an important hint about a character's tendencies or traits? Compare and contrast the use of subordinate actions in each short story that you are preparing to write about.

## COMMENTS AND EXAMPLES

The main plot of a story can be economically stated. Susan Quick's identification of the main movements of *Young Goodman Brown* and *Gold Coast* illustrate this point:

GOLD COAST

*Gold Coast* centers essentially on the speaker's relationship to the old janitor, a relationship which starts out as a distant pity for old Sullivan, progresses to an identification with his desperation, and concludes with Robert's fear of that desperation and his running from it.

YOUNG GOODMAN BROWN

Hawthorne tells the story of a man's disillusionment with the piety of his fellow Christians. Young Goodman Brown takes a dream-like journey into the woods with the devil to observe a devil-worship ceremony. Hesitating the whole way, Goodman Brown is finally converted when he sees all the upstanding Puritans in Salem including his wife, Faith, attend an evil ceremony. Whether the experience was a dream or not is left open to question, but Goodman Brown returns to town the next day a changed man. No longer does he trust the good-in-men, instead becomes a cynic to the end of his days.

*Susan Quick*

Susan's prewriting accounts well for the change each character undergoes: Young Goodman Brown develops into a cynic; Robert runs from further commitment to Sullivan.

Brenda Rhyne's prewriting of the same exercise also briefly identifies the plot. But it goes one step further and shows how traits in the characters initiate actions in each story:

GOLD COAST

Robert starts out in the story ambitious enough to talk to the Old Man Sullivan and put up with his filth. He seems to want to know everything about everything: his writer's curiosity drives him on. From there he goes into an "I can't stand it anymore" phase. Hates being janitor, the old man, everything. But curiously this takes place after the old dog has been taken away. Then he goes into a kind of love for the guy and sentimental. After he leaves and then sees Sullivan again a touch of conflict ends the story — longing to help Sullivan but an understanding not to want to get tangled in Sullivan's life again.

*Brenda Rhyne*

YOUNG GOODMAN BROWN

A trusting, yet highly curious young Christian man goes into the forest one evening, leaves his sweet little wife behind and meets the devil in a challenge to sell his soul. Through the course of fighting a mental battle with the devil he finds that most all of the people of his church already seem to be sold to the Devil. He goes out of the forest back into his life a very cynical and untrusting soul who doesn't step into Church for the rest of his life. Did he see it? Did the Devil win?

*Brenda Rhyne*

Notice that Brenda sees the main character's curiosity as the force that drives the plots of both stories. She has established a significant comparative aspect that the two stories share.

Finally, in relating a subordinate action to the main plot, the final aspect of your prewriting exercise, it's possible to discover other common denominators between two stories. Pam Robinette's identification and analysis of a smaller action in *Gold Coast* and *Young Goodman Brown* illustrate this point:

> 1 *Gold Coast* — The taking away of Sullivan's dog through the scheming spiteful actions of Miss O'Hara. This incident fits into the main action because it gives an important hint about Sullivan's and Meg's traits. They are sensitive, lonely people. Although they could show no affection to one another, each felt love and affection for the dog. The dog, although vicious to outsiders, was the only common bond between husband and wife.
>
> 2 *Young Goodman Brown* — When he meets Goody Cloyse on the forest road. This meeting sets up Brown's final removal from the society. Goody Cloyse, his god-fearing catechism teacher, is not the devout Christian he thought she was. She deceived him. She is a witch in disguise. This meeting convinces Brown that something is amiss in his community. This meeting also suggests the similar traits and characteristics of the community as a whole.
>
> Pam Robinette

What Pam has discovered in this exercise is another common bond between the two stories: in addition to both main characters being driven by curiosity, we see Robert and Young Goodman Brown in light of the communities they live in. Robert is defined partly by the values that he shares or doesn't share with the Sullivans. Young Goodman Brown discovers that he shares his perception of evil with his community, a startling realization because he thought the community entirely innocent.

It is these insights, then, about the main and subordinate actions and about what drives the main plots that establish a set of assumptions from which to begin a paper.

# 13

# Character in Fiction

## 24 · DISCOVERING CHARACTER IN SURVIVAL STORIES

Look first at the survival story that you wrote for chapter 12, and study it primarily for the way it reveals an aspect of your character. Do you appear fearful except for this one moment of bravery that the story tells? Did obeying a strict code of ethics help you survive?

Then, go on to sketch briefly three or four other episodes from your life that would make good stories if you were to tell them in full. Provide only brief outlines of these; you needn't write them out entirely, nor do they need to be survival stories. Merely list three or four narratives that might be part of an autobiography. Set these sketches for stories alongside your survival story, comparing and contrasting them with these questions in mind:

*DISCUSSION* Discuss your stories in class, using these questions:

1. What character traits emerge most strongly in the survival story? What other traits do you have that lie hidden from view in the survival episode but that show up in the other narratives? What does each story reveal about your attitudes, your system of ethics, or your weaknesses that the survival stories don't show? Focus especially on the longings revealed in each story; for example, a longing to be an athlete or to be a musician.
2. By what means, either in the survival story or the new ones you have sketched, do you reveal your character? Actions, including the main

actions of each narrative? Habits? Dress? Conversations? Attitudes? Companions? Family background?
3 What emerge in these stories as primary longings? Do you wish to please your parents? Are you driven by desires for fame, love, money, or a political cause? Do you look for new kicks all the time, or do you enjoy the comfort of what is already tested and true?
4 If it is possible to organize the survival story and the sketches into a sequence that reveals some way you have developed or changed, what would be that sequence? Do you find evidence of a change or development in your character? Increased capacity for understanding people? A fresh affirmation or denial of a law or code of morality you always held to be true?

---

## COMMENTS AND EXAMPLES

We tend to admire complex characters in fiction more than we do simple ones — those who have believable longings motivating them and those who act in keeping with their established natures.

In looking at yourself as a character in your autobiographical writings, you have a chance to present through a number of stories the major traits you have: loyalty, fear, a seldom revealed sarcastic side, a love of ceremony, a hatred of order, an ability to trust, being easily bored, and so forth.

In the same way, a single trait may be what a fiction writer wishes to emphasize in a character. But to avoid stereotyping, the writer tries to show characters in their complexity even though the story may stress a dominant trait: how the main action of murder, let's say, is shaped by a character's jealousy.

A good way to begin to understand characters is to look at what drives them. For example, what we long for often defines us as people. One story idea that appears again and again uses what's known as "the monkey's paw motif": a man and woman possess a charmed monkey's paw, which will allow them to have a wish granted. They long for their son to be brought back from death. He is brought back all right but as mutilated as he went into the grave. This story has retained its universality partly because most of us have made vain wishes, wishes that shouldn't come true because if they did, the satisfaction would be more unsatisfying than the longing. By describing characters' actions and language, a writer often wants you to understand their longings.

Brenda Rhyne's survival paper nicely illustrates the point that a person's longings are a good way to comprehend the concept of character:

Friday morning, and only a few people were sitting around drinking the black habit. Morning is the only time the tables are all clean, not littered with classical studies meetings, the Daily Bull, those white styrofoam cups that keep anything hot and cold, stinky cigarette butts on the floor, and ashtrays tipped over spilling their guts on the coffee-stained tables. My best friend sat across the table from me. We had gone through junior high and high school together, always together doing everything but never sharing our minds or hearts.

There we were, skipping our 8:00 class, drinking hot tea and eating warm donuts when she read this job ad from the *Moses Lake Herald*. It was one of those "see the world and earn a guaranteed income" promises. We wanted to leave Tumble-Weed Tech, which to us was just a glorified high school with ashtrays, and make it on our own. By noon we had talked to a man who to show class was staying in one of the better motels in town. We would be traveling around selling magazines. The job sounded good to me, but Donna decided not to go.

The ride was an hour's drive from Moses Lake, and it was already dark. The man who was representing the company (I'll just call him Mr. Good-Driver) handled the car well at night on windy, curvy roads. That is what I noticed first about him to keep my mind off the fears my mind was subjecting itself to as we traveled the very long drive to Wenatchee, the town where I was to begin my career.

Donna was to withdraw me from school on Monday. I was surprised we said goodbye so easily that Friday. So I just dropped everything and went off with a man I had never met before.

Saturday morning my folks changed their minds from their initial approval. My education was more important to them and should be to me also. The idea of my selling magazines suddenly sent them into a frenzy and they tried to find me. Mr. Good-Driver's name did not correspond to the one he had checked us in under at the Wenatchee Your-Host Motel. You can clearly see how this would make my folks, who are strict, believe that I, their eldest daughter of eight children, was unscrupulously and savagely sold into, yes, that merciless, unclean, most possibly inexcusable of all systems, white slavery.

Sliding under the crisp clean sheets smelling of motel cleanness, I said a hopeful goodnight to a girl who had been recruited from Spokane and then said a quick reassuring prayer that I was doing what He wanted.

On Sunday when we started selling, the snow was piled up waist high in some of the yards. We had to tramp it down as we boldly knocked on doors. My partner for the morning was really good with her spiel. Being a novice, myself, I even began to believe that people were getting *Good Housekeeping* at a bargain. But I couldn't get the hang of selling and began to feel lonely and at a loss for words.

Sunday night I called home, which proved to be the turning point in my career as a magazine salesgirl. After sobbing into the phone for five minutes and talking my dad out of sending the police to put Mr.

Good-Driver in jail, my career ended when my father drove over from Moses Lake, in more snow, to take his ex-salesgirl home.

*Brenda Rhyne*

When Brenda came to analyze this paper using the discussion questions above in exercise 24, she said about her own paper, "My primary longing was to leave Moses Lake and do something different." She went on to say that the act represented "subtle rebellion, to be on my own — to make a life for myself." Brenda concluded with this observation about taking the magazine job: "Also a denial of a code of morality I had held to be true." That is, she longed to test the codes she had never challenged. In trying to sell magazines and make a fast buck, she found out how her codes held up, so much so, as a matter of fact, that she couldn't sell with a clear conscience, and gave it up.

Longings, however, are only one way to assess character. Other kinds of actions, attitudes, and emotional traits are equally important. Compare, for example, Susan Quick's sketches for other autobiographical stories with her survival story "The Abortion" in chapter 12.

1 Working as a receptionist for Banquet Foods Corporation on the top of the Executive Building in downtown St. Louis, I rode the bus to work reading science fiction, took coffee breaks reading science fiction. I escaped my startling reality quite a lot. Got involved in company gossip with the other secretaries — laughing at their pettiness. Everyone envied me because I was going to leave and they couldn't.

2 Living in the Tetons in a log cabin in the woods; rode my horse every day and read a lot. Took hikes till it got too cold and the ice was two inches thick on my windows. Chopped a lot of wood and stocked the fire every morning. Left when it just got too cold for me to want to stay. Worked as a waitress in a local hamburger joint and fed the cowboys their morning cups of "mud."

3 The first time I got drunk was with my best friend in high school. Stole a fifth of cheap bourbon and drank it straight from the bottle walking around the track of the junior high. We talked about what we were going to do with our lives and all the shit we'd been through already. We sounded like two old winos from Pioneer Square. We were both gonna be poets and lead scattered lives in dreams of the ideal.

4 The last time I got drunk — this time with a new friend and a college professor. Although I now mix my bourbon with 7-Up and drink an occasional "white cadillac," I'm still talking about dreams, my eyes are still clouded with visions of the ideal. Conversation about alternatives in education and living on the land and old lovers.

Susan's sketches for stories reveal different sides of her character and different means of revealing character besides talking about their longings. She says that the abortion story shows that she has "a tragic view of my condition — there are no ideals left"; yet the same story indicates that she has a hope that "maybe I'm wrong." Her other stories reveal that "I dislike the big city; but am not satisfied in the country. I also like to articulate and to self-indulge in analysis of my own motives; e.g., the drinking examples."

Susan's sketches show us a person walking, talking, and drinking with friends, all important ways to understand character. She also shows us herself at work — contrasting jobs in vastly different sections of the country.

The entire set of descriptions, running from the survival paper through the four sketches, indicates a much more complex person than the narrative by itself can show us. Character, we begin to see, in autobiography as well as in fiction, needs complexity. We expect fictional characters to resemble the motivations and behavior of people we know or can imagine.

## 25 · PREWRITING: CHARACTER IN FICTION

Like exercise 23, this is another prewriting assignment that asks you to gather materials for your documented paper. This time you will be looking at character. Again you will compare and contrast two pieces of fiction.

Begin with a conception introduced in the chapter on plot — we tend to admire plots that emerge out of character; that is, actions that have their beginnings in the way people are. Let's say, for example, a social-climbing family longs to marry its one daughter to a wealthy man and thereby to elevate itself one more rung up the social ladder. But she runs away to marry a poor student, the central action of the story, which reveals her character and also the shock and disappointment of the family. So the plot of humiliation and defeat begins in the family's central character trait: the longing to rise socially, a motivation that sets its loss in motion.

PREWRITING Use these questions first to gather material for your eventual paper and then for class discussion once your prewriting is done:

1 For the major characters in each of the two stories you are studying, identify the central longing or longings that drive each character. Is it a desire for fame? To be loved? Are there conflicting desires within the

characters — is a woman torn between her wish to have a career and her family responsibilities?

2 How do the minor characters relate to the main ones in each story? Do they show parallel or contrasting motivations — rebellious major characters versus minor characters who accept things the way they are?

3 Do the characters seem to be complex? For instance, is a character's rebelliousness emphasized to the point where you lose other senses of him as a person?

4 Given the characters' traits, do they make choices that are in keeping with their natures? For example, would a proud woman, established as one who never crawls, actually humble herself in a given situation in order to protect someone else's feelings?

5 How are the characters revealed? Does the writer concentrate on the way characters speak and show themselves in actions? Or are they revealed in various ways: who they know, what they wear, what their attitudes are, how they dress, what others think of them, or still other ways?

*DISCUSSION* Once completed, examine in class your prewriting in light of the above questions.

## COMMENTS AND EXAMPLES

A study of character in fiction, we have noted, begins in an analysis of what drives the characters, that is, how the action of a story grows out of a character's longings. Once the motivations are identified, you can then move on to considerations of (1) other traits possessed by the characters; (2) their relative complexity and believability, and (3) the relationship between major and minor characters. As illustrations of these points, look at some students' prewriting that examines *Young Goodman Brown* and *Gold Coast* in terms of what each main character longs for and of what choices each makes in light of that primary longing. Pam Robinette speaks of the primary motivations of Young Goodman Brown and of Robert.

> The force driving Robert is a desire to find himself as a writer — this includes his professional purpose in life and also his desire to be loved for what he is, a human being, not a racial stereotype.
>
> The force driving Young Goodman Brown is a desire to find, in spite of himself, the meaning of faith and to discover what is the difference

between good and evil. That is, he is a questioning person, even against his own will.

*Pam Robinette*

Notice that Pam has a clear basis here for comparison and contrast: Robert's conscious motives versus Young Goodman Brown's unconscious ones. Brown's search is for religious meaning; Robert's is for a sense of identity. Once she has a view of each character's primary longing, then Pam is able to talk about the choices open to each character, choices that go with or against the grain of the primary motives:

> In *Gold Coast,* the choices the character makes seem sensible. The black guy is young and still has a more or less optimistic view of life, and he still has his whole life to explore with. His choice of moving on and finding "something" is reasonable since he knows he wants to write. Sullivan's refusal to leave is sensible also. He is old, and alcoholic, and he is ill and dying so why change now? He has nothing to lose if he stays the same and really, nothing to gain if he does change because life is passing him by and he already has lived his life, e.g., the hippie passing him and his wife and calling them "Mr. and Mrs. Speedy Molasses."
>
> Given Brown's trait as an unconscious questioner, what he does is sensible. He becomes a changed man because he is driven by his desire to seek out the truth of good and evil and has no choice but to change. He changes because he cannot distinguish between fact and fiction and every concept and idea learned or believed in becomes a confusing distortion. That is, he becomes cynical when he thinks he has seen his wife at the black mass in the woods.

*Pam Robinette*

Again, Pam draws a sharp contrast between the two characters: Robert, who lives in a world of rational choices, decides to get on with life and neglect his commitment to the Sullivans. As a writer, he has learned something as a janitor. But he has to move on. On the other hand, Young Goodman Brown can't escape his unconscious drive to know good and evil. The longing for knowledge propels him into the forest; what he learns there forces him to give up his idealism and to fall all the way to cynicism: to know that people, including his wife, are a mixture of good and evil. This knowledge is Brown's undoing because he has believed that people are good, and he can't accept them as full of the same mixed motives and longings as he possesses.

Paul Faber reinforces much of what Pam sees in each of these characters when he talks about the relative complexity and credibility of each. For example, Paul mentions that Brown is complex because of his believable struggle: "Brown is fighting with himself, wanting to go to the meeting, but knowing it may not be the best thing to do — I would disagree with his choice, but because he was curious, and wanted to learn, his choice is one that he could have made in the end." Paul doesn't see Robert struggling in the same way, for Robert "makes his decision to leave, a choice I would agree with, and learns to live with it without much fighting with himself." Paul interjects some strong personal opinions about what the characters do. In effect, he can put himself in the place of each character; and even though he may not admire Brown's decision the way he does Robert's, he can admit that the reasons for deciding are complex enough to be believed as human actions.

Finally, Susan Quick examines the minor characters of each story in comparison to what drives the major ones:

> In *Gold Coast*, Robert's motivation for working as a janitor is to gain insights and inspirations for his writing. His motivation to love Jean is that they both transcend their race identity in their relationship. Sullivan's motivation for befriending Robert is to have a young apprentice, thus salvaging some pride in his work; also he is motivated to have stimulating and sympathetic company as his only companions are a mad wife and a mean dog. He is extremely lonely due to his realization of his age. Robert wants to be his companion because he feels a human pity for old Sullivan, but also wants his privacy to think, write and be with Jean. Miss O'Hara is motivated to hate old Sullivan because he stands for everything she is afraid of in herself: he is Irish, filthy, lower class, has bad habits, and is old. It is the same basic motivation Robert has in the end of rejecting Sullivan. Jean's motives for loving Robert seem to be superficial — because he is black and a writer, but then she can't stand the pressures of those same things that attracted her in the first place.
>
> In *Young Goodman Brown,* the devil has a contrasting motivation to that of Brown in that he wants Brown to worship him but Brown knows that is evil even though he desires to distinguish good from evil. The people have interesting motivations for what they want Brown to do. In town they try to enforce Brown's piety; in the dream-vision they try to enforce his change to devil-worship. In both cases, they are motivated to change Brown to be like themselves.
>
> *Susan Quick*

Susan's main points then are that the major characters in *Young Goodman Brown* and *Gold Coast* live in a world where they are defined by community attitudes and motives. Brown lives in a larger world where an entire community shapes his attitudes, first toward piety, then toward skepticism. Robert is likewise affected by a community, but the small one of an apartment house full of old people whose shaping influence he is able to withstand once he has tapped them for interesting stories for his writing.

In preparing to write an extended paper comparing and contrasting two pieces of fiction, you have analyzed and done prewriting on plot and on character. That is, you have moved from action to motives for the action. So far you have been concerned mainly with the people in the story, not with the storyteller. The next chapter, on point of view, asks you to look at the storyteller and for the way that narrator affects meaning.

# 14

# Point of View in Fiction

## 26 · DISCOVERING POINT OF VIEW IN SURVIVAL STORIES

*WRITING* For this assignment rewrite a paragraph of your survival story from chapter 12 using the voices of two narrators, neither of whom is the one you used to tell it originally. Attempt to find two voices unlike your own to retell your story. Here are some suggestions for rewriting:

1 How would someone who dislikes you tell the story? What unsavory aspects of your character would come out? Could this same story be turned into gossip in the hands of some people?
2 How would someone who completely misreads your character retell the story; someone who has a stereotype of you different from the way you see yourself?
3 How would a person tell it who likes you too much and who sees nothing of your flaws, uncertainties, or conflicts?
4 How would a totally neutral voice — a third person who has no strong feelings about you except as a good story to tell — relate your narrative?
5 If you have a gift for parody, how would your story be retold by a favorite writer of yours, such as Kurt Vonnegut Jr., or by a movie director such as Sam Peckinpah or by Walt Disney Studios?
6 How would a sociologist, a psychologist, or a professional social worker write it up as a case-study? What kind of jargon might one of these voices use?
7 Can you imagine your story as popular ballad written by Judy Collins or Bob Dylan?

*DISCUSSION* In class, discuss the way shifts in voice affect the story you are telling. Use these questions to guide your discussion:

1 What shifts in character (motivation and revelation especially) and plot (selection of incidents and emphases in particular) occur when the point of view is changed?
2 Which of the three versions is most sympathetic to the main character of the narratives? Why? Which is most hostile or neutral? Why?
3 What kinds of details come to the eye of each narrator? What kinds do some narrators overlook? How does selection of details give you some indication of the nature of the narrator?
4 How far can you go in viewing each narrator as a character in the story? How much does that narrator define himself or herself while telling the story?
5 Does each narrator imply a different set of values as he or she tells the story? Does one admire raw physical courage, for example, and another dismiss it?

## COMMENTS AND EXAMPLES

Now that you have had a chance to rewrite sections of your survival stories using a variety of voices, you have gone some way toward understanding the concept of *point of view* in fiction. For each time that a narrator changes, there is going to be a corresponding shift in the attitudes toward the characters, in the details that come to the narrator's eye, and in the value systems described by each voice. In some stories, characters emerge so strongly that their voices dominate even that of the narrator. Perhaps this idea can be best demonstrated in a narrative that uses largely a *dramatic* point of view; that is, even though in Cole Flegel's paper there is an "I" telling about the horrors of a family reunion, the voices of his relatives are so strong that they characterize themselves as they talk. Cole doesn't need to reveal them. It wouldn't be hard to imagine, for example, the same reunion retold from the angles of Cole's Uncle Bill, his Granny, his Aunt Meg, or his mother since each is so carefully individualized:

> Granny leaned over to where I was sitting. Her Nuit d'Amour perfume nearly knocked me over. Why do all little old ladies wear so much? Oblivious to my uneasiness she whispered "Why don't you go say hello to your cousin Sue. She's such a dear sweet girl."
> Why do I do it? I always feel obligated to come to these awful family reunions. They're worse than funerals. They are worse than weddings. At least there is lots of free booze.
> I'm on my third Scotch-on-the-rocks and Uncle Bill pulls me aside,

"That your motorcycle out front? Sure is big." He said the same about my Honda about half the size of this Harley. My witty reply is "Well, I like it."

My mother, the perfect hostess, is telling Aunt Meg, the retired high school vice principal, her mating call of the clam joke. It will not be appreciated.

I'm on my fifth Scotch-on-the-rocks now. My brother, lucky being in the Army, is at Fort Knox. One helluva excuse for not coming to this gathering.

Next I'm offered the initiation fee for a fraternity, asked again about my bike, and how I like school. My answer to the first is, "No thanks," and "They're OK" to the second pair.

Granny is talking my ear off about my flunking my draft physical, and how that's why I was never very athletic. At least my girlfriend isn't with me, so I don't have to have the sleeping arrangements okayed by Granny or listen to Uncle Bill's questions about her.

"On the rocks or straight up?" is Uncle Bill's question as he sees I'm having difficulty pouring number 6.

"No more rocks," I say; but I think, "No more folks."

*Cole Flegel*

Other narratives, however, depend strongly on the emergence of a strong narrator, one who gives shape to all the events in the story. Notice, for example, the vast changes in Susan Quick's "The Abortion" when a section of it is retold first by an objective third person voice and, secondly, by one of the other people in that story, Tony.

1. CHANGE IN VOICE FROM FIRST PERSON TO THIRD PERSON

She hung on to the receiver as she put it back in its place as though she were clinging to a window ledge five stories off the ground. Finally, staggering back she confronted herself in the mirror. Her face, the one that had always been called beautiful, hung limply now and pale.

"Jesus," she groaned, squinting at the image and fumbling with the bottle of pills. She gulped two down dry and fell back on the bed like some tossed doll. The curtains were heavily drawn, enclosing the mood. Hanging around her were pieces of her life; some from her childhood and some from her newly found womanhood. At the foot of the bed lay "Bunny," an ancient blue-stuffed blind rabbit, worn from countless embraces. A poster of a mountain stream and wildflowers stared from across the room at the floor which was smothered with an oriental rug and strewn with heavy hiking boots and dirty wool socks. Dripping from the closet were long dresses and blue jeans and an old flannel shir·. The radiator hissed at the cigarette ashes and half-smoked remnants laying on the desk which was cluttered with attempted manuscripts and open volumes on the Victorian poets. Silently the door opened and closed; a young man stepped onto the rug and stared back at the mountain scene. His light hair hung loosely around his shoulders; his heavy clothes hung limply around his body. In a single movement he slid out of his coat and sat on the edge of the bed, hesitating to touch the crumpled form in the midst of tangled blankets. His eye caught hold of the drawings and his mind flashed the image of her as she looked at him that day. It was a look he could summon whenever he closed his eyes: he remembered the sunny day in the mountains, laying in the tall grass, reaching over to touch her, and those eyes peering at him through the golden grass. They rolled down the hill, watching mountains tumble in the sky above them. He opened his eyes, lowered them from the drawing to the form on the bed. She was so pale; he felt slightly sick to his stomach. He wanted to take her shape in his arms and sculpt the flowing symmetry which would support her. She looked so fragile; he couldn't imagine seeing her pull her legs and arms together, stand up and walk out of the room with him and into the snowy cold. She would surely crack. His hand, unable to hesitate any longer, brushed a solitary strand of hair from her eyes. She stirred slightly; touching into reality, she opened her eyes. Her muddy gaze flowed into the clarity of his eyes. His soft voice broke the suspension.

"Hey, don't worry. . . . I know. . . . I'm here."

## 2. CHANGE FROM VOICE OF SUSAN TO TONY

The weather that day was the worst I'd seen in Colorado. First of all it was overcast, and for Colorado that's unusual. I remember when I first moved here, an old timer from Leadville told me it only rained on alternate Tuesdays in months beginning with "J." If you figure that out that's only seven days; one week out of 52. And I think that guy was right, out of the whole time I've lived here I can't recall many cloudy days. But that day it was not only overcast, but snowing in a slippery way; cold in the way it gets back East where it penetrates into your bones and the chill stays with you till spring. I knew it was not going to be one of my better days in Colorado when I woke up that morning and was insulted when I looked out my window. I had just gotten back to my room and scraped the peanut butter from my roommate's lunch off my desk, just ready to get into Kant for Philosophy 101 when John appeared standing next to me. John is the kind of guy who just vaporizes when he wants to go somewhere. I really don't think he uses his legs, he just floats down the street. He claims his "aura" (and everybody notices his spiritual mystique) is due to the time he spent a month taking LSD every day in the mountains and painting his masterpiece — in his head of course. Anyway, this time I knew he didn't want to talk to me about the metaphysical poets or impressionist painters; something was really wrong, I could tell by his "aura."

He spoke, "Susan and I are incapable of functioning very rationally in our present emotional states. Our minds are somewhere else entirely. She is really sick and you and I must take her to the hospital in Denver." He spoke as though he'd rehearsed it several times or tape-recorded it when he was rational and was playing it back for me.

"You know you can count on me, man. Anything you need or she needs — you got it." I never said anything I meant more. I wasn't really sure what was wrong, but I knew it was heavy and they were my best friends. I felt honored to help. I didn't need to ask any questions. "I'll see if I can borrow my roommate's car," I said calmly, staring into John's eyes. He was feeling such pain, I tried to take some of it from him so his load wouldn't be too heavy.

"It's already taken care of; Susan's brother gave us his," he said. As I put on my boots and coat, I could sense he was not really in the room with me, his body hung there soulless, like it didn't belong. He was with her. I stared into his eyes and for an instant joined them. He moved (for the first time since he came into the room) to put his arm around me. He too felt the union, "Now all we gotta do is hold on to each other so we can make it down to Denver without sinking."

We walked out into the cold. The chill set in and wouldn't leave. Susan was sitting in the car staring straight ahead. As we approached she smiled slightly. That smile, even though it was little, saved me from sinking. I was really afraid as we approached the car that she was just gonna sit there staring straight ahead like *rigor mortis* had already set in. But she smiled and I knew we'd make it. I climbed in back, although I thought I should drive, John wanted to keep a semblance of normality. I never drove places, John always drove when the three of us went places. That way Susan and I could talk to each other and entertain John, that was just part of the bargain, the triad. As we pulled on to the freeway those clouds really let loose on us. We could hardly see the road. It was so strange, this wasn't Colorado; this wasn't John and Susan and Tony cruising down to Denver. But then I realized it was us; the ties went deeper than that. I leaned up and put my arms around them, understanding our unity even more now. Turning to Susan who was trying so hard to hold on, I gave her a handle: "How're you feeling kid?" I grinned.

In the third person version, details appear describing the room and the emotions felt by John and Susan that couldn't show up logically in the original version. In the first version, the narrator's vision and voice blurred by pain and drugs aren't capable of describing things like the poster, the blue-stuffed rabbit, and the sound of the radiator. Nor can Susan's voice describe the sunny day in the mountains, the sick feeling in John's stomach, nor Tony's feelings about the triad.

In each of the three versions the story of the abortion is central, but its significance changes when a different narrator is introduced to tell it. The concept of point of view illustrates, then, a point most of us already are aware of: "Truth is relative to the beholder."

## 27 · PREWRITING: POINT OF VIEW IN FICTION

*PREWRITING AND DISCUSSION* The main purpose of this third prewriting exercise is to identify whose voices tell the stories that you are studying and then to compare how these voices affect the stories. (Before you complete this assignment, read the section of Comments and Examples.)

Use the following set of questions as a way of turning up evidence about the contrasting features of the two stories you are researching and, secondly, as a basis for class discussion so that you check your readings with other people's.

1. Whose voice tells the story? Is it one of the chief actors in the story — like Huckleberry Finn describing actions he has taken part in? Is it someone who has stood on the sidelines and taken only a minor role — a young man recounting stories of his father's generation? Or is it a voice that appears not to have been on the scene of the action but seems to know a great deal about the characters, seems to know what they are thinking, and even seems to move about freely from one character to another? Contrast and compare the two stories on these bases.
2. What special view does the narrator have of the events and characters in the story? Do the characters see and know the same things as the narrator? Can you imagine how the story would change if told from a different angle?
3. Do the narrator's values emerge as he tells the story, and do they conflict with those of the characters?
4. Do you question the narrator's authority as he tells the story? In other words, do you find his moral judgment or his view of a character flawed?

## COMMENTS AND EXAMPLES

As you saw in exercise 26, writers must decide which is the most suitable voice to tell a story. That choice, or point of view, provides a special angle to view the plot and characters from. It would be hard to imagine, for example, *The Adventures of Huckleberry Finn* in anybody else's voice but Huck's.

> The widow she cried over me, and called me a poor lost lamb, and she called me a lot of other names, too, but she never meant no harm by it. She put me in them new clothes again, and I couldn't do nothing but sweat and sweat, and feel all cramped up. Well, then, the old thing commenced again. The widow rung a bell for supper, and you had to

come to time. When you got to the table you couldn't go right to eating, but you had to wait for the widow to tuck down her head and grumble a little over the victuals, though there warn't really anything the matter with them. That is, nothing only everything was cooked by itself. In a barrel of odds and ends it is different; things get mixed up, and the juice kind of swaps around, and the things go better.

After supper she got out her book and learned me about Moses and the Bulrushers; and I was in a sweat to find out all about him; but by-and-by she let it out that Moses had been dead a considerable long time; so then I didn't care no more about him; because I don't take no stock in dead people.

Pretty soon I wanted to smoke, and asked the widow to let me. But she wouldn't. She said it was a mean practice and wasn't clean, and I must try to not do it any more. That is just the way with some people. They get down on a thing when they don't know nothing about it. Here she was a bothering about Moses, which was no kin to her, and no use to anybody, being gone, you see, yet finding a power of fault with me for doing a thing that had some good in it. And she took snuff too; of course that was all right, because she done it herself.[1]

Huck lacks the malice of most of the people in his society, but Twain's best way of pointing out that malice is to have a rascally child, who is nonetheless forgiving and kind, become so fed up with the likes of Widow Douglas that by the end of the novel he leaves for the West — he's had it with civilization, and will take his chances with savages.

In identifying point of view, it is useful to have some terms in hand when you talk about this technique in fiction.

1 *Participant in the action*

    a *First person:* a witness, recorder, or actor in the story. This voice, characterized by the use of "I," may let you see less but more deeply than another storyteller could. For example, one section of Faulkner's *The Sound and the Fury* is told by an idiot, whose language and vision are scrambled but whose version of things you come to trust as one picture of reality. Or the first person point of view may serve chiefly to characterize the person telling the story. For instance, if a priest tells you a vicious story about another clergyman's vices, the point of view may reveal the narrator's own lack of charity, possibly a greater vice than any he finds in his fellow priest.

    b *Third person:* also a witness or recorder who tells the story but talks about himself or herself in the action as "he," "she," or "the author," but not as "I."

---

1. Mark Twain, *The Adventures of Huckleberry Finn,* ed. H. Hill and W. Blair (San Francisco: Chandler, 1969), p. 18.

a *Third person:* an all-knowing voice who can look into minds, make guesses about the characters' motivations, record conversations, and leap from continent to continent, if necessary, to continue the story. This voice, to insure a kind of credibility, may stay closest to one character and attempt to look at little else outside the main character's mind, conversations, and contacts.

A famous instance of the third person observer occurs in Dostoevsky's *Crime and Punishment,* a novel told in first draft as a confession in the voice of Raskolnikov. The first draft required "too much naiveté and frankness" on the part of Raskolnikov, so Dostoevsky, as his notebooks record, decided on another plan: "Narrative from the author's point of view, as if by an invisible but omniscient being, but not leaving him [Raskolnikov] for even a minute."[2] This shift in point of view in the second draft allowed the novelist to make Raskolnikov a more concealing and cunning person, one whose self-deceptions and changes could be described by the narrator but could be hidden from the character. This shift then from the first person to the *third-person limited omniscient point of view* helped Dostoevsky reshape his great novel.

The narrative voice may not stick close to one character, as Dostoevsky's did to Raskolnikov, but move from person to person, cite historical or literary parallels to what is happening in the plot, and turn out to be like the voice in Fielding's *Tom Jones.* Fielding's narrator is alternately a mocker, scoffer, clown, and wise man. For example, after he describes a battle between Tom Jones and his two principal, boyhood antagonists Thawackim and Blifel, Fielding mocks novels that have murmuring brooks just for the sake of pastoral descriptions. Fielding says the brook in his novel has unusual importance because Jones for the first time has earned the good wishes of Squire Weston and his daughter Sophia. Tom has been injured, and Squire Weston has just urged him to bathe in the gentle stream. As he's bathing, Sophia sees his wounds and expresses her first tender feelings toward Tom.

This is Fielding's description of the brook, which captures his tone and shows the narrator as one who mocks other novels and who enjoys stepping out of the story to talk to the reader:

> The Reader may remember, that in our Description of the Grove we mentioned a murmuring Brook, which Brook did not come there, as such gentle Streams flow through vulgar Romances, with no other purpose than to murmur. No; Fortune had decreed to ennoble this little

---

2. Feodor Dostoevsky, *Crime and Punishment,* ed. by George Gibson (New York: W.W. Norton, Co., 1964), p. 534.

Brook with a higher Honour than any of those which wash the Plains of Arcadia, ever deserved.[3]

What you have seen in rewriting your survival stories from different points of view is that truth is relative to the beholder. Each new narrator will project his or her personality on the story and will select details, conversations, and an organizational scheme that fits his or her version of the tale. Let's look at some prewriting comparing and contrasting *Young Goodman Brown* and *Gold Coast* for the way two quite different narrators shape those stories. These are Pam Robinette's notes on *Young Goodman Brown* and *Gold Coast:*

*GOLD COAST* — FIRST PERSON — THE PARTICIPANT IN THE ACTION

The narrator of *Gold Coast* is the first person: he knows the characters because he talks to them. In this story, the characters see the same incidents as does the narrator, but they do not know how he really feels because he does not verbalize his feelings to them — only to the reader. The reader is inside his head. If the story were told from Miss O'Hara's point of view we would have, for example, a very different view of Sullivan, the janitor, because she hates him so badly. The narrator's values emerge; but they don't conflict until the end of the story when because he does like Sullivan, it's tough for him to leave his responsibility to the man.

I don't question the narrator's authority as he tells the story because he doesn't really have anything to gain or lose by not telling the truth. I think his emotions are stirred in the story, so he tends to look at the other characters with a sense of compassion — a pity for them — until he realizes he must escape and find himself, before he becomes like them and before he begins to lose his desire to write.

*YOUNG GOODMAN BROWN* — THIRD PERSON — OBSERVER

This narrator of *Young Goodman Brown* is a third person observer, who is not quite omniscient — he sees all but does not know all because after reading the story, one is still as confused as the narrator as to what really happened and what was fantasy: was Faith in the woods? Did she drop her ribbons returning from the dark ritual in the forest?

The characters see the same incidents as the narrator but they do not know, like he does, what the main character is thinking, feeling, or what changes take place in him, or for what reasons. For example, they don't know the source of his bitterness at the end. If the story was told by Rev. Deacon Gookin's point of view it would be changed drastically — it would be less effective on the reader because the Reverend could see but the outside of Brown's character, especially since Brown is not a confessional person and wouldn't even tell his minister his doubts.

---

3. Henry Fielding, *Tom Jones*, ed. Sheridan Baker (New York: W. W. Norton, 1973), p. 201.

> There seems to be a difference between Brown's values and the narrator's. The narrator believes in a balanced view, optimism tinted with pessimism; Brown's values are less forgiving — he can't forgive or forget; once he becomes pessimistic, everything is tinted ugly.
>
> Pam Robinette

Pam concludes, "Both Brown and Robert in the two stories escaped from responsibilities. Robert runs faithfully to a new one, but Brown can't handle his old responsibilities once he has lost his faith."

Notice that Pam first identifies the point of view in each story. Then she goes on to explain how the writer's selection of a voice affects what is seen, the values in each story, and the narrator's credibility. This prewriting is especially good in the subtle distinction Pam draws between an all-seeing and an all-knowing narrator in *Young Goodman Brown,* a story with a third-person limited omniscient point of view. The narrator's perplexity keeps us close to Brown's and our own confusion: was it dream or reality in the woods? Pam also ties the two prewriting comments together nicely when she observes that both stories comment on human responsibility — how people behave once they have questioned judgment, an idea that could well serve as the center for a paper comparing and contrasting the stories.

By the same token, Susan Quick's prewriting keeps comparisons and contrasts before the reader:

> Point of View: in *Gold Coast,* the author chooses two points of view; he writes in first person (I), yet he tells the story from a historical perspective. That is, the "I" in the story is himself when he was young and naive compared to the voice telling the story. Thus he becomes a participator in the action (first person) and also an observer (third person). The reader can see the naiveté of the man in the story through the cynical eyes of the wiser man reflecting on "That spring when I had a great deal of potential and no money at all . . . when I was still very young." This device allows the reader to identify with the experience of the "I" in the story, understanding these experiences will result in a loss of naiveté forming the present cynical narrator.
>
> In *Young Goodman Brown,* the narrator chooses the part of an observer yet stays very close to the character, Young Goodman Brown. Hawthorne takes you through Brown's disillusionments as Brown himself experiences them. Yet there is no doubt that Brown is not Hawthorne himself, such as at the end of the story where the narrator sums up the rest of Brown's unhappy life. The narrator has a subtle mocking tone such as when he describes Goody Cloyse mumbling "a prayer doubtless," but the reader knows she is a worshipper of the devil. Later he calls the deacons "holy men" when again the reader knows of their "wickedness." This may be seen as the author's intent to reflect the naiveté of Goodman Brown, but keeping the reader more informed than Brown. The reader suspects the narrator's wisdom in spite of his attempt at being as naive as Brown, and I note a subtle sarcasm in the narrator's tone. His play on

words such as *Faith* and *Goodman* and describing the devil in "grave" attire indicates this ironic tone. The language of the narrator is that of a New England Puritan as he calls the Bible "the sacred truths of our religion," and uses words such as "Howbeit," "prithee," "sayest thou," etc. It is a very formal style to an audience of Puritans. It is as though this is an old tale which the narrator has heard many times (and this the subtle cynicism) when he says, "Some affirm that the lady of the Governor was there," and is told to a sensitive audience, "With reverence be it spoken, the figure bore no slight similitude to some grave divine of the New England churches." Thus the narrator is telling a folk tale with a moralistic sarcastic tone; shyly mocking professed Puritan pieties with his questions as to whether it was all just a dream.

*Susan Quick*

As Pam did in her prewriting, Susan also makes some subtle distinctions. In one example she points out that the narrator in *Gold Coast* has aged a bit when he tells his story. His youth justifies his gullibility, the time and energy that he gives old Sullivan. Notice also that Susan sees that *Gold Coast* could scarcely be as good a portrait of a young writer growing up if another point of view were to tell it: it's important to have the writer's own testimony about his experience. He certainly takes the blame for his failure of commitment, and doesn't emerge totally guiltless in deserting Sullivan. Even an omniscient point of view couldn't have been more honest about that than Robert is. Finally, there is in Susan's prewriting, as in Pam's, the seeds of a good essay. For instance, she could base one on what the stories would be from different points of view, and then go on to show why the first person for *Gold Coast* and third-person limited for *Young Goodman Brown* fit the writers' intentions so well.

# 15

# Language in Fiction

## 28 · DISCOVERING LANGUAGE IN SURVIVAL STORIES

*WRITING* Do a short, written analysis of one of your classmate's survival papers on its use of language. Begin by using a perception from chapter 14: narrators tend to develop and reveal their own personalities as they talk; so do characters as they talk. In other words, study the voices in the survival story that you are examining for what their language reveals. Use these questions to guide your analysis.

1. What are the peculiar language features that distinguish one voice from another in the story you are analyzing? Is one speaker fond of comparisons, clichés, slang, professional jargon? Can you tell the difference between old and young and male or female voices?
2. Does one talk in a bookish way? Another at a street level? Are there other ways of distinguishing the kinds of language employed by the various speakers in the story: prudish, obscene; lively, dull; complicated, simple; elegant, plain; pained, joyful? Can these differences be compared to the voice tones that may be used in reading the narratives aloud?
3. Are there implied as well as direct statements made in the narrative? In other words, is an important idea concealed in an understated conversation?

*DISCUSSION* Use the same list of questions as the basis for a class discussion once you have completed your study.

## COMMENTS AND EXAMPLES

With each new voice in a narrative, whether it be a piece of fiction or one of your survival stories, there should be captured a special sense of that speaker's character; the features that set that person apart from his or her companions in the story, and that separate him or her from the rest of us. Since our language gives away our attitudes, our backgrounds, our ages, and our professions, the writer to remain credible seizes the ways that we ordinarily judge each other by language to individualize people in stories. Look, for example, at a survival paper by Perry Bedard, which is an example of these principles of how we view people through their language:

"Just up the stairs, third door to your left."

I thanked the man; I think he would have preferred a drink. It had been too many years. We tend to get wrapped up in ourselves, I guess. The hall was dark and dingy, very narrow, lightbulbs hanging from the ceiling, fly-catchers, the smell of sleeping people.

I knocked. A large man opened the door without getting out of bed. The room was dark, one solitary lightbulb with a pull string, a narrow bed, a sink, a window that looked out to a brick wall, boots and clothes on the floor, no chairs, no closet, tiny, close. A constant noise of people drinking and shouting came from below the floor. The walls were bare, except for one spot in the center — here was a printed list:

(oldest son) Jim (Feb. 1)
(wife) Agnes (May 22)
Greg (Feb. 29)
Tony (Oct. 16)
Mike (Jun. 7)
~~1146 East 16th Street Calgary~~
102 Maple Street Calgary
(the list repeats for each of his four sons)

It was the names of all his children, their wives, and his grand-children. Dates of birth for all. Addresses neatly crossed out and rewritten for every time they moved — nothing more.

"Is that you, son?"

"Hi Pop," was all I managed to say, a thousand pleasant memories of my childhood burst in my mind. The piggy-back rides when I was small. The going fishing when I grew a little older. The falling of trees when he said I had become a man. It had been a long time.

We spent that day together, just me and him. I bought him the best steak in town. We did a lot of talking. He asked how I was and what I was doing. How was my wife, and especially how was my daughter? He had four sons; and until my daughter, he had had only grandsons. She was very special to him. I could see my words being transformed into photographic images in the back of his mind, images that he could hold on to when I was gone. My stay was very short. I wrote this poem on the way back home:

> They said he didn't care
> That he was a drunk
> That he would curse and swear
> But late each night
> Only God could hear his prayer
>
> Someone said he had a family
> Living somewhere over there
> But that he really didn't care.
>
> He chose to live alone
> In his tiny room
> Above the roar
> Of the drinking and shouting
> Under his floor,
> And they said
> He really didn't care.
>
> But on his wall
> He knew where all
> His children slept each night
> When he knelt to say his prayer.
> *Perry Bedard*

In Perry's narrative, there are only three voices: the landlord's, his father's, and his own. Yet each one is highly individualized. Perry himself, for example, analyzes the voice of the landlord to be saying something they both understand even though it isn't uttered out loud: "Just up the stairs, third door to your left" is spoken in such a way that Perry knows that the man would rather have a drink than a thank-you. This brief conversation which opens the narrative provides a key to the rest of it — Perry's father is down and out because of booze, but all of this is implied, never stated directly. In other words, neither Perry nor his father discuss "the problem" that separated the father from his family in the first place. This is all handled through understated language.

Perry's voice continually talks about his father in forgiving tones. The reader hears about "a constant noise of people drinking and shouting from below the floor," a comment that intensifies the reader's understanding of the flophouse environment. Yet Perry's vision of his father falls not on his father's role in that world but on his father's concern and love for his family — the up-to-date list of names, birthdates, and addresses on the wall. This list is a crucial piece of language evidence, for it tells us first about the father and then something about Perry when he repeats it. The list indicates more than anything else in the narrative that the father and son have a shared attitude — a sense of love and loss over the association they once had and can never regain.

In other words, what might appear to be an insignificant piece of language evidence — a penciled list of names on a wall — becomes the major key to Perry's and his father's attitudes towards each other.

## 29 · PREWRITING: LANGUAGE IN FICTION

*PREWRITING* In addition to identifying and examining the kinds of language in the short stories or novels that you are comparing and contrasting, this exercise asks you to look at outside critical opinions for the first time. Your major focus in looking at the short stories will again be the narrators; your minor focus will be the language traits of the characters. You will study outside critical opinions for what the writers have to say about the major aspects that you have been systematically prewriting on: plot, character, point of view, and language.

Examine your two pieces of fiction in light of the following questions.

1 How do the narrators of the two stories differ in their usage of language?
   a Do they talk on the same level — street or classroom talk? Rich and ornate or plain? Prudish or obscene? Pained or joyful? Is one a fast talker; the other, slow and deliberate?
   b Does one employ imagery or literary references? Does the other talk plain language — the straightforward language of the businessman or soldier who avoids images?
   c Is there a pattern of images used by one of the narrators: dark, light; spirit, flesh; dry, wet; crazy, sane? Does this pattern reveal something about the narrator, or does it relate to a character or major action in the story?
   d Given the narrator's language, would you say that one of the major features of the story is the author's interest in the narrator as a character? That is, is the narrator on stage more than his characters? Or does the narrator's particular view of the events or characters indicate that the author is interested in using the story to reveal the narrator's character?
2 Now go on to examine the other characters' language.
   a How do they differ from each other? Do they speak at a number of levels, from street talk to professional jargon?
   b How much of the characters' revelations are dependent upon what they say in conversation (either talking to themselves or to other

people) as opposed to what they do? Does one author emphasize dialogue more than the second? For what purpose?

c Do the stories differ in the way authors give their characters rich and imagistic language?

DISCUSSION OF LANGUAGE Bring your notes to class and use the same questions as a basis for group discussion.

DISCUSSION OF OUTSIDE READING As mentioned early in this section on fiction, the purpose of bringing in outside reading is to teach you the techniques of documentation and to allow you to weigh outside opinions against your own critical judgments. The essay that you are going to write should not be considered a research paper. Its scope is much more limited than that. But you do need a list of sources where you can find articles or books about the two pieces of fiction that you are comparing and contrasting. These are some steps that you might follow in locating at least one article about each of the two works:

1 Check the card catalogue of your library under the name of the author or the title of the book. Look for works that deal critically with the work.
2 If the work has been published within the past ten years, check the author's name in the *Book Review Index* (Detroit: Gale Research Co., 1965–present). Attempt to find review articles in places like the *New York Times Book Review, Time,* or *Saturday Review,* which have analyzed the new fiction.
3 If the work has been published for over ten years, go one step beyond an examination of the card catalogue or the *Book Review Index*. Most of the following sources will be found either in your reference library or in the periodicals where bibliographies are annually printed:

"Articles in American Studies," *American Quarterly*. 1954–present.

"Annual Bibliography of Short Fiction Explication," *Studies in Short Fiction*. Denver: Alan Swallow, 1964–present.

Bell, Inglish F., and Donald Baird. *The English Novel 1578–1956: A Checklist of Twentieth Century Criticisms*. Denver: Alan Swallow, 1958.

Leary, Lewis. *Articles on American Literature 1950–1967*. Durham, N.C.: Duke University Press, 1970.

Gerstenberger, Donna, and George Hendrick. *The American Novel, 1789–1959: A Checklist of Twentieth Century Criticism*. Denver: Alan Swallow, 1961. (Volume II covers 1960–68.)

*Publication of the Modern Language Association of America: Annual Bibliography.*

Thurston, Jarris, et al. *Short Fiction Criticism: A Checklist of Interpretations since 1925 of Stories and Novelettes (American, British and Continental) 1800–1958*. Denver: Alan Swallow, 1960.

Walker, Warren S. *Twentieth-Century Short Story Explication: Interpretations, 1900–1966, of Short Fiction since 1800.* 2nd ed. Hamden, Conn.: Shoe String Press, 1967.

Woodress, James, ed. *American Literary Scholarship: An Annual.* Durham, N.C.: Duke University Press, 1965–present.

4 Be sure to keep track precisely of the bibliographical information concerning each work:

| ARTICLE | BOOK |
| --- | --- |
| author | author |
| title of article | title |
| title of journal | place of publication |
| volume number | publisher |
| inclusive page numbers of article | date of publication |
| date of journal | page numbers of material used |

5 Be sure to quote exactly any material you use from the sources studied. Also indicate any material that you have put into your own words, or paraphrased from the works. In other words, it's your obligation to cite borrowed words or ideas.

6 Once you have found at least two articles or sections from books, use these questions to take notes:
   a Do the readings have something specifically to say about each aspect of fiction that you have studied so far? 1) Plot? 2) Character? 3) Point of view? 4) Language?
   b Does your perception differ or agree with that of the writers of the outside readings?
   c What kinds of evidence do the critics offer for their judgments? Quotations? Summaries of plot action? What is their major evidence for the way that they read the short stories?

---

## COMMENTS AND EXAMPLES

This prewriting exercise completes the last step in your examination of two pieces of fiction for the way they compare and contrast in aspects of plot, character, point of view, and language. Let's look at some students' prewriting on language in *Young Goodman Brown* and *Gold Coast:* the first, a short story rich in imagery and in its sense of Puritan speakers; the latter, a story plainer in style but rich in its sense of the development of Robert's character.

For example, Jane Ferrier talks about how Goodman Brown's own language indicates how close he is to accepting the devil's view when he begins to doubt his own family and the people in his community:

What pulls Young Goodman Brown steadily over the line is seeing how closely related wife, father, grandfather, Goody Cloyse are to his own sinful tendencies. When Goody Cloyse's staff appears to be a serpent, Goodman is shocked; for he exclaims in surprise, "That old woman taught me my catechism." The narrator adds, "There was a world of meaning in this simple comment."

Jane carefully distinguishes the narrator from Goodman himself:

> The narrator's language casts an attitude of uncertainty on the story by emphasizing its dream-like qualities. Use of verbs of seeming when he describes something even he isn't sure Goodman saw: the narrator talks about the baptismal basin in the rock at the ceremony and asks, "Did it contain water, reddened by the lurid light? or was it blood? or, perchance, a liquid flame?"
>
> *Jane Ferrier*

In contrast to this world of ambiguity and a language to support it in *Young Goodman Brown,* Pam Robinette points out that in *Gold Coast* the narrator and the main character, Robert, uses a plain unadorned style that is "not formal, yet it is not illiterate." She goes on to say that despite this lack of richness in language, the narrator indicates certain changes in his attitude by his change in language at the end of the story. Even though he describes the filth of the Sullivans' apartment, one doesn't get the impression that Robert himself dislikes his surroundings until the end. Pam goes on to say that "I notice that Robert mentions the smallness and closeness of his room and the dark, damp basement where he works. I think this begins to tell something about the narrator, especially when he talks about these aspects of the building toward the end of the story — right before he leaves."

These aspects of language then connect directly to a reader's perception of not only the narrators but also the characters of short stories. Careful prewriting about language furnishes the writer with evidence to flesh out earlier, perhaps skeletal, insights into character and point of view.

# 16

# Theme in Fiction

## 30 · DISCOVERING THEME IN SURVIVAL STORIES

*WRITING* Attempt a one-line definition of the theme of a classmate's survival story, preferably the one that you analyzed in chapter 15 for its language features. Theme, which you are identifying in this assignment, refers to the underlying, general statement about life that the story makes.

These one-line definitions correspond roughly to theme in fiction, that is, an underlying, governing idea that helps give a story its shape. Themes may be highly complex statements on religious or political philosophies and imply a message for how we ought to conduct our lives. For example, I might state the theme of *Young Goodman Brown* like this: "Each of us must reenact the fall of man. That is, be cast out of our innocent state; live a life of exile, pain, and guilt; and then be readmitted to Paradise if we have suffered enough to earn a place and if we are forgiving of other people's guilt." Themes may also be simple statements without moral messages about the nature of human life, complex only in the way that the author chooses to bring an old theme to life: "Life is brief; beauty, fleeting," or perhaps "Courtship is Heaven; marriage, Hell." Use the following questions to help you discover the themes of the survival stories.

1  What statements about life do your survival stories make? Can you see an attitude toward life expressed or implied in the story?
   NOTE: The themes of your survival stories, the central ideas that implicitly or explicitly govern them, are not attempts to

reduce your stories to one-line formulas. Rather they are an attempt to discover the essence of one's thinking or attitudes, often an act which may show that almost any story you told about yourself would result in a variation on one of your major themes. For example, if you are a person who advocates enjoying each day, celebrating the flesh, that attitude or idea would show up in most stories that you told. On the other hand, if you believe in denying the flesh, planning your future carefully, your stories would be shot through with this notion.

2  Are there any famous one-line sayings that capture the theme of the story you are working with? "Familiarity breeds contempt"; "Beauty is only skin deep"; or "You can't make a silk purse out of a sow's ear."

DISCUSSION  Use the questions above as the basis for a class discussion of theme.

## COMMENTS AND EXAMPLES

The theme of a story, its underlying statement about some aspect of life, may be explicit or implicit. That is, writers may let you know what that statement is, or they may allow you to come to your own conclusion. Also it's possible to come to different conclusions about the theme of a story. Look, for instance, at Wayne Olson's survival narrative and the variety of statements of theme concerning it:

> Waking after a restless night's sleep, my eyes focused on the ceiling of my van. Immediately flinging the side door open, I staggered out, baked by a July, Texas sun. I fell into the camp's swimming pool. I had been stranded in Houston for the last week. A letter with money was coming, but until it came there was nothing I could do but sit and sweat in a town of over 1-1/2 million strangers.
> 
> I pulled myself out of the pool and squinted to find my way back to my van through the maze of the apartment building complexes. Finding the van I put my glasses on. A row of blurred reflections turned into rows of parked cars. I started across the asphalt to the gas station around the corner.
> 
> The clock showed ten o'clock Standard Station Time. The thermometer read 90°; the humidity was unbearable. My daily stroll to the Post Office went past a very scenic plaza, several gas stations, and a pair of twin glass skyscrapers. I thought the design of this city was to reflect enough heat on the pedestrians so that everyone would drive a car, which would give Houston oil companies and car dealers a better living.

FICTION

I pushed the Post Office door open and entered.

"Ya?" asked the stranger behind the General Delivery Counter.

"Is there a letter here for Wayne Olson?" My pulse reflected my anticipation. "Ah, nope. Sorry, not today."

"Another day in Hell!" I mumbled to myself while shuffling through the faceless crowd. Deciding to visit the only familiar faces in town, I set course for the Wanted posters. One particular criminal wanted for mail fraud reminded me of the man who had dismissed me from his counter.

By now it was time to find dinner. After half an hour, I drifted across the blazing concrete into a large, bustling supermarket which I had never seen. I grabbed a cart and packed it quickly with anything in sight. However when passing the fruit counters I'd gorge myself with cherries, berries, carrots, and apples, and bananas. Leaving the cart, I would buy a carton of milk on the way out.

The rest of the day I spent in a hospital lobby reading old magazines. Hours later finishing a decrepit *Better Homes and Gardens*, I noticed darkness had slipped in.

Stepping out the door the night traffic caught me off guard.

"You wouldn't have a spare dime?" I inquired to a woman while waiting at a crosswalk. I glanced into her eyes. She was looking at my face. This small human exchange stunned me! She dropped a quarter in my open hand and trotted across the street.

*Wayne Olson*

Linda Adamczyk, in commenting on Wayne's paper, said that she saw three possible statements of theme. Two concerned Wayne's way of making do and of finding food and shelter: "Where there's a will there's a way," and "Necessity is the mother of invention." But she went on to say that these two proverbs didn't adequately point out what the story had to say. Since those two proverbs say nothing about human needs for companionship, Linda offered this more complex statement as the third alternative: "When a person is attempting to survive in times of stress, ordinary gestures like eye contact with a stranger take on special importance as do the small crimes a person may commit simply to feed oneself. Everything is heightened that would be overlooked at other times." So even in one person's view of a fairly straightforward survival story, there are a variety of things the narrative says about human nature.

Therefore, in trying to state the theme of one of your classmate's stories or of a fictional work by a professional writer, it isn't necessary to come up with the "right" perception. Just try to see the story in its totality and to come to some overall judgment about what the story itself says — as if it had a voice of its own; as if in listening to it closely, you could hear its statement about itself.

## 31 · WRITING A DOCUMENTED PAPER ON FICTION

*PREWRITING* Contrast and compare the statements about life, the themes, of the two stories you are soon to write about. Discuss these statements of theme in class.

Paul Faber, for example, sees both *Gold Coast* and *Young Goodman Brown* as making statements about aspects of human perception. "In *Gold Coast,* Robert finally perceives that he has become bound to Sullivan for the wrong reason — pity. While he still has choices, Robert has freedom denied to the old man. Hence Robert can choose to leave; Old Sullivan can't." Then about *Young Goodman Brown:* "Man adjusts his attitude to what he thinks he sees, or perhaps wants to see, not to what really exists. Hence Goodman, on the basis of what he appears to have seen, chooses a cynical outlook for the balance of his life."

*WRITING* Now that you have completed five prewriting assignments, write your essay comparing and contrasting the two pieces of fiction that you have been studying. The following suggestions may help in organizing your paper:

1 In the first approach, you might discuss three or four aspects of fiction — plot, character, point of view, language, or theme — in an extended paper. This way you could go back through your prewriting and find the most telling comparisons and contrasts. Then you could organize these from, let's say, the least telling to the most telling feature. If your notes on plot, for example, are more extensive than on language, that might indicate the weight could be given to plot in your essay. It would also indicate that plot should be placed at one of the climactic points in your organizational scheme.
2 Another approach would be to take an aspect of character such as motivation, and to show how point of view, plot, and language help shape a comparative reading of the motivation of characters in the two stories. Or you could look back at your prewriting for the idea that seems most striking to you — your favorite insight into the two works — and then you could organize a paper around that idea.
3 Note on comparison and contrast papers: These papers tend to be more successfully organized if you identify features that both stories share or don't share rather than if you discuss one story fully in one half of the paper, then go on to the second in the last half. For example, let's say that you have identified the plot of *Gold Coast* as simple and that of *Young Goodman Brown* as complex. Then, in a part of the paper devoted to plot, you would talk about both stories, stressing and

supporting the contrasting features. For example, you could show how the action in *Gold Coast* is simple: Robert's decision to give up on a good commitment gone bad. *Young Goodman Brown,* on the other hand, describes the complex action of a man who can't decide easily what he wants to do; who doesn't know whether what he has done is dream or reality, and who finally goes on living with his halfhearted decision and his seeming vision as if he had discovered the blackest truth at the heart of the world.

This kind of organization, keeping plot in one section of your paper, holds the paper more tightly together than if those two insights about plot are scattered at either end of a long paper. The reader needs a bridge between the two insights. A comparison and contrast scheme which sets the two stories side by side under common headings can best provide that bridge.

4 Providing the information for footnoting a paper is not difficult if you have kept track of the bibliographical information as you have done your outside reading. Following is the information which a note should include:

  a Cite your first reference to a book or article in full:

    1 BOOK: author's name in normal order, title in full and in italics (publication data in parentheses and in this order: place of publication, publisher, date of publication), page number or numbers of cited and paraphrased material. Sample: [1]Frederick Crews, *The Sins of the Fathers: Hawthorne's Psychological Themes* (New York: Oxford University Press, 1966), pp. 106–110.

    2 ARTICLE: author's name in normal order, title of article in full and in quotation marks, title of journal in full and in italics, volume number (date of publication in parentheses), page number or numbers of cited and paraphrased material. Sample: [2]R. V. Cassill, "Tales of an Old World and a New," *Book World,* 18(May 25, 1969), 4.

  b Cite immediate second references to a work as *Ibid.,* followed by the page number.

  c If a new work intervenes, cite the second reference by indicating the author's last name:
Sample: [3]Crews, p. 115.

---

# COMMENTS AND EXAMPLES

The essay assigned in exercise 31 culminates your study of fiction. Here you use the preliminary work done throughout part 3. This assignment emphasizes selecting a topic out of a wealth of material and incorporating, if it's worthwhile, reading from the outside that contributes to your own ideas.

Jane Ferrier chose motivation as a topic in her examination of *Young Goodman Brown* and *Gold Coast*. Jane's paper demonstrates how careful prewriting furnishes you a way to think through a complex paper.

CURIOSITY IN *YOUNG GOODMAN BROWN* AND *GOLD COAST*

The fact that curiosity can be a damaging motivation is reflected in the old saying, "Curiosity killed a cat." In this paper, I want to look at two characters who don't die of it but who are radically altered by their curiosity.

Young Goodman Brown, the main character of Hawthorne's story by the same name, is a man who prides himself for his pious life. To be sure, he is young and married to a woman equally as pious, but Goodman Brown has one small trait that doesn't fit into Puritan Massachusetts; Brown is guilty of curiosity. Oh, not just plain curiosity, but curiosity about *sin*. Goodman Brown was motivated by a desire to see the "other side" of life. For what other reason would he have made an appointment to travel to meet with the Devil that night? Curiosity — that was what forced him onto the course at first and what gave the Devil the excuse to keep him there. Robert, the main character in McPherson's *Gold Coast*, is driven by the same force as the basis for his actions.

Robert is a black man in *Gold Coast* who wishes to create a certain life for himself. Specifically, he does not want the stereotyped position of the intellectual black man incarcerated in an ivory tower. He too has that basic curiosity about the segment of the society he has previously had little to do with. Instead of contact with the devil, he wants to experience the great varieties of life so that as a writer he can grow.

His answer is to work as a janitor in an apartment building full of old or disappointed people. His curiosity about people propelled him to this decaying old building; but curiosity alone can't keep him there. His role as a developing writer compels him to stay on, a compulsion to tough things out not shared by Young Goodman Brown. I can't imagine Goodman jotting his new cynical views in a notebook, for example.

The two characters, Goodman and Robert, are similar in that curiosity drives them both into situations which didn't quite turn out as they'd expected. In the case of Goodman Brown, curiosity about evil brings him as far as the forest rite. For example, he was inquisitive about tidbits of information that the Devil dropped that kept him hiking into the woods. In one case, the Devil coaxed him by resembling Goodman's grandfather. The fiend also mentions having been alongside Brown's father and grandfather during Indian massacres. Both incidents suggest family ties. In response to Brown's worries about his ability to face the village again, the Devil causes him to meet some of the most pious church members, all making for the same fiendish meeting. Brown stays curious until he thinks he sees Faith, his wife, at the evil gathering, a completely unexpected situation, one he hadn't bargained for. The possibility that she is just as curious about sin as he drives him mad. Frederick Crews gives *Young Goodman Brown* a much more sexual interpretation than I do. Even though I can't fully buy his point, we do agree that curiosity is at the basis of Brown's first decision to go into the woods: "Thus, Goodman Brown, a curiously preoccupied bridegroom, escapes from his wife's embraces to a vision of general nastiness. The accusation that Brown's Devil makes against all mankind . . . clearly issues from Brown's own horror of adulthood, his inability to accept the place of sexuality in married love."[1] Whatever the source of Goodman's curiosity, Crew's version or mine, the effect on Brown's character is the same: a vision of evil so complete that he lives out his days a cynical, suspicious man.

Robert's motivation also drives him into a new posture and a set of unexpected situations, but his character is influenced differently. He chooses to examine a side of society foreign to him — like Goodman. But unlike Goodman, he doesn't find the new side distasteful. For here, he is in a building full of material for his writing. What Robert doesn't expect is that he will be drawn into the web of life in the building. After all, he's just a janitor. But when he becomes aware of just how involved he's gotten with the lives of the tenants, he wants out. He can't be independent — they are turning him into one of them. He's losing his writer's distance. The next change had to come for Robert: his desire is to break out of the janitor mold, just as he'd wanted to break out of the "black" mold. For instance, he can't just stand by and observe the Sullivans, man, wife, and dog. He gets more than he bargains for — just like Goodman Brown — and he finds that the death of Sullivan's dog affects far more than his writer's curiosity. It affects his humanity. R. V. Cassill makes a similar observation when he says that "the young writer in *Gold Coast* endures a season of small gains and belated discoveries to earn nothing more comfortable than a Sisyphean vision of the treadmill turned by the human heart."[2] In other words, a writer can't just give up his human responsibilities and merely watch. The writer too walks on the treadmill that Cassill talks about.

So it seems that the force behind each of the characters in the beginning is curiosity, and curiosity then gives way to other motivations. Brown, who starts with a curiosity about the nature of sin, is subsequently motivated by the tempting information that the Devil drops about people Brown knows. But then he is driven by doubts about any goodness at all in the world; he sees only sin. On the other hand, Robert, who is also curious about a life different from his previous experience, loses his initial purpose of accumulating writing material. For Robert, his purpose backfires when he finds himself

---

[1] *The Sins of the Fathers: Hawthorne's Psychological Themes* (New York: Oxford Univ. Press, 1966), p. 102.
[2] "Tales of an Old World and a New," *Book World* (May 25, 1969), 4.

trapped by the realization that he's caught in the entangled web of lives in the building. He wants out, but the force holding him to the people is too strong. They aren't "characters" now; they are people who need him, if only to drink beer with and to bemoan their condition with him. When he runs away, it is both to save his writing and disentangle himself from the bad bargains he has made. Both characters are alone at the end of their stories. Curiosity drives Robert and Goodman Brown to know people and to get involved in the messy sides of human nature. But, the themes of both stories go on to say, both characters get fed up with what they see and choose to be no longer involved.

Curiosity then drives both Robert and Goodman up crooked paths and into unexpected situations: what you look for may not be what you get.

*Jane Ferrier*

The topic for Jane's paper spins off from her study of character, stressing especially the characters' motives. Her paper is nicely focused on the topic of curiosity, but doesn't confine itself to a study of character. For instance, the effects of curiosity on Robert and Goodman Brown can be measured only in terms of plot — the actions that result when curiosity compels each into surprising situations. That is, Jane had to be able to see the actions that resulted because Robert and Goodman were inquisitive before she could talk about how their characters change when they learn things that startle them.

Jane's paper also coherently develops into a comparison and contrast statement of the theme shared by the two stories — that curious people can see too much. Neither character can live with human responsibilities after he has seen what he thought he wanted to learn. In other words, Jane had to be able to spot the themes of both stories in order to balance so carefully her comments about each: (1) both main characters share curiosity as a driving force; (2) both are driven into unexpected situations; (3) but both react differently to the new situations and to the motivations that replace curiosity; (4) and finally both share a common theme.

Jane's paper, then, is a good example of a comparison and contrast essay on fiction. Not only does she trust her own perceptions and keep the quotations from outside sources to a minimum, but she also has done such thorough preparation that her paper is largely a matter of selecting a specific topic from a large batch of material.

# FICTION READINGS

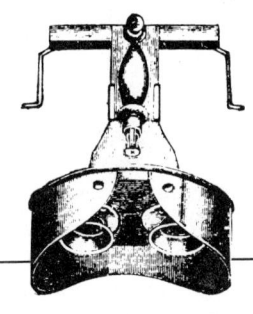

## YOUNG GOODMAN BROWN

—— *Nathaniel Hawthorne*

Young Goodman Brown came forth at sunset into the street at Salem village; but put his head back, after crossing the threshold, to exchange a parting kiss with his young wife. And Faith, as the wife was aptly named, thrust her own pretty head into the street, letting the wind play with the pink ribbons of her cap while she called to Goodman Brown.

"Dearest heart," whispered she, softly and rather sadly, when her lips were close to his ear, "prithee put off your journey until sunrise and sleep in your own bed to-night. A lone woman is troubled with such dreams and such thoughts that she's afeared of herself sometimes. Pray tarry with me this night, dear husband, of all nights in the year."

"My love and my Faith," replied young Goodman Brown, "of all nights in the year, this one night must I tarry away from thee. My journey, as thou callest it, forth and back again, must needs be done 'twixt now and sunrise. What, my sweet, pretty wife, dost thou doubt me already, and we but three months married?"

"Then God bless you!" said Faith, with the pink ribbons; "and may you find all well when you come back."

"Amen!" cried Goodman Brown. "Say thy prayers, dear Faith, and go to bed at dusk, and no harm will come to thee."

So they parted; and the young man pursued his way until, being about to turn the corner by the meeting-house, he looked back and saw the head of Faith still peeping after him with a melancholy air, in spite of her pink ribbons.

"Poor little Faith!" thought he, for his heart smote him. "What a wretch am I to leave her on such an errand! She talks of dreams, too. Methought as she spoke there was trouble in her face, as if a dream had warned her what work is to be done to-night. But no, no; 't would kill her to think it. Well, she's a blessed angel on earth; and after this one night I'll cling to her skirts and follow her to heaven."

With this excellent resolve for the future, Goodman Brown felt himself justified in making more haste on his present evil purpose. He had taken a dreary road, darkened by all the gloomiest trees of the forest, which barely stood aside to let the narrow path creep through, and closed immediately behind. It was all as lonely as could be; and there is this peculiarity in such a solitude, that the traveller knows not who may be concealed by the innumerable trunks and the thick boughs overhead; so that with lonely footsteps he may yet be passing through an unseen multitude.

"There may be a devilish Indian behind every tree" said Goodman Brown to himself; and he glanced fearfully behind him as he added, "What if the devil himself should be at my very elbow!"

His head being turned back, he passed a crook of the road, and, looking forward again, beheld the figure of a man, in grave and decent attire, seated at the foot of an old tree. He arose at Goodman Brown's approach and walked onward side by side with him.

"You are late, Goodman Brown," said he. "The clock of the Old South was striking as I came through Boston, and that is full fifteen minutes agone."

"Faith kept me back a while," replied the young man, with a tremor in his voice, caused by the sudden appearance of his companion, though not wholly unexpected.

It was now deep dusk in the forest, and deepest in that part of it where these two were journeying. As nearly as could be discerned, the second traveller was about fifty years old, apparently in the same rank of life as Goodman Brown, and bearing a considerable resemblance to him, though perhaps more in expression than features.

Still they might have been taken for father and son. And yet, though the elder person was as simply clad as the younger, and as simple in manner too, he had an indescribable air of one who knew the world, and who would not have felt abashed at the governor's dinner table or in King William's court, were it possible that his affairs should call him thither. But the only thing about him that could be fixed upon as remarkable was his staff, which bore the likeness of a great black snake, so curiously wrought that it might almost be seen to twist and wriggle itself like a living serpent. This, of course, must have been an ocular deception, assisted by the uncertain light.

"Come, Goodman Brown," cried his fellow-traveller, "this is a dull pace for the beginning of a journey. Take my staff, if you are so soon weary."

"Friend," said the other, exchanging his slow pace for a full stop, "having kept covenant by meeting thee here, it is my purpose now to return whence I came. I have scruples touching the matter thou wot'st of."

"Sayest thou so?" replied he of the serpent, smiling apart. "Let us walk on, nevertheless, reasoning as we go; and if I convince thee not thou shalt turn back. We are but a little way in the forest yet."

"Too far! too far!" exclaimed the goodman, unconsciously resuming his walk. "My father never went into the woods on such an errand, nor his father before him. We have been a race of honest men and good Christians since the days of the martyrs; and shall I be the first of the name of Brown that ever took this path and kept —"

"Such company, thou wouldst say," observed the elder person, interpreting his pause. "Well said, Goodman Brown! I have been as well acquainted with your family as with ever a one among the Puritans; and that's no trifle to say. I helped your grandfather, the constable, when he lashed the Quaker woman so smartly through the streets of Salem; and it was I that brought your father a pitch-pine knot, kindled at my own hearth, to set fire to an Indian village, in King Philip's war. They were my good friends, both; and many a pleasant walk have we had along this path, and returned merrily after midnight. I would fain be friends with you for their sake."

"If it be as thou sayest," replied Goodman Brown, "I marvel they never spoke of these matters; or, verily, I marvel not, seeing that the least rumor of the sort would have driven them from New England. We are a people of prayer, and good works to boot, and abide no such wickedness."

"Wickedness or not," said the traveller with the twisted staff, "I have a very general acquaintance here in New England. The deacons of many a church have drunk the communion wine with me; the selectmen of divers towns make me their chairman; and a majority of the Great and General Court are firm supporters of my interest. The governor and I, too — But these are state secrets."

"Can this be so?" cried Goodman Brown, with a stare of amazement at his undisturbed companion. "Howbeit, I have nothing to do with the governor and council; they have their own ways, and are no rule for a simple husbandman like me. But, were I to go on with thee, how should I meet the eye of that good old man, our minister, at Salem village? Oh, his voice would make me tremble both Sabbath day and lecture day."

Thus far the elder traveller had listened with due gravity; but now burst into a fit of irrepressible mirth, shaking himself so violently that his snake-like staff actually seemed to wriggle in sympathy.

"Ha! ha! ha!" shouted he again and again; then composing himself, "Well, go on, Goodman Brown, go on; but, prithee, don't kill me with laughing."

"Well, then, to end the matter at once," said Goodman Brown, considerably nettled, "there is my wife, Faith. It would break her dear little heart; and I'd rather break my own."

"Nay, if that be the case," answered the other, "e'en go thy ways, Goodman Brown. I would not for twenty old women like the one hobbling before us that Faith should come to any harm."

As he spoke he pointed his staff at a female figure on the path, in whom Goodman Brown recognized a very pious and exemplary dame, who had taught him his catechism in youth, and was still his moral and spiritual adviser, jointly with the minister and Deacon Gookin.

"A marvel, truly, that Goody Cloyse should be so far in the wilderness at nightfall," said he. "But with your leave, friend, I shall take a cut through the woods until we have left this Christian woman behind. Being a stranger to you, she might ask whom I was consorting with and whither I was going."

"Be it so," said his fellow-traveller. "Betake you the woods, and let me keep the path."

Accordingly the young man turned aside, but took care to watch his companion, who advanced softly along the road until he had come within a staff's length of the old dame. She, meanwhile, was making the best of her way, with singular speed for so aged a woman, and mumbling some indistinct words — a prayer, doubtless — as she went. The traveller put forth his staff and touched her withered neck with what seemed the serpent's tail.

"The devil!" screamed the pious old lady.

"Then Goody Cloyse knows her old friend?" observed the traveller, confronting her and leaning on his writhing stick.

"Ah, forsooth, and is it your worship indeed?" cried the good dame. "Yea, truly is it, and in the very image of my old gossip,

Goodman Brown, the grandfather of the silly fellow that now is. But — would your worship believe it? — my broomstick hath strangely disappeared, stolen, as I suspect, by that unhanged witch, Goody Cory, and that, too, when I was all anointed with the juice of smallage, and cinquefoil, and wolf's bane —"

"Mingled with fine wheat and the fat of a new-born babe," said the shape of old Goodman Brown.

"Ah, your worship knows the recipe," cried the old lady, cackling aloud. "So, as I was saying, being all ready for the meeting, and no horse to ride on, I made up my mind to foot it; for they tell me there is a nice young man to be taken into communion to-night. But now your good worship will lend me your arm, and we shall be there in a twinkling."

"That can hardly be," answered her friend. "I may not spare you my arm, Goody Cloyse; but here is my staff, if you will."

So saying, he threw it down at her feet, where, perhaps, it assumed life, being one of the rods which its owner had formerly lent to the Egyptian magi. Of this fact, however, Goodman Brown could not take cognizance. He had cast up his eyes in astonishment, and, looking down again, beheld neither Goody Cloyse nor the serpentine staff, but his fellow-traveller alone, who waited for him as calmly as if nothing had happened.

"That old woman taught me my catechism," said the young man; and there was a world of meaning in this simple comment.

They continued to walk onward, while the elder traveller exhorted his companion to make good speed and persevere in the path, discoursing so aptly that his arguments seemed rather to spring up in the bosom of his auditor than to be suggested by himself. As they went, he plucked a branch of maple to serve for a walking stick, and began to strip it of the twigs and little boughs, which were wet with evening dew. The moment his fingers touched them they became strangely withered and dried up as with a week's sunshine. Thus the pair proceeded, at a good free pace, until suddenly, in a gloomy hollow of the road, Goodman Brown sat himself down on the stump of a tree and refused to go any farther.

"Friend," said he, stubbornly, "my mind is made up. Not another step will I budge on this errand. What if a wretched old woman do choose to go to the devil when I thought she was going to heaven: is that any reason why I should quit my dear Faith and go after her?"

"You will think better of this by and by," said his acquaintance, composedly. "Sit here and rest yourself a while; and when you feel like moving again, there is my staff to help you along."

Without more words, he threw his companion the maple stick, and was as speedily out of sight as if he had vanished into the deepening gloom. The young man sat a few moments by the roadside, applauding himself greatly, and thinking with how clear a conscience he should meet the minister in his morning walk, nor shrink from the eye of good old Deacon Gookin. And what calm sleep would be his that very night, which was to have been spent so wickedly, but so purely and sweetly now, in the arms of Faith! Amidst these pleasant and praiseworthy meditations, Goodman Brown heard the tramp of horses along the road, and deemed it advisable to conceal himself within the verge of the forest, conscious of the guilty purpose that had brought him thither, though now so happily turned from it.

On came the hoof tramps and the voices of the riders, two grave old voices, conversing soberly as they drew near. These mingled sounds appeared to pass along the road, within a few yards of the young man's hiding-place; but, owing doubtless to the depth of the gloom at that particular spot, neither the travellers nor their steeds were visible. Though their figures brushed the small boughs by the wayside, it could not be seen that they intercepted, even for a moment, the faint gleam from the strip of bright sky athwart which they must have passed. Goodman Brown alternately crouched and stood on tiptoe, pulling aside the branches and thrusting forth his head as far as he durst without discerning so much as a shadow. It vexed him the more, because he could have sworn, were such a thing possible, that he recognized the voices of the minister and Deacon Gookin, jogging along quietly, as they were wont to do, when bound to some ordination or ecclesiastical council. While yet within hearing, one of the riders stopped to pluck a switch.

"Of the two, reverend sir," said the voice like the deacon's, "I had rather miss an ordination dinner than to-night's meeting. They tell me that some of our community are to be here from Falmouth and beyond, and others from Connecticut and Rhode Island, besides several of the Indian powwows, who, after their fashion, know almost as much deviltry as the best of us. Moreover, there is a goodly young woman to be taken into communion."

"Mighty well, Deacon Gookin!" replied the solemn old tones of the minister. "Spur up, or we shall be late. Nothing can be done, you know, until I get on the ground."

The hoofs clattered again; and the voices, talking so strangely in the empty air, passed on through the forest, where no church had ever been gathered or solitary Christian prayed. Whither, then, could these holy men be journeying so deep into the heathen wilderness? Young Goodman Brown caught hold of a tree for support, being ready to sink down on the ground, faint and overburdened with the heavy sickness of his heart. He looked up to the sky, doubting whether there really was a heaven above him. Yet there was the blue arch, and the stars brightening in it.

"With heaven above and Faith below, I will yet stand firm against the devil!" cried Goodman Brown.

While he still gazed upward into the deep arch of the firmament and had lifted his hands to pray, a cloud, though no wind was stirring, hurried across the zenith and hid the brightening stars. The blue sky was still visible, except directly overhead, where this black mass of cloud was sweeping swiftly northward. Aloft in the air, as if from the depths of the cloud, came a confused and doubtful sound of voices. Once the listener fancied that he could distinguish the accents of townspeople of his own, men and women, both pious and ungodly, many of whom he had met at the communion table, and had seen others rioting at the tavern. The next moment, so indistinct were the sounds, he doubted whether he had heard aught but the murmur of the old forest, whispering without a wind. Then came a stronger swell of those familiar tones, heard daily in the sunshine at Salem village, but never until now from a cloud of night. There was one voice, of a young woman, uttering lamentations, yet with an uncertain sorrow, and entreating for some favor, which, perhaps, it would grieve her to obtain; and all the unseen multitude, both saints and sinners, seemed to encourage her onward.

"Faith!" Shouted Goodman Brown, in a voice of agony and desperation; and the echoes of the forest mocked him, crying, "Faith! Faith!" as if bewildered wretches were seeking her all through the wilderness.

The cry of grief, rage, and terror was yet piercing the night, when the unhappy husband held his breath for a response. There was a scream, drowned immediately in a louder murmur of voices, fading into far-off laughter, as the dark cloud swept away, leaving the clear and silent sky above Goodman Brown. But something fluttered lightly down through the air and caught on the branch of a tree. The young man seized it, and beheld a pink ribbon.

"My Faith is gone!" cried he, after one stupefied moment. "There is no good on earth; and sin is but a name. Come, devil; for to thee is this world given."

And, maddened with despair, so that he laughed loud and long, did Goodman Brown grasp his staff and set forth again, at such a rate that he seemed to fly along the forest path rather than to walk or run. The road grew wilder and drearier and more faintly traced, and vanished at length, leaving him in the heart of the dark wilderness, still rushing onward with the instinct that guides mortal man to evil. The whole forest was peopled with frightful sounds — the creaking of the trees, the howling of wild beasts, and the yell of Indians; while sometimes the wind tolled like a distant church bell, and sometimes gave a broad roar around the traveller, as if all

Nature were laughing him to scorn. But he was himself the chief horror of the scene, and shrank not from its other horrors.

"Ha! ha! ha!" roared Goodman Brown when the wind laughed at him. "Let us hear which will laugh loudest. Think not to frighten me with your deviltry. Come witch, come wizard, come Indian powwow, come devil himself, and here comes Goodman Brown. You may as well fear him as he fear you."

In truth, all through the haunted forest there could be nothing more frightful than the figure of Goodman Brown. On he flew among the black pines, brandishing his staff with frenzied gestures, now giving vent to an inspiration of horrid blasphemy, and now shouting forth such laughter as set all the echoes of the forest laughing like demons around him. The fiend in his own shape is less hideous than when he rages in the breast of man. Thus sped the demoniac on his course, until, quivering among the trees, he saw a red light before him, as when the felled trunks and branches of a clearing have been set on fire, and throw up their lurid blaze against the sky, at the hour of midnight. He paused, in a lull of the tempest that had driven him onward, and heard the swell of what seemed a hymn, rolling solemnly from a distance with the weight of many voices. He knew the tune; it was a familiar one in the choir of the village meeting-house. The verse died heavily away, and was lengthened by a chorus, not of human voices, but of all the sounds of the benighted wilderness pealing in awful harmony together. Goodman Brown cried out, and his cry was lost to his own ear by its unison with the cry of the desert.

In the interval of silence he stole forward until the light glared full upon his eyes. At one extremity of an open space, hemmed in by the dark wall of the forest, arose a rock, bearing some rude, natural resemblance either to an altar or a pulpit, and surrounded by four blazing pines, their tops aflame, their stems untouched, like candles at an evening meeting. The mass of foliage that had overgrown the summit of the rock was all on fire, blazing high into the night and fitfully illuminating the whole field. Each pendent twig and leafy festoon was in a blaze. As the red light arose and fell, a numerous congregation alternately shone forth, then disappeared in shadow, and again grew, as it were, out of the darkness, peopling the heart of the solitary woods at once.

"A grave and dark-clad company," quoth Goodman Brown.

In truth they were such. Among them, quivering to and fro between gloom and splendor, appeared faces that would be seen next day at the council board of the province, and others which, Sabbath after Sabbath, looked devoutly heavenward, and benignantly over the crowded pews, from the holiest pulpits in the land. Some affirm that the lady of the governor was there. At least there were high dames well known to her, and wives of honored husbands, and widows, a great multitude, and ancient maidens, all of excellent repute, and fair young girls, who trembled lest their mothers should espy them. Either the sudden gleams of light flashing over the obscure field bedazzled Goodman Brown, or he recognized a score of the church members of Salem village famous for their especial sanctity. Good old Deacon Gookin had arrived, and waited at the skirts of that venerable saint, his revered pastor. But, irreverently consorting with these grave, reputable, and pious people, these elders of the church, these chaste dames and dewy virgins, there were men of dissolute lives and women of spotted fame, wretches given over to all mean and filthy vice, and suspected even of horrid crimes. It was strange to see that the good shrank not from the wicked, nor were the sinners abashed by the saints. Scattered also among their pale-faced enemies were the Indian priests, or powwows, who had often scared their native forest with more hideous incantations than any known to English witchcraft.

"But where is Faith?" thought Goodman Brown; and, as hope came into his heart, he trembled.

Another verse of the hymn arose, a slow and mournful strain, such as the pious love, but joined to words which expressed all that our nature can conceive of sin, and darkly hinted at far more. Unfathomable to mere mortals is the lore of fiends. Verse after verse was sung; and still the chorus of the desert swelled between like the deepest tone of a mighty organ; and with the final peal of that dreadful anthem there came a sound, as if the roaring wind, the rushing streams, the howling beasts, and every other voice of the unconcerted wilderness were mingling and according with the voice of guilty man in homage to the prince of all. The four blazing pines threw up a loftier flame, and obscurely discovered shapes and visages of horror on the smoke wreaths above the impious assembly. At the same moment the fire on the rock shot redly forth and formed a glowing arch above its base, where now appeared a figure. With reverence be it spoken, the figure bore no slight similitude, both in garb and manner, to some grave divine of the New England churches.

"Bring forth the converts!" cried a voice that echoed through the field and rolled into the forest.

At the word, Goodman Brown stepped forth from the shadow of the trees and approached the congregation, with whom he felt a loathful brotherhood by the sympathy of all that was wicked in his heart. He could have well-nigh sworn that the shape of his own dead father beckoned him to advance, looking downward from a smoke wreath, while a woman, with dim features of despair, threw out her hand to warn him back. Was it his mother? But he had no power to retreat one step, nor to resist, even in thought, when the minister and good old Deacon Gookin seized his arms and led him to the blazing rock. Thither came also the slender form of a veiled female, led between Goody Cloyse, that pious teacher of the catechism, and Martha Carrier, who had received the devil's promise to be queen of hell. A rampant hag was she. And there stood the proselytes beneath the canopy of fire.

"Welcome, my children," said the dark figure, "to the communion of your race. Ye have found thus young your nature and your destiny. My children, look behind you!"

They turned; and flashing forth, as it were, in a sheet of flame, the fiend worshippers were seen; the smile of welcome gleamed darkly on every visage.

"There," resumed the sable form, "are all whom ye have reverenced from youth. Ye deemed them holier than yourselves, and shrank from your own sin, contrasting it with their lives of righteousness and prayerful aspirations heavenward. Yet here are they all in my worshipping assembly. This night it shall be granted you to know their secret deeds: how hoary-bearded elders of the church have whispered wanton words to the young maids of their households; how many a woman, eager for widows' weeds, has given her husband a drink at bedtime and let him sleep his last sleep in her bosom; how beardless youths have made haste to inherit their fathers' wealth; and how fair damsels — blush not, sweet ones — have dug little graves in the garden, and bidden me, the sole guest, to an infant's funeral. By the sympathy of your human hearts for sin ye shall scent out all the places — whether in church, bed-chamber, street, field, or forest — where crime has been committed, and shall exult to behold the whole earth one stain of guilt, one mighty blood spot. Far more than this. It shall be yours to penetrate, in every bosom, the deep mystery of sin, the fountain of all wicked arts, and which inexhaustibly supplies more evil impulses than human power — than my power at its utmost — can make manifest in deeds. And now, my children, look upon each other."

They did so; and, by the blaze of the hell-kindled torches, the wretched man beheld his Faith, and the wife her husband, trembling before that unhallowed altar.

"Lo, there ye stand, my children," said the figure, in a deep and solemn tone, almost sad with its despairing awfulness, as if his once angelic nature could yet mourn for our miserable race. "Depending upon one another's hearts, ye had still hoped that virtue were not all a dream. Now are ye undeceived. Evil is the nature of mankind. Evil must be your only happiness. Welcome again, my children, to the communion of your race."

"Welcome," repeated the fiend worshippers, in one cry of despair and triumph.

And there they stood, the only pair, as it seemed, who were yet hesitating on the verge of wickedness in this dark world. A basin was hollowed, naturally, in the rock. Did it contain water, reddened by the lurid light? or was it blood? or, perchance, a liquid flame? Herein did the shape of evil dip his hand and prepare to lay the mark of baptism upon their foreheads, that they might be partakers of the mystery of sin, more conscious of the secret guilt of others, both in deed and thought, than they could now be of their own. The husband cast one look at his pale wife, and Faith at him. What polluted wretches would the next glance show them to each other, shuddering alike at what they disclosed and what they saw!

"Faith! Faith!" cried the husband, "look up to heaven, and resist the wicked one."

Whether Faith obeyed he knew not. Hardly had he spoken when he found himself amid calm night and solitude, listening to a roar of the wind which died heavily away through the forest. He staggered against the rock, and felt it chill and damp; while a hanging twig, that had been all on fire, besprinkled his cheek with the coldest dew.

The next morning young Goodman Brown came slowly into the street of Salem village, staring around him like a bewildered man. The good old minister was taking a walk along the graveyard to get an appetite for breakfast and meditate his sermon, and bestowed a blessing, as he passed, on Goodman Brown. He shrank from the venerable saint as if to avoid an anathema. Old Deacon Gookin was at domestic worship, and the holy words of his prayer were heard through the open window. "What God doth the wizard pray to?" quoth Goodman Brown. Goody Cloyse, that excellent old Christian, stood in the early sunshine at her own lattice, catechizing a little girl who had brought her a pint of morning's milk. Goodman Brown snatched away the child as from the grasp of the fiend himself. Turning the corner by the meeting-house, he spied the head of Faith, with the pink ribbons, gazing anxiously forth, and bursting into such joy at sight of him that she skipped along the street and almost kissed her husband before the whole village. But Goodman Brown looked sternly and sadly into her face, and passed on without a greeting.

Had Goodman Brown fallen asleep in the forest and only dreamed a wild dream of a witch-meeting?

Be it so if you will; but, alas! it was a dream of evil omen for young Goodman Brown. A stern, a sad, a darkly meditative, a distrustful, if not a desperate man did he become from the night of that fearful dream. On the Sabbath day, when the congregation were singing a holy psalm, he could not listen because an anthem of sin rushed loudly upon his ear and drowned all the blessed strain. When the minister spoke from the pulpit with power and fervid eloquence, and, with his hand on the open Bible, of the sacred truths of our religion, and of saint-like lives and triumphant deaths, and of future bliss or misery unutterable, then did Goodman Brown turn pale, dreading lest the roof should thunder down upon the gray blasphemer and his hearers. Often, awaking suddenly at midnight, he shrank from the bosom of Faith; and at morning or eventide, when the family knelt down at prayer, he scowled and muttered to himself, and gazed sternly at his wife, and turned away. And when he had lived long, and was borne to his grave a hoary corpse, followed by Faith, an aged woman, and children and grandchildren, a goodly procession, besides neighbors not a few, they carved no hopeful verse upon his tombstone, for his dying hour was gloom.

# GOLD COAST

——*James Alan McPherson*

That spring, when I had a great deal of potential and no money at all, I took a job as a janitor. That was when I was still very young and spent money very freely, and when, almost every night, I drifted off to sleep lulled by sweet anticipation of that time when my potential would suddenly be realized and there would be capsule biographies of my life on dust jackets of many books, all proclaiming: ". . . He knew life on many levels. From shoeshine boy, free-lance waiter, 3rd cook, janitor, he rose to . . ." I had never been a janitor before and I did not really have to be one and that is why I did it. But now, much later, I think it might have been because it is possible to be a janitor without really becoming one, and at parties or at mixers when asked what it was I did for a living, it was pretty good to hook my thumbs in my vest pockets and say comfortably: "Why, I am an apprentice janitor." The hippies would think it degenerate and really dig me and it made me feel good that people in Philosophy and Law and Business would feel uncomfortable trying to make me feel better about my station while wondering how the hell I had managed to crash the party.

"What's an apprentice janitor?" they would ask.

"I haven't got my card yet," I would reply. "Right now I'm just taking lessons. There's lots of complicated stuff you have to learn before you get your card and your own building."

James Alan McPherson, "Gold Coast." From *Hue and Cry* by James Alan McPherson. Copyright © 1968, 1969 by James Alan McPherson. Reprinted by permission of Little, Brown and Co. in association with the Atlantic Monthly Press.

"What kind of stuff?"

"Human nature, for one thing. *Race* nature, for another."

"Why race?"

"Because," I would say in a low voice looking around lest someone else should overhear, "you have to be able to spot Jews and Negroes who are passing."

"That's terrible," would surely be said then with a hint of indignation.

"It's an art," I would add masterfully.

After a good pause I would invariably be asked: "But you're a Negro yourself, how can you keep your own people out?"

At which point I would look terribly disappointed and say: "*I don't keep them out. But if they get in it's my job to make their stay just as miserable as possible. Things are changing.*"

Now the speaker would just look at me in disbelief.

"It's Janitorial Objectivity," I would say to finish the thing as the speaker began to edge away. "Don't hate me," I would call after him to his considerable embarrassment. "Somebody has to do it."

It was an old building near Harvard Square. Conrad Aiken had once lived there and in the days of the Gold Coast, before Harvard built its great Houses, it had been a very fine haven for the rich; but that was a world ago and this building was one of the few monuments of that era which had survived. The lobby had a high ceiling with thick redwood beams and it was replete with marble floor, fancy ironwork, and an old-fashioned house telephone that no longer worked. Each apartment had a small fireplace, and even the large bathtubs and chain toilets, when I was having my touch of nature, made me wonder what prominent personage of the past had worn away all the newness. And, being there, I felt a certain affinity toward the rich.

It was a funny building; because the people who lived there made it old. Conveniently placed as it was between the Houses and Harvard Yard, I expected to find it occupied by a company of hippies, hopeful working girls, and assorted graduate students. Instead, there were a majority of old maids, dowagers, asexual middle-aged men, homosexual young men, a few married couples and a teacher. No one was shacking up there, and walking through the quiet halls in the early evening, I sometimes had the urge to knock on a door and expose myself just to hear someone breathe hard for once.

It was a Cambridge spring: down by the Charles happy students were making love while sad-eyed middle-aged men watched them from the bridge. It was a time of activity: Law students were busy sublimating, Business School people were making records of the money they would make, the Harvard Houses were clearing out, and in the Square bearded pot-pushers were setting up their restaurant tables in anticipation of the Summer School faithfuls. There was a change of season in the air, and to comply with its urgings, James Sullivan, the old superintendent, passed his three beaten garbage cans on to me with the charge that I should take up his daily rounds of the six floors, and with unflinching humility, gather whatever scraps the old-maid tenants had refused to husband.

I then became very rich, with my own apartment, a sensitive girl, a stereo, two speakers, one tattered chair, one fork, a job, and the urge to acquire. Having all this and youth besides made me pity Sullivan: he had been in that building thirty years and had its whole history recorded in the little folds of his mind, as his own life was recorded in the wrinkles of his face. All he had to show for his time there was a berserk dog, a wife almost as mad as the dog, three cats, bursitis, acute myopia, and a drinking problem. He was well over seventy and could hardly walk, and his weekly check of twenty-two dollars from the company that managed the building would not support anything. So, out of compromise, he was retired to superintendent of my labor.

My first day as a janitor, while I skillfully lugged my three overflowing cans of garbage out of the building, he sat on his bench in the lobby, faded and old and smoking in patched, loose blue pants. He watched me. He was a chain smoker and I noticed right away that he very carefully dropped all of the ashes and butts on the floor and crushed them under his feet until there was a yellow and gray smear. Then he laboriously pushed the mess under the bench with his shoe, all the while eyeing me like a cat in silence as I hauled the many cans of muck out to the big disposal unit next to the building. When I had finished, he gave me two old plates to help stock my kitchen and his first piece of advice.

"Sit down, for Chrissake, and take a load off your feet," he told me.

I sat on the red bench next to him and accepted the wilted cigarette he offered me from the crushed package he kept in his sweater pocket.

"Now I'll tell you something to help you get along in the building," he said.

I listened attentively.

"If any of these sons-of-bitches ever ask you to do something extra, be sure to charge them for it."

I assured him that I absolutely would.

"If they can afford to live here, they can afford to pay. The bastards."

"Undoubtedly," I assured him again.

"And another thing," he added. "Don't let any of these girls shove any cat shit under your nose. That ain't your job. You tell them to put it in a bag and take it out themselves."

I reminded him that I knew very well my station in life, and that I was not about to haul cat shit or anything of that nature. He looked at me through his thick-lensed glasses. He looked like a cat himself. "That's right," he said at last. "And if they still try to sneak it in the trash be sure to make the bastards pay. They can afford it." He crushed his seventh butt on the floor and scattered the mess some more while he lit up another. "I never hauled out no cat shit in the thirty years I been here and you don't do it either."

"I'm going to wash my hands," I said.

"Remember," he called after me, "don't take no shit from any of them."

I protested once more that, upon my life, I would never, never do it, not even for the prettiest girl in the building. Going up in the elevator, I felt comfortably resolved that I would never do it. There were no pretty girls in the building.

I never found out what he had done before he came there, but I do know that being a janitor in that building was as high as he ever got in life. He had watched two generations of the rich pass the building on their way to the Yard, and he had seen many governors ride white horses thirty times into that same Yard to send sons and daughters of the rich out into life to produce, to acquire, to procreate and to send back sons and daughters so that the cycle would continue. He had watched the cycle from when he had been able to haul the cans out for himself, and now he could not, and he was bitter.

He was Irish, of course, and he took pride in Irish accomplishments when he could have none of his own. He had known Frank O'Connor when that writer had been at Harvard. He told me on many occasions how O'Connor had stopped to talk every day on his way to the Yard. He had also known James Michael Curley, and his most colorful memory of the man was a long ago day when he and James Curley sat in a Boston bar and one of Curley's runners had come in and said: "Hey Jim, Sol Bernstein the Jew wants to see you." And Curley, in his deep, memorial voice had said to James Sullivan: "Let us go forth and meet this Israelite Prince." These were his memories, and I would obediently put aside my garbage cans and laugh with him over the hundred or so colorful, insignificant little details which made up a whole lifetime of living in the basement of Harvard. And although they were of little value to me then, I knew that they were the reflections of a lifetime and the happiest moments he would ever have, being sold to me cheap, as youthful time is cheap, for as little time and interest as I wanted to spend. It was a buyer's market.

## II

In those days I believed myself gifted with a boundless perception and attacked my daily garbage route with a gusto superenforced by the happy knowledge that behind each of the fifty or so doors in our building lived a story which could, if I chose to grace it with the magic of my pen, become immortal. I watched my tenants fanatically, noting their perversions, their visitors, and their eating habits. So intense was my search for material that I had to restrain myself from going through their refuse scrap by scrap; but at the topmost layers of muck, without too much hand-soiling in the process, I set my perceptions to work. By late June, however, I had discovered only enough to put together a skimpy, rather naïve Henry Miller novel. The most colorful discoveries being:

(1) The lady in #24 was an alumna of Paducah College.
(2) The couple in #55 made love at least five hundred times a week and the wife had not yet discovered the pill.
(3) The old lady in #36 was still having monthly inconvenience.
(4) The two fatsos in #56 consumed nightly an extraordinary amount of chili.
(5) The fat man in #54 had two dogs that were married to each other, but he was not married to anyone at all.
(6) The middle-aged single man in #63 threw out an awful lot of flowers.

Disturbed by the snail's progress I was making, I confessed my futility to James one day as he sat on his bench chain-smoking and smearing butts on my newly waxed lobby floor. "So you want to know about the tenants?" he said, his cat's eyes flickering over me.

I nodded.

"Well the first thing to notice is how many Jews there are."

"I haven't noticed many Jews," I said.

He eyed me in amazement.

"Well, a few," I said quickly to prevent my treasured perception from being dulled any further.

"A few, hell," he said. "There's more Jews here than anybody."

"How can you tell?"

He gave me that undecided look again. "Where do you think all that garbage comes from?" He nodded feebly toward my bulging cans. I looked just in time to prevent a stray noodle from slipping over the brim. "That's right," he continued. "Jews are the biggest eaters in the world. They eat the best too."

I confessed then that I was of the chicken-soup generation and believed that Jews ate only enough to muster strength for their daily trips to the bank.

"Not so!" he replied emphatically. "You never heard the expression: 'Let's get to the restaurant before the Jews get there'?"

I shook my head sadly.

"You don't know that in certain restaurants they take the free onions and pickles off the tables when they see Jews coming?"

I held my head down in shame over the bounteous heap.

He trudged over to my can and began to turn back the leaves of noodles and crumpled tissues from #47 with his hand. After a few seconds of digging he unmucked an empty paté can. "Look at that," he said triumphantly. "Gourmet stuff, no less."

"That's from #44," I said.

"What else?" he said all-knowingly. "In 1946 a Swedish girl moved in up there and took a Jewish girl for her roommate. Then the Swedish girl moved out and there's been a Jewish Dynasty up there ever since."

I recalled that #44 was occupied by a couple that threw out a good number of S. S. Pierce cans, Chivas Regal bottles, assorted broken records, and back issues of *Evergreen* and the *Realist*.

"You're right," I said.

"Of course," he replied as if there was never any doubt. "I can spot them anywhere, even when they think they're passing." He leaned closer and said in a you-and-me voice: "But don't ever say anything bad about them in public, the Anti-Defamation League will get you."

Just then his wife screamed for him from the second floor, and the dog joined her and beat against the door. He got into the elevator painfully and said: "Don't ever talk about them in public. You don't know who they are and that Defamation League will take everything you got."

Sullivan did not really hate Jews. He was just bitter toward anyone better off than himself. He liked me because I seemed to like hauling garbage and because I listened to him and seemed to respect what he said and seemed to imply, by lingering on even when he repeated himself, that I was eager to take what wisdom he had for no other reason than that I needed it in order to get along.

He lived with his wife on the second floor and his apartment was very dirty because both of them were sick and old, and neither could move very well. His wife swept dirt out into the hall, and two hours after I had mopped and waxed their section of the floor, there was sure to be a layer of dirt, grease, and crushed-scattered tobacco from their door to the end of the hall. There was a smell of dogs and cats and age and death about their door, and I did not ever want to have to go in there for any reason because I feared something about it I cannot name.

Mrs. Sullivan, I found out, was from South Africa. She loved animals much more than people and there was a great deal of pain in her face. She kept little pans of meat posted at strategic points about the building, and I often came across her in the early morning or late at night throwing scraps out of the second-floor window to stray cats. Once, when James was about to throttle a stray mouse in their apartment, she had screamed at him to give the mouse a sporting chance. Whenever she attempted to walk she had to balance herself against a wall or a rail, and she hated the building because it confined her. She also hated James and most of the tenants. On the other hand, she loved the *Johnny Carson Show,* she loved to sit outside on the front steps (because she could get no further unassisted), and she loved to talk to anyone who would stop to listen. She never spoke coherently except when she was cursing James, and then she had a vocabulary like a sailor. She had great, shrill lungs, and her screams, accompanied by the rabid barks of the dog, could be heard all over the building. She was never really clean, her teeth were bad, and the first most pathetic thing in the world was to see her sitting on the steps in the morning watching the world pass, in a stained smock and a fresh summer blue hat she kept just to wear downstairs, with no place in the world to go. James told me, on the many occasions of her screaming, that she was mentally disturbed and could not control herself. The admirable thing about him was that he never lost his temper with her, no matter how rough her curses became and no matter who heard them. And the second most pathetic thing in the world was to see them slowly making their way in Harvard Square, he supporting her, through the hurrying crowds of miniskirted summer girls, J-Pressed Ivy Leaguers, beatniks, and bused Japanese tourists, decked in cameras, who would take pictures of every inch of Harvard Square except them. Once, he told me, a hippie had brushed past them and called back over his shoulder: "Don't break any track records, Mr. and Mrs. Speedy Molasses."

Also on the second floor lived Miss O'Hara, a spinster who hated Sullivan as only an old maid can hate an old man. Across from her lived a very nice, gentle, celibate named Murphy who had once served with Montgomery in North Africa and who was now spending the rest of his life cleaning his little apartment and gossiping with Miss O'Hara. It was an Irish floor.

I never found out just why Miss O'Hara hated the Sullivans with such a passion. Perhaps it was because they were so unkempt and she was so superciliously clean. Perhaps it was because Miss O'Hara had a great deal of Irish pride and they were stereotyped Irish. Perhaps it was because she merely had no reason to like them. She was a fanatic about cleanliness and put out her little bit of garbage wrapped very neatly in yesterday's *Christian Science Monitor* and tied in a bow with a fresh piece of string. Collecting all those little neat packages, I would wonder where she got the string and imagined her at night picking meat-market locks with a hairpin and hobbling off with yards and yards of white cord concealed under the gray sweater she always wore. I could even imagine her back in her little apartment chuckling and rolling the cord into a great white ball by candlelight. Then she would stash it away in her breadbox. Miss O'Hara kept her door slightly open until late at night, and I suspected that she heard everything that went on in the building. I had the feeling that I should never dare to make love with gusto for fear that she would overhear and write down all my happy-time phrases, to be maliciously recounted to me if she were ever provoked.

She had been in the building longer than Sullivan, and I suppose that her greatest ambition in life was to outlive him and then attend his wake with a knitting ball and needles. She had been trying to get him fired for twenty-five years or so and did not know when to quit. On summer nights when I painfully mopped the second floor, she would offer me root beer, apples, or cupcakes while trying to pump me for evidence against him.

"He's just a filthy old man, Robert," she would declare in a little-old-lady whisper. "And don't think you have to clean up those dirty old butts of his. Just report him to the Company."

"Oh, I don't mind," I would tell her, gulping the root beer as fast as possible.

"Well, they're both a couple of lushes, if you ask me. They haven't been sober a day in twenty-five years."

"Well, she's sick too, you know."

"Ha!" She would throw up her hands in disgust. "She's only sick when he doesn't give her the booze."

I fought to keep down a burp. "How long have *you* been here?"

She motioned for me to step out of the hall and into her dark apartment. "Don't tell him," — she nodded towards Sullivan's door — "but I've been here for thirty-four years." She waited for me to be taken aback. Then she added: "And it was a better building before those two lushes came."

She then offered me an apple, asked five times if the dog's barking bothered me, forced me to take a fudge brownie, said that the cats had wet the floor again last night, got me to dust the top of a large chest too high for her to reach, had me pick up the minute specks of dust which fell from my dustcloth, pressed another root beer on me, and then showed me her family album. As an afterthought, she had me take down a big old picture of her great-grandfather, also too high for her to reach, so that I could dust that too. Then together we picked up the dust from it which might have fallen to the floor. "He's really a filthy old man, Robert," she said in closing, "and don't be afraid to report him to the property manager any time you want."

I assured her that I would do it at the slightest provocation from Sullivan, finally accepted an apple but refused the money she offered, and escaped back to my mopping. Even then she watched me, smiling, from her half-opened door.

"Why does Miss O'Hara hate you?" I asked James once.

He lifted his cigaretted hand and let the long ash fall elegantly to the floor. "That old bitch has been an albatross around my neck ever since I got here," he said. "Don't trust her, Robert. It was her kind that sat around singing hymns and watching them burn saints in this state."

There was never an adequate answer to my question. And even though the dog was noisy and would surely kill someone if it ever got loose, no one could really dislike the old man because of it. The dog was all they had. In his garbage each night, for every wine bottle, there would be an equally empty can of dog food. Some nights he took the brute out for a long walk, when he could barely walk himself, and both of them had to be led back to the building.

III

In those days I had forgotten that I was first of all a black and I had a very lovely girl who was not first of all a black. We were both young and optimistic then, and she believed with me in my potential and liked me partly because of it; and I was happy because she belonged to me and not to the race, which made her special. It made me special too because I did not have to wear a beard or hate or be especially hip or ultra-Ivy Leaguish. I did not have to smoke pot or supply her with it, or be for any other cause at all except myself. I only had to be myself, which pleased me; and I only had to produce, which pleased both of us. Like many of the artistically inclined rich, she wanted to own in someone else what she could not own in herself. But this I did not mind, and I forgave her for it because she forgave me moods and the constant smell of garbage and a great deal of latent hostility. She only minded James Sullivan and all the valuable time I was wasting listening to him rattle on and on. His conversations, she thought, were useless, repetitious, and promised nothing of value to me. She was accustomed to the old-rich whose conversations meandered around a leitmotiv of how well off they were and how much they would leave behind very soon. She was not at all cold, but she had been taught how to tolerate the old-poor and perhaps toss them a greeting in passing. But nothing more.

Sullivan did not like her when I first introduced them because he saw that she was not a hippie and could not be dismissed. It is in the nature of things that liberal people will tolerate two interracial hippies more than they will an intelligent, serious-minded mixed couple. The former liaison is easy to dismiss as the dregs of both races, deserving of each other and the contempt of both races; but the latter poses a threat because there is no immediacy or overpowering sensuality or "you-pick-my-fleas-I'll-pick-yours" apparent on the surface of things, and people, even the most publicly liberal, cannot dismiss it so easily.

"That girl is Irish, isn't she?" he had asked one day in my apartment soon after I had introduced them.

"No," I said definitely.

"What's her name again?"

"Judy Smith," I said, which was not her name at all.

"Well, I can spot it," he said. "She's got Irish blood, all right."

"Everybody's got a little Irish blood," I told him.

He looked at me cattily and craftily from behind his thick lenses. "Well, she's from a good family, I suppose."

"I suppose," I said.

He paused to let some ashes fall to the rug. "They say the Colonel's Lady and Nelly O'Grady are sisters under the skin." Then he added: "Rudyard Kipling."

"That's true," I said with equal innuendo, "that's why you have to maintain a distinction by marrying the Colonel's Lady."

An understanding passed between us then, and we never spoke more on the subject.

Almost every night the cats wet the second floor while Meg Sullivan watched the *Johnny Carson Show* and the dog howled and clawed the door. During commercials Meg would curse James to get out and stop dropping ashes on the floor or to take the dog out or something else, totally unintelligible to those of us on the fourth, fifth and sixth floors. Even after the *Carson Show* she would still curse him to get out, until finally he would go down to the basement and put away a bottle or two of wine. There was a steady stench of cat functions in the basement, and with all the grease and dirt, discarded trunks, beer bottles, chairs, old tools and the filthy sofa on which he sometimes slept, seeing him there made me want to cry. He drank the cheapest sherry, the wino kind, straight from the bottle; and on many nights that summer at 2:00 A.M. my phone would ring me out of bed.

"Rob? Jimmy Sullivan here. What are you doing?"

There was nothing suitable to say.

"Come on down to the basement for a drink."

"I have to be at work at eight-thirty," I would protest.

"Can't you have just one drink?" he would say pathetically.

I would carry down my own glass so that I would not have to drink out of the bottle. Looking at him on the sofa, I could not be mad because now I had many records for my stereo, a story that was going well, a girl who believed in me and belonged to me and not to the race, a new set of dishes, and a tomorrow morning with younger people.

"I don't want to burden you unduly," he would always preface.

I would force myself not to look at my watch and say: "Of course not."

"My Meg is not in the best health, you know," he would say, handing the bottle to me.

"She's just old."

"The doctors say she should be in an institution."

"That's no place to be."

"I'm a sick man myself, Rob. I can't take much more. She's crazy."

"Anybody who loves animals can't be crazy."

He took another long draw from the bottle. "I won't live another year. I'll be dead in a year."

"You don't know that."

He looked at me closely, without his glasses, so that I could see the desperation in his eyes. "I just hope Meg goes before I do. I don't want them to put her in an institution after I'm gone."

At 2:00 A.M. with the cat stench in my nose and a glass of bad sherry standing still in my hand because I refused in my mind to touch it, and when all my dreams of greatness were above him and the basement and the building itself, I did not know what to say. The only way I could keep from hating myself was to talk about the AMA or the Medicare program or hippies. He was pure hell on all three. To him, the medical profession was "morally bankrupt," Medicare was a great farce which deprived oldsters like himself of their "rainy-day dollars," and hippies were "dropouts from the human race." He could rage on and on in perfect phrases about all three of his major dislikes, and I had the feeling that because the sentences were so well constructed and well turned, he might have memorized them from something he had read. But then he was extremely well read and it did not matter if he had borrowed a phrase or two from someone else. The ideas were still his own.

It would be 3:00 A.M. before I knew it, and then 3:30, and still he would go on. He hated politicians in general and liked to recount, at these times, his private catalogue of political observations. By the time he got around to Civil Rights it would be 4:00 A.M., and I could not feel sorry or responsible for him at that hour. I would begin to yawn and at first he would just ignore it. Then I would start to edge toward the door, and he would see that he could hold me no longer, not even by declaring that he wanted to be an honorary Negro because he loved the race so much.

"I hope I haven't burdened you unduly," he would say again.

"Of course not," I would say, because it was over then and I could leave him and the smell of the cats there and sometimes I would go out in the cool night and walk around the Yard and be thankful that I was only an assistant janitor, and a transient one at that. Walking in the early dawn and seeing the Summer School fellows sneak out of the girls' dormitories in the Yard gave me a good feeling, and I thought that tomorrow night it would be good to make love myself so that I could be busy when he called.

IV

"Why don't you tell that old man your job doesn't include baby-sitting with him?" Jean told me many times when she came over to visit during the day and found me sleeping.

I would look at her and think to myself about social forces and the pressures massing and poised, waiting to attack us. It was still July then. It was hot and I was working good. "He's just an old man," I said. "Who else would listen to him?"

"You're too soft. As long as you do your work you don't have to be bothered with him."

"He could be a story if I listened long enough."

"There are too many stories about old people."

"No," I said, thinking about us again, "there are just too many people who have no stories."

Sometimes he would come up and she would be there, but I would let him come in anyway, and he would stand in the room looking dirty and uncomfortable, offering some invented reason for having intruded. At these times something silent would pass between them, something I cannot name, which would reduce him to exactly what he was: an old man, come out of his basement to intrude where he was not wanted. But all the time this was being communicated, there would be a surface, friendly conversation between them. And after five minutes or so of being unwelcome, he would apologize for having come, drop a few ashes on the rug and back out the door. Downstairs we could hear his wife screaming.

We endured and aged and August was almost over. Inside the building the cats were still wetting, Meg was still screaming, the dog was getting madder, and Sullivan began to drink during the day. Outside it was hot and lush and green, and the summer girls were wearing shorter miniskirts and no panties and the middle-aged men down by the Charles were going wild on their bridge. Everyone was restless for change, for August is the month when undone summer things must be finished or regretted all through the winter.

V

Being imaginative people, Jean and I played a number of original games. One of them we called "Social Forces," the object of which was to see which side could break us first. We played it with the unknown nightriders who screamed obscenities from passing cars. And because that was her side I would look at her expectantly, but she would laugh and say: "No." We played it at parties with unaware blacks who attempted to enchant her with skillful dances and hip vocabulary, believing her to be community property. She would be polite and aloof, and much later, it then being my turn, she would look at me expectantly. And I would force a smile and say: "No." The last round was played while taking her home in a subway car, on a hot August night, when one side of the car was black and tense and hating and the other side was white and of the same mind. There was not enough room on either side for the two of us to sit and we would not separate; and so we stood, holding on to a steel post through all the stops, feeling all the eyes, between the two sides of the car and the two sides of the world. We aged. And, getting off finally at the stop which was no longer ours, we looked at each other, again expectantly, and there was nothing left to say.

I began to avoid the old man, would not answer the door when I knew it was he who was knocking, and waited until very late at night, when he could not possibly be awake, to haul the trash down. I hated the building then; and I was really a janitor for the first time. I slept a lot and wrote very little. And I did not give a damn about Medicare, the AMA, the building, Meg or the crazy dog. I began to consider moving out.

In that same month, Miss O'Hara finally succeeded in badgering Murphy, the celibate Irishman, and a few other tenants into signing a complaint about the dog. No doubt Murphy signed because he was a nice fellow and women like Miss O'Hara had always dominated him. He did not really mind the dog: he did not really mind anything. She called him "Frank Dear," and I had the feeling that when he came to that place, fresh from Montgomery's Campaign, he must have had a will of his own; but she had drained it all away, year by year, so that now he would do anything just to be agreeable.

One day soon after the complaint, the Property Manager came around to tell Sullivan that the dog had to be taken away. Miss O'Hara told me the good news later, when she finally got around to my door.

"Well, that crazy dog is gone now, Robert. Those two are enough."

"Where is the dog?" I asked.

"I don't know, but Albert Rustin made them get him out. You should have seen the old drunk's face," she said. "That dirty useless old man."

"You should be at peace now," I said.

"Almost," was her reply. "The best thing would be to get rid of those two old boozers along with the dog."

I congratulated Miss O'Hara again and then went out. I knew that the old man would be drinking and would want to talk. I did not want to talk. But very late that evening he called on the telephone and caught me in.

"Rob?" he said. "James Sullivan here. Would you come down to my apartment like a good fellow? I want to ask you something important."

I had never been in his apartment before and did not want to go then. But I went down anyway.

They had three rooms, all grimy from corner to corner. There was a peculiar odor in that place I did not want to ever smell again, and his wife was dragging herself around the room talking in mumbles. When she saw me come in the door, she said: "I can't clean it up. I just can't. Look at that window. I can't reach it. I can't keep it clean." She threw up both her hands and held her head down and to the side. "The whole place is dirty and I can't clean it up."

"What do you want?" I said to Sullivan.

"Sit down." He motioned me to a kitchen chair. "Have you changed that bulb on the fifth floor?"

"It's done."

He was silent for a while, drinking from a bottle of sherry, and he offered me some and a dirty glass. "You're the first person who's been here in years," he said. "We couldn't have company because of the dog."

Somewhere in my mind was a note that I should never go into his apartment. But the dog had not been the reason. "Well, he's gone now," I said, fingering the dirty glass of sherry.

He began to cry. "They took my dog away," he said. "It was all I had. How can they take a man's dog away from him?"

There was nothing I could say.

"I couldn't do nothing," he continued. After a while he added: "But I know who it was. It was that old bitch O'Hara. Don't ever trust her, Rob. She smiles in your face but it was her kind that laughed when they burned Joan of Arc in this state."

Seeing him there, crying and making me feel unmanly because I wanted to touch him or say something warm, also made me eager to be far away and running hard. "Everybody's got problems," I said. "I don't have a girl now."

He brightened immediately, and for a while he looked almost happy in his old cat's eyes. Then he staggered over to my chair and held out his hand. I did not touch it, and he finally pulled it back. "I know how you feel," he said. "I know just how you feel."

"Sure," I said.

"But you're a young man, you have a future. But not me. I'll be dead inside of a year."

Just then his wife dragged in to offer me a cigar. They were being hospitable and I forced myself to drink a little of the sherry.

"They took my dog away today," she mumbled. "That's all I had in the world, my dog."

I looked at the old man. He was drinking from the bottle.

VI

During the first week of September one of the middle-aged men down by the Charles got tired of looking and tried to take a necking girl away from her boyfriend. The police hauled him off to jail, and the girl pulled down her dress tearfully. A few days later another man exposed himself near the same spot. And that same week a dead body was found on the banks of the Charles.

The miniskirted brigade had moved out of the Yard and it was quiet and green and peaceful there. In our building another Jewish couple moved into #44. They did not eat gourmet stuff and, on occasion, threw out pork-and-beans cans. But I had lost interest in perception. I now had many records for my stereo, loads of S. S. Pierce stuff, and a small bottle of Chivas Regal which I never opened. I was working good again and did not miss other things as much; or at least I told myself that.

The old man was coming up steadily now, at least three times a day, and I had resigned myself to it. If I refused to let him in he would always come back later with a missing bulb on the fifth floor. We had taken to buying cases of beer together, and when he had finished his half, which was very frequently, he would come up to polish off mine. I began to enjoy talking about politics, the AMA, Medicare, and hippies, and listening to him recite from books he had read. I discovered that he was very well read in history, philosophy, literature and law. He was extraordinarily fond of saying: "I am really a cut above being a building superintendent. Circumstances made me what I am." And even though he was drunk and dirty and it was very late at night, I believed him and liked him anyway because having him there was much better than being alone. After he had gone I could sleep and I was not lonely in sleep; and it did not really matter how late I was at work the next morning, because when I really thought about it all, I discovered that nothing really matters except not being old and being alive and having potential to dream about, and not being alone.

Whenever I passed his wife on the steps she would say: "That no-good bastard let them take my dog away." And whenever her husband complained that he was sick she said: "That's good for him. He took my dog away."

Sullivan slept in the basement on the sofa almost every night because his wife would think about the dog after the *Carson Show* and blame him for letting it be taken away. He told her, and then me, that the dog was on a farm in New Hampshire; but that was unlikely because the dog had been near mad, and it did not appease her. It was nearing autumn and she was getting violent. Her screams could be heard for hours through the halls and I knew that beyond her quiet door Miss O'Hara was plotting again. Sullivan now had little cuts and bruises on his face and hands, and one day he said: "Meg is like an albatross around my neck. I wish she was dead. I'm sick myself and I can't take much more. She blames me for the dog and I couldn't help it."

"Why don't you take her out to see the dog?" I said.

"I couldn't help it Rob," he went on. "I'm old and I couldn't help it."

"You ought to just get her out of here for a while."

He looked at me, drunk as usual. "Where would we go? We can't even get past the Square."

There was nothing left to say.

"Honest to God, I couldn't help it," he said. He was not saying it to me.

That night I wrote a letter from a mythical New Hampshire farmer telling them that the dog was very fine and missed them a great deal because he kept trying to run off. I said that the children and all the other dogs liked him and that he was not vicious any more. I wrote that the open air was doing him a lot of good and added that they should feel absolutely free to come up to visit the dog at any time. That same night I gave him the letter.

One evening, some days later, I asked him about it.

"I tried to mail it, I really tried," he said.

"What happened?"

"I went down to the Square and looked for cars with New Hampshire license plates. But I never found anybody."

"That wasn't even necessary, was it?"

"It had to have a New Hampshire postmark. You don't know my Meg."

"Listen," I said. "I have a friend who goes up there. Give me the letter and I'll have him mail it."

He held his head down. "I'll tell you the truth. I carried that letter in my pocket so much it got ragged and dirty and I got tired of carrying it. I finally just tore it up."

Neither one of us said anything for a while.

"If I could have sent it off it would have helped some," he said at last. "I know it would have helped."

"Sure," I said.

"I wouldn't have to ask anybody if I had my strength."

"I know."

"If I had my strength I would have mailed it myself."

"I know," I said.

That night we both drank from his bottle of sherry and it did not matter at all that I did not provide my own glass.

## VII

In late September the Cambridge police finally picked up the bearded pot-pusher in the Square. He had been in a restaurant all summer, at the same table, with the same customers flocking around him; but now that summer was over, they picked him up. The leaves were changing. In the early evening students passed the building and Meg, blue-hatted and waiting on the steps, carrying sofas and chairs and coffee tables to their suites in the Houses. Down by the Charles the middle-aged men were catching the last phases of summer sensuality before the grass grew cold and damp, and before the young would be forced indoors to play. I wondered what those hungry, spying men did in the winter or at night when it was too dark to see. Perhaps, I thought, they just stood there and listened.

In our building Miss O'Hara was still listening. She had never stopped. When Meg was outside on the steps it was very quiet and I felt good that Miss O'Hara had to wait a long, long time before she heard anything. The company gave the halls and ceilings a new coat of paint, but it was still old in the building. James Sullivan got his yearly two-week vacation and they went to the Boston Common for six hours: two hours going, two hours sitting on the benches, and two hours coming back. Then they both sat on the steps, watching, and waiting.

At first I wanted to be kind because he was old and dying in a special way and I was young and ambitious. But at night, in my apartment, when I heard his dragging feet in the hall outside and knew that he would be drunk and repetitious and imposing on my privacy, I did not want to be kind any more. There were girls outside and I knew that I could have one now because that desperate look had finally gone somewhere deep inside. I was young and now I did not want to be bothered.

"Did you read about the lousy twelve per cent Social Security increase those bastards in Washington gave us?"

"No."

He would force himself past me, trying to block the door with my body, and into the room. "When those old pricks tell me to count my blessings, I tell them, 'You're not one of them.'" He would seat himself at the table without meeting my eyes. "The cost of living's gone up more than twelve per cent in the last six months."

"I know."

"What unmitigated bastards."

I would try to be busy with something on my desk.

"But the Texas Oil Barons got another depletion allowance."

"They can afford to bribe politicians," I would mumble.

"They tax away our rainy-day dollars and give us a lousy twelve per cent."

"It's tough."

He would know that I did not want to hear any more and he would know that he was making a burden of himself. It made me feel bad that it was so obvious to him, but I could not help myself. It made me feel bad that I disliked him more every time I heard a girl laugh on the street far below my window. So I would nod occasionally and say half-phrases and smile slightly at something witty he was saying for the third time. If I did not offer him a drink he would go sooner and so I gave him Coke when he hinted at how dry he was. Then, when he had finally gone, saying, "I hope I haven't burdened you unduly," I went to bed and hated myself.

VIII

If I am a janitor it is either because I have to be a janitor or because I want to be a janitor. And if I do not have to do it, and if I no longer want to do it, the easiest thing in the world, for a young man, is to step up to something else. Any move away from it is a step up because there is no job more demeaning than that of a janitor. One day I made myself suddenly realize that the three dirty cans would never contain anything of value to me, unless, of course, I decided to gather material for Harold Robbins or freelance for the *Realist*. Neither alternative appealed to me.

Toward dawn one day, during the first part of October, I rented a U-Haul truck and took away two loads of things I had accumulated. The records I packed very carefully, and the stereo I placed on the front seat of the truck beside me. I slipped the Chivas Regal and a picture of Jean under some clothes in a trunk I will not open for a long time. And I left the rug on the floor because it was dirty and too large for my new apartment. I also left the two plates given to me by James Sullivan, for no reason at all. Sometimes I want to go back to get them, but I do not know how to ask for them or explain why I left them in the first place. But sometimes at night, when there is a sleeping girl beside me, I think that I cannot have them again because I am still young and do not want to go back into that building.

I saw him once in the Square walking along very slowly with two shopping bags, and they seemed very heavy. As I came up behind him I saw him put them down and exercise his arms while the crowd moved in two streams around him. I had an instant impulse to offer help and I was close enough to touch him before I stopped. I will never know why I stopped. And after a few seconds of standing behind him and knowing that he was not aware of anything at all except the two heavy bags waiting to be lifted after his arms were sufficiently rested, I moved back into the stream of people which passed on the left of him. I never looked back.

# Index

Alliteration, 47
Audience, convincing the, 106–107

Benedikt, Michael, "The Energy Chest," 62
*Beowulf*, 31
Brautigan, Richard
  "Adrenalin Mother," 56
  "The Pill Versus the Springhill Mine Disaster," 62
Browning, Robert, "Soliloquy of the Spanish Cloister," 58–59

Character in drama, 73–80
  conflict, 85
  credibility of, 77–80
  motivation of, 74–77
  revelation of, 74–77
  writing about, 73–80
    critical, 76–80
    experience and observation, 73–76
Character in fiction, 222–230
  change of, 223
  complexity of, 223
  motivations of, 222–229
  stereotyping, 223
  writing about, 222–230
    critical essay, 226–230
    experience and observation, 222–226
Childress, William
  "Lobo," 65
  "Hunting the Trolls," 66
Clichés, 17
Clifton, Lucile, "Good Times," 63
Coleridge, Samuel Taylor, 45
Comparison and contrast, 26–27
  definition of, 26
  writing about
    fiction, 211, 218
    symbols in poetry, 26–29
    theme in poetry, 34–40
Conflict in drama, 81–88
  character, 85
  writing about, 81–88
    critical, 83–88
    experience and observation, 81–83
Contrast, *see* Comparison and contrast
Convincing an audience, 106–107
Credibility in drama
  characters, 77–80
  conflict, 84–88
  definition of, 78
  language, 97, 102–107
  plot, 92–95
  staging, 108–112

287

Details, 6
Documentation, techniques of, 246–247, 253–256
Documented paper, 218
Dostoevsky, Feodor, *Crime and Punishment*, 238
Drama
 character in, 73–80
 conflict in, 81–88
 language in, 97–107
 personifications in, 73–76
 plot in, 89–96
 prewriting, 76, 83, 92, 102
 staging in, 108–112
 *see also* Credibility in drama
Dramatic point of view in fiction, 232
Dramatic situations in poetry, 8–14
 images, 17–20
 writing about, 8–14
  critical, 12–14
  experience and observation, 8–11

*Everyman*, 113–139
Explicit themes, 250–251

Fiction, 211, 218
 character in, 222–230
 dramatic point of view, 232
 language in, 242–248
 plot in, 213–221
 point of view in, 231–241
 prewriting, 218, 226, 236, 245, 252
 reference books for, 246
 theme in, 249–256
Fielding, Henry, *Tom Jones*, 239
First person, 237
Footnoting, 253–256
Forster, E. M., *Aspects of the Novel*, 214
Free verse, 46

*Gawain and the Green Knight*, 46

Hansberry, Lorraine, *A Raisin in the Sun*, 134–210
Hawthorne, Nathaniel, *Young Goodman Brown*, 257–268

Imagery, 245
Images, 15–22
 definition of, 16
 types of
  clichés, 17
  metaphor, 17
  personification, 3–7
  simile, 17
 writing about, 15–22
  critical, 15–18
  experience and observation, 18–22
Implicit themes, 250–251
Internal rhyme, 48

Jefferson, Todd Davis, "Cows," 32–33

Language in drama, 97–107
 credibility, 97, 102–107
 critical, 102–103
 experience and observation, 97–101
 writing about, 97–107
Language in fiction, 242–248
 imagery, 245
 individualizing features of, 245–246
 level of, 242, 245
 writing about, 242–248
  critical essays, 245–248
  experience and observation, 242–245
Larkin, Phillip, "If, My Darling," 69
Lewis, C. S., 16

McPherson, James Alan, *Gold Coast*, 268–286
Memorable sayings, 32
Metaphor, 17
Meter, 44
Motivation, character, 74–77, 222–229

Observer point of view, 238
Omniscient point of view, 238

Participant point of view, 237
Personifications in drama, 73–76
Personifications in poetry, 3–7
 definition of, 4
 writing about, 2–7
  critical, 5–7
  experience and observation, 3–4

288   INDEX

*Piers Plowman,* 48
Plot in drama, 89–96
  main action, 92–94
  subordinate action, 92–94
  writing about, 89–96
    critical, 92–96
    experience and observation, 89–92
Plot in fiction, 213–221
  definition of, 214
  main action, 214–221
  subordinate action, 219–221
  writing about, 213–221
    critical essay, 218–221
    experience and observation, 213–218
Poetry
  comparison and contrast in, 26–29, 34–40
  dramatic situations in, 8–14
  free verse, 46
  internal rhyme, 48
  meter, 44
  personifications in, 3–7
  prewriting, 19, 26, 34, 48
  sound in, 41–55
  rhyme, 47
  rhythm, 41–55
Point of view in fiction, 231–241
  definition of, 232
  dramatic point of view, 232
  first person, 237
  observer of action, 238
  omniscient, 238
  participant in action, 237
  third person, 238
  writing about, 231–241
    critical essay, 236–241
    experience and observation, 231–235
Prewriting
  definition of, 5
  drama, 76, 83, 92, 102
  fiction 218, 226, 236, 245, 252
  poetry, 19, 26, 34, 48

Reference books for fiction, 246–247
Revelation, of dramatic character, 74–77
Rhyme, 47
Rhythm, 41–55
  definition of, 43–44
  free verse, 46

  meter, 44
  stressed verse, 30
Roethke, Theodore, "The Geranium," 49–50

Shakespeare, William, *Henry IV, Part One,* 44–45
Simic, Charles, "Bestiary for the Fingers of My Right Hand," 57
Simile, 17
Sound in poetry, 41–55
  writing about, 41–55
    critical essay, 47–55
    experience and observation, 41–46
Speaking pictures, 11
Staging in drama, 108–112
Stereotyping, fictional character, 223
Stressed verse, 46
  and rhythm, 30
Symbols, 23–29
  definition of, 24
  writing about symbols, 23–29
    critical essay, 26–29

Tate, James, "The Lost Pilot," 63
Theme in fiction, 249–256
  definition of, 250
  explicit, 250–251
  implicit, 250–251
  writing about, 249–256
    critical essay, 252–256
    experience and observation, 249–252
Theme in poetry, 30–40
  definition of, 31
  writing about, 30–40
    critical, 34–40
    experience and observation, 30–33
Third person, 238
Twain, Mark, *The Adventures of Huckleberry Finn,* 236–237

Verse
  free, 46
  stressed, 46
  *see also* Poetry

Wakoski, Diane, "No More Soft Talk," 67–68
Williams, William Carlos, "Tract," 60–61